NED'S NAVY

NED'S NAVY

The Private Letters of
EDWARD CHARLTON
from Cadet to Admiral

A WINDOW ON THE
BRITISH EMPIRE
FROM 1878
TO 1924

FRANK URBAN

Airlife
England

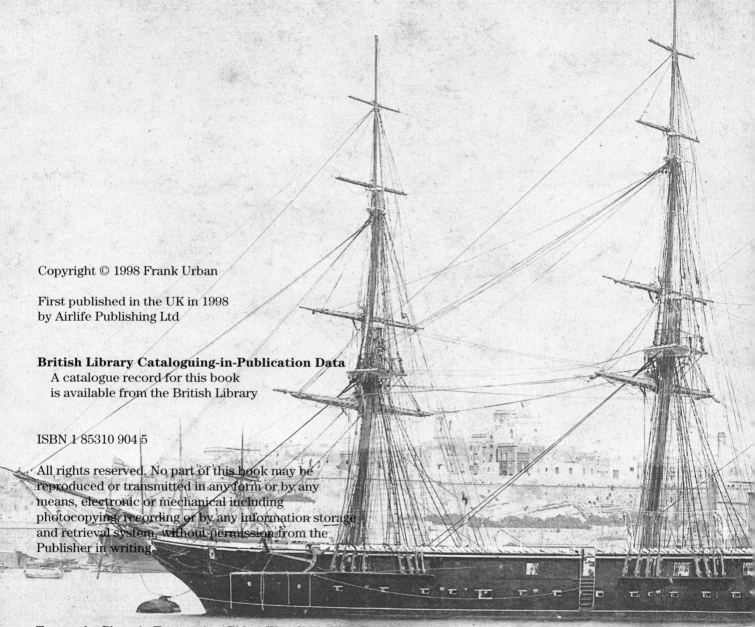

First published in the UK in 1998
by Airlife Publishing Ltd

British Library Cataloguing-in-Publication Data
A catalogue record for this book
is available from the British Library

ISBN 1 85310 904 5

Typeset by Phoenix Typesetting, Ilkley, West Yorkshire, England
Printed in England by Butler and Tanner Ltd, London and Frome

Airlife Publishing Ltd
101 Longden Road, Shrewsbury, SY3 9EB, England

Contents

Acknowledgements

The eight large folio volumes left by Admiral Edward Charlton have been called 'diaries' by his family but, with the exception of 1881, they are in essence a collection of numerous personal letters, thousands of photographs, a few official reports and several newspaper clippings. They cover half a century and weigh thirty-three kilograms.

Ned's letters record events of international moment . . . and humdrum meals. His photographs include historic occasions . . . and untitled, faded portraits of persons and ships unknown. The sentiments expressed are sometimes sublime . . . and sometimes bigoted by today's mores. This book includes no more than a tenth of his letters. The delicate scroll-work surrounding the letters in Ned's earlier folios reveals an artist's hand, perhaps that of his sister Elise. The folio for 1914/1918 was probably compiled by Ned himself. Many letters and photographs were kept loose. In 1992 the folios were given by Admiral Charlton's eldest child, Audrey Urban, to the writer to compile and this has been attempted without concentrating unduly either on his successes or his shortcomings.

Ned's daughters – Audrey, Laura and Rosemary – and nephew Oscar all kindly provided personal recollections.

One of Ned's aunts, Barbara Charlton, mistress of Hesleyside, wrote memoirs describing her life between 1815 and 1866. These were compiled by L.E.O. Charlton and published in 1949 as *The Recollections of a Northumbrian Lady*. Barbara describes how, during the Napoleonic wars, her mother-to-be was interned in a convent school in Paris. When she reached seventeen her parents sought permission to send her to Britain but this was refused. When an English nun died, the difficulty of her mother's passage to Britain 'was very simply overcome by the substitution of herself in the crated coffin placed at her disposal'. One might wonder whether this influenced Barbara's idiosyncratic recollections on Mrs William Wordsworth ('the long-suffering widow of the verbose and cantankerous poet'), on a lapsed convert ('her religion was that of farmyard poultry who pick up anything that catches the eye'), and on the failure of Ned's father, Doctor Edward Charlton, to prevent the death of his first wife from consumption ('The stethoscope did not seem to be his strong point').

Most sincere thanks to the following for information and encouragement:

In Britain:	Rosemary Acton,	In South Africa:	Michael and Wyn Urban
	E. Oscar Charlton,	In the USA:	Bob Forrest
	Sister Laura Charlton	In Australia:	Colin and Sarah Macdonald,
	William Charlton		Donald Scott-Orr,
	Maldwin Drummond OBE		Members of the Fellowship
	Gerard de Lisle,		of Australian Writers
	Claire Reid,		(Hastings Region), and
	Roderick Suddaby		especially my wife, Patricia.
	Martin and Jill Urban		

Bread upon the Waters

Mariner, mariner, home from the sea,
What has your tall ship brought for me?
Oh, we've brought you wool and we've brought you wheat,
And there's fish coming in from the drifter fleet;
For a cruiser watched that we all sailed free,
And guarded the mariners home from the sea.

From verses by
Rear-Admiral R.A. Hopwood
pasted into the first page of
Admiral Charlton's scrapbook.

Background Brief

Northumbria and the Royal Navy

For no fewer than ten thousand generations the nomadic ancestors of the British people battled for survival on a peninsula that formed part of Western Europe. The success achieved by these palaeolithic people in evading and eventually triumphing over man's larger and more dangerous sabre-toothed predators is a portent of their descendants' tenacity.

An event of cataclysmic significance to the future history of Britain occurred about 7000 BC when the low-lying landbridge joining the British peninsula to the Continent of Europe was swept away by storm and rising sea levels. Britain became an island, the English Channel a natural moat. No longer would intruders be able to invade Britain on foot: the islanders would be prudent to establish a navy to counter threats from the sea.

In the millennia before Christ the Celts invaded Britain and used Bronze Age weapons to overcome the flintstone weapons of the natives. Using Iron Age weapons, Julius Caesar invaded in 55 BC but failed to establish a permanent foothold. Nearly nine decades later the Romans again invaded and, after many battles, in AD 61 General Suetonius overcame the courageous resistance offered by the British Queen Boadicea. After conquering the southern half of the island, the Romans proceeded to defend it successfully against incursion from the Picts and Scots by building Hadrian's formidable rock wall across the narrow waist of the island. The defence of Roman Britain included a navy. With sails, hulls and seamen's clothing all camouflaged sea-green, the Classis Britannica fleet guarded the island's coastline.

The Roman Empire gradually crumbled and Rome encouraged Teutonic and British soldiers to man Hadrian's Wall, granting them a piece of land or a pension after twenty-five years' service. Intermarriage occurred between Romans and Britons. In AD 410 the Roman legions departed and a large part of Britain was immediately invaded by Picts, Scots, Saxons and Angles, the last-named being people from the former German state of Angle, now part of Schleswig-Holstein. Sir Winston Churchill suggests that for the bulk of the British people, who lived in the countryside, this represented little more than a change of master. He cites as evidence the retention of Celtic names for natural features even though the Roman names of many towns were replaced by Anglo-Saxon equivalents.

The departure of the Romans heralded dark centuries of insecurity and ignorance. A flash of light is provided by the Venerable Bede, the first Briton to write a history of Britain. Bede lived all his life in Northumbria and had access at Jarrow to the finest library then in existence on the island. In his *Ecclesiastical History of the English People*, Bede tells us of Edwin, the first Christian ruler of Northumbria, who was baptised on Easter Day AD 627. Bede attended the great Synod of Whitby in 663 where, in Churchill's words, 'the hinging issue was whether British Christianity should conform to the general life-plan of Christendom or whether it should be expressed by the monastic orders which had founded the Celtic Churches . . . the decision was taken that the Church of Northumbria should be a definite part of the Church of Rome and the Catholic system . . . there was opened to every member of the English Church the broad vista of a world-state and universal communion.'

Anglo-Saxon Britain had no navy and initially provided an easy target for the Vikings who ravaged all but the southern kingdom of the island. The Danes settled in eastern Britain but were eventually beaten by King Alfred the Great and his successors. King Alfred earned the title 'Great' not only for attacking the Vikings from his small southern base, but also in recognition of the magnanimity with which, on occasions, he treated them when he defeated them in battle, in some cases baptising and releasing them. But these were not his only attributes. He also founded a Royal Navy and instigated the *Anglo-Saxon-Chronicles*, the primary record of a period from which scant written material is available. The *Chronicles* report on Britain's history between AD 892 and 1154. The first major battle fought by King Alfred's Royal Navy against the Vikings is reported thus: 'King Alfred caused some long ships, of 40 oars or more, to be got ready against the aforesaid ships of the Danes. And whilst six of the Danish ships were lying near the coast of Devonshire, they were surprised by nine of the King's ships. The Danes seeing this, moved against them with

Ned with his Father, aged about three.

7

three only of their ships, for the other three were stranded and could not move because the tide was out. Six ships, therefore, of the English fought against three of the Danes, whilst the other three went against the three Danish ships that were stranded. The three Danish ships fought long and desperately against the six, but numbers at last prevailed, and two of the Danish ships were taken; the third fled, after all her crew had been killed except five.'

At the great Battle of Hastings in 1066 Britain was invaded and conquered for the last time. The Normans established permanent domicile, initially as foreign-speaking aristocrats but finally integrating with the populace and adopting English.

The modern Royal Navy traces its history directly from the navy of Queen Elizabeth I. It was not just an organisation with royal patronage but a direct extension of the sovereign's powerful sword arm beyond the shores of Britain . . . initially over the 'English' Channel, then to the Caribbean and the Mediterranean and finally to every ocean. For the first two hundred years senior naval officers were almost exclusively aristocratic friends of the sovereign, and even in the eighteenth century most flag officers depended on political patronage for their appointments.

Because of its situation at the narrow 'waist' of Britain, Northumbria frequently provided a magnet for marauders. In the time of Bede it was the premier kingdom in Britain, but its significance gradually bowed to the milder climate of the south. This area is where Edward Charlton, 'Ned', was born and raised. Of necessity the people remaining, including Ned's ancestors, are of hardy and resourceful stock.

The Charlton Family from 1157

The origin of the family name 'Charlton' lies in Old English, prior to both Anglo-Saxon and Norman. The first recorded Charlton, Hugh de Charleton, lived on the family land 'Hesleyside' during the reign of Richard I (1157–1199). He was succeeded by his son William de Charleton I, who was succeeded in turn by his son Alexander, his brother Adam I, his son Adam II and his son, William de Charlton II. William's son Edward occupied a defensible 'pele tower' at Hesleyside in 1343. In those days a pele tower provided the only alternative to living a life of continual movement, herding one's livestock before one, to escape successive onslaughts by English or Scots in cross-border raids. Hesleyside Hall, now a three-storey home just north of Hadrian's Wall, incorporates an ancient pele tower and stands beside the Hesley Burn which provides it with its own water supply.

In 1415 a Charlton from Hesleyside fought at Agincourt. By 1536 the Charltons had dropped the 'de' and an Edward was the leader in North Tynesdale of 'The Pilgrimage of Grace', a campaign by a number of Northumberland families to restore the Catholic faith. Edward was succeeded by his son William who became Commissioner for the Enclosures on the Middle Marches, in effect a land registrar. He was also a 'reiver', a cattle rustler, who with five hundred men led a raid on the Scott family, now Dukes of Buccleuch, at Cavers in Scotland on 12 October 1540, capturing the 'Buccleuch Sword'. During this time the 'Charlton spur' was, when occasion demanded,

served on a plate by the Lady of Hesleyside to the menfolk to indicate that meat supplies were low and, consequently, beef or mutton should be 'reived' from the Scots.

An Edward Charlton was commissioned in 1607 to raise one hundred men for service in Ireland. He was succeeded by his brother Matthew, who in turn was succeeded by his son Edward, who was knighted. Sir Edward Charlton raised a Troop of Horse for King Charles I; had his estates confiscated, then restored; and was proposed as Governor of Hartlepool but was not appointed after objections were raised that he was a Catholic. As his sons had died in infancy his title lapsed on his death and his brother William became head of the family.

Edward Charlton, born 1665, was on the Commission of the Peace for Northumberland in 1687; was tried for treason in 1689 and acquitted; and was succeeded by his son, William, who was High Sheriff of Northumberland, in 1722. In 1713 Hesleyside Hall was extended and a priest's hiding hole was discovered. The Charltons took no part in the Jacobite risings, a fact which saved the life of John Charlton, when he was pardoned by Queen Anne for fighting a duel.

Once again a William was succeeded by an Edward who was then succeeded by a series of Williams; William John, High Sheriff; William Henry, the instigator of a railway from Hexham to serve the North Tyne Valley; William Oswald, a diplomat; William Henry, High Sheriff in 1932 and a Captain in the Northumberland Hussars. He died in 1950 and Hesleyside passed to Mrs Mamie Charlton, who served in the Women's Royal Naval Service, and her husband and distant cousin Major John Charlton, formerly surnamed Anne, who served in Normandy and Burma and became the fifth Charlton to serve as High Sheriff of Northumberland.

The Charltons of Hesleyside have an unbroken succession of eight hundred years during which they maintained an allegiance to both the Crown and Catholic beliefs, a dichotomy that must have surely sometimes seen serious strain. When Henry VIII rejected the papal ruling against divorce the Charltons remained Catholic. All Catholic churches in Britain were confiscated. Catholics were frequently fined and some lost their land; a number were executed. They were not permitted to worship in public until 1829. They were excluded from 'Parliament, voting at elections, the Magistracy, holding public office, keeping school and teaching in any way'. At Hesleyside a secret chapel was built in 1810 to enable the Charltons to practise the Catholic form of worship.

While the Charlton succession is not the longest continuous Catholic family in Britain, its tradition of dual loyalty to King and Catholicism must have been a powerful influence on the young Edward Charlton. The family motto is 'Sans Varier' – 'Without Change'. Ned included the family crest, a lion rampant, on the cover of all his folios.

William John Charlton, born 1784, married Katherine Henrietta Cholmeley in 1809. In addition to their heir, William Henry, a second son Edward was born in 1814. Edward was educated first at Ushaw College and then for six years at the University of Edinburgh where he was awarded the degree of Doctor of Medicine in 1836.

After graduating Dr Edward continued his studies for two years in Paris and contributed a thesis entitled 'Pneumonia as it Affects the Aged'. He then lectured at the Newcastle-upon-Tyne School of Medicine at Durham University on Medical Jurisprudence and Practice of Physics. He was awarded an honorary Doctorate of Medicine and Civil Law by Durham University and was made an honorary member of the Royal Swedish Academy of Medicine. In 1870 Dr Edward Charlton became President of the British Medical Association and, in 1872, was elected Professor of Medicine and President of the Newcastle College of Medicine. He published articles on Lead Colic, Scarlatina and Leprosy as well as on historical subjects as diverse as 'Vestiges of the Catholic Faith in Scandinavia', 'Witchmania of the Last Four Centuries', 'Saxon Cross from Rothbury', 'Roman Copper Vessel Found Near Capheaton', and 'Danish and German Poetry and Romance'. On 25 May 1913 Dr John Hedley wrote to Ned: 'I was your father's clinical clerk in Newcastle Infirmary. He was considered the best physician in the North, and was besides, a most accomplished linguist. All the foreign sailors were sent into our wards . . . I remember (hearing of) his interview with Pope Pius IX, who paid him the compliment of consulting him professionally.'

Doctor Edward Charlton married in 1842 and became a widower without issue twenty years later. In 1864 he married Margaret Jane Bellasis. They had six sons and one daughter, the youngest being born after Dr Charlton died in 1874. The seven children were: Edward 'Ned' (1865–1937), William 'Willie' (1867–1922), Elise (1868–1949), Henry (born 1869, died as a child 1872), Oswin (1871–1941), George (1873–1943) and Frank (1874–1908). Ned's folios do not include a *curriculum vitae* for his mother, the daughter of Sergeant Bellasis, a Parliamentary lawyer whose duties included pleading in the House of Lords. However it is evident that Margaret Charlton was a remarkable woman educating six children, mostly as a widow, and launching five sons successfully into careers.

She died in 1914 aged seventy-six.

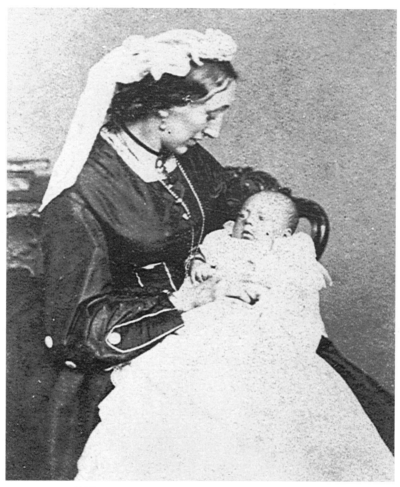

Eddie aged three months and Mrs Margaret Charlton, 1865.

Cadet Edward Charlton, aged 12.

Cadet Charlton
Joins the Royal Navy – 1878

Edward Francis Benedict Charlton was born on 21 March 1865 at Newcastle-upon-Tyne. He attended Ushaw Catholic College at Durham in Northumbria. His mother recorded an important incident:

Ushaw College; an experience in 1875: Dr Charlton (her late husband) having expressed a wish in writing that, if I could afford it, I was to educate my boys at Ushaw, I carried out his wishes and sent Edward, aged 10.

My mother came on a visit. We were sitting in the drawing room awaiting our dinner bell about 7pm when Eddie (Ned) opened the front door, rushed up the stairs and flung his arms round my neck exclaiming 'I could not help it! I could not help it. I have run away from the College. The boys would have killed me had I stopped!' It appears there were a good number of rough boys in his class recently entered and not observing the rule they were never to go beyond bounds without a Prefect. They had been to a small shop buying sweets, jam, sardines etc. and made Edward carry their purchases. He, being laden, dropped first one and then another, upon which the boys got angry. Dropping everything he rushed down into a quarry hard by where the lads pelted him with stones and sticks. Seeing a chance to escape he made for the station taking a ticket for Newcastle from Durham. I felt it was an error of judgement but I was bound to take him back as soon as possible; taking a flag (horse-drawn taxi) for Durham and arriving at the College about 10pm.

One of the Priests had been sent to Newcastle to inform me he was missing; the boys had described the scene at the quarry. My mother told the Priest that his (Ned's) mother had taken him back to Durham.

Hearing from the Head Master he had been flogged for running away I went to Ushaw and interviewed the Principals informing them I would remove Edward immediately, which I did. Theirs was the blame for allowing new boys to go beyond bounds unaccompanied by a Prefect. The Duchess of Norfolk obtained a nomination to the Royal Navy from Admiral Sir Hastings Yelverton. I sent him to 'Burneys' at Gosport from whence he passed brilliantly into Britannia at Dartmouth.

In August 1877 Ned took the required entrance examination at the Royal Naval Academy, Greenwich. The Admiralty informed him: 'In the event of your passing the examination it is to be understood that your Parents or Guardians will be prepared to allow the sum of fifty Pounds a year to you as a private allowance'. Churchill states that following the suffering and disgrace of the Crimean War, reforms at the War Office were long overdue. As a consequence, after a hard fight against Service opinion, the

'Eddie' (Ned) Charlton, aged 5.

purchase of commissions was prohibited by Gladstone's government in 1871. It appears, however, that some financial assistance by the family was still a prerequisite for young men aspiring to become officers. From August to December 1877 Ned studied at the Royal Academy, Gosport. When he left, Edward Burney wrote of him: 'No boy could have behaved better or made more satisfactory progress than he did here. Trust he will do as well in the *Britannia.*'

Edward Charlton joined the Royal Navy at the age of twelve years ten months: 'The Lords Commissioners of the Admiralty having appointed you Supernumerary Naval Cadet of Her Majesty's Ship *Britannia* . . . direct you to repair on board at Dartmouth, on 25 Jan 1878.' The training ship *Britannia*, the first Royal Naval Officer Training ship, was a wooden-sided battleship of 2,600 tons. It was roughly similar in design to Nelson's flagship HMS *Victory* and, as a man-of-war, had been known as the *Prince of Wales*. It was later extended and converted from sail to steam but, as a training college, its days were spent moored in the estuary of the River Dart in Devonshire.

Cadet Edward Charlton in 1878, aged 13.

Ned lists all the 1878 entrants to *Britannia* in his first folio and gives notes on their subsequent progress:

'The number of naval cadets commencing naval officer training in 1878 was 43.'
In addition, Princes Albert and George were there as regular cadets and were known as 'Sprat' and 'Herring'. One day an officer entered a rowdy class and asked who was the noisy culprit. One of the boys said it was Charlton but Ned was not, in his view, to blame. He picked up an inkpot and threw it at the squealer; unfortunately it missed its target and hit Prince George, who as King George V, jovially reminded him of the incident in later life.

'In the initial year nine cadets were "ploughed out" of *Britannia* [failed examinations] leaving 34.'
In the next four years as Midshipmen, three were dismissed, three resigned, one died and one, Edward Hay, a friend of Ned's, was killed in the Niger Expedition of 1883.

'The number appointed Sub-Lieutenant in 1884 was 26.'
The career of one of those who failed suggests that he was not naval officer material. T.S. Newbold was dismissed for forgery, became a cowboy in Texas, posed as a stockbroker and suicided. But in the next four years most of the Sub-Lieutenants were promoted to Lieutenant. In the next eight years eight more resigned, generally to settle and marry.

'The number promoted to Commander was 18.'
Of these E.L. Boyle became a Captain in the Royal Naval Reserve and won the CMG; C.E. Biscoe participated in the Pioneer Column to Rhodesia in 1892: 'The Union Jack was run up an improvised flagstaff by Lieutenant Tyndale-Biscoe

RN and formal possession of the country was taken in the name of Queen Victoria.' (*The Morning Post*, 12 September 1930); Harry Jones died of Bright's disease and F. Hammond of Malta Fever. I.T. Brandreth became Deputy-Governor of Bodmin Prison.

'The number continuing to Captain was 13.'
Another eight retired or died over the next few years.

'The number reaching Flag Officer rank was 5.'
Their class place in 1879, name, rank, and position held near retirement were:

2nd   Admiral E.F. Charlton, KCB KCMG. President, Naval Commission of Control, Berlin.
8th   Vice-Admiral D.R. de Chair, KCB MVO. Governor of New South Wales.
12th   Rear-Admiral S.A.G. Calthorpe, KCB CVO. Commander-in-Chief, Mediterranean.
18th   Admiral R.F. Phillimore, KCB KCMG MVO. Commander-in-Chief, Plymouth Station.
38th   Rear-Admiral E.F. Gaunt, KCB KBE. C-in-C, East Indies.

———— ∞ ————

Ned's folios include only one letter home from *Britannia*:
Dartmouth, 26 Oct 1879.

My dear Mamma, If you come down before prize day I shall be able to get leave to be with you. We are working very hard for exams now; most of us turn out at five in the morning instead of half-past six, and have an extra hour of seamanship in the evening.
P.S. A little money would be very acceptable.

———— ∞ ————

At the time Ned joined the Navy it was undergoing more significant transformations than had occurred in the previous two centuries. The changes included: replacement of sail by coal-fired steam engines; replacement of wooden hulls by ironclads; and replacement of rows of smooth-bored cannons ranged along both sides of the ship by rifled gun-turrets placed amidships. The first ship to incorporate most of the new elements, HMS *Captain*, was launched in 1870. Unfortunately the designer was compelled against his wish to include sails. This made the ship top-heavy; it capsized in a storm and most of its crew were lost including the son of Hugh Childers, First Lord of the Admiralty.

———— ∞ ————

At fourteen, Midshipman Charlton left Britain to complete his officer training overseas. The day he left he wrote:
HMS *Inconstant*, Portsmouth, 25 Feb 1880.

My dear Mother, I went on shore yesterday and had a grand dinner, the last in old England for three years. There is a great squash on board as there are 35 in the gunroom (about 25 feet by 12).

Ned's primary base for the next three years was to be Malta where he had relatives. Malta was one of a series of

Above: HMS Hindustan *and HMS* Britannia *at Dartmouth, Devonshire, 1879.*

Below: Seamanship Study, starboard side.

Above: Cadets landing boats.

Below: Cutter's Racing Crew.

major British military bases around the world and served as home port for the Royal Navy's Mediterranean Fleet.

———— ∞ ————

HMS *Hibernia* (base accommodation), Malta, 19 Mar 1880.

My dear Mother, When we got here, I went ashore and hunted out cousin Amy and Sir Adrian (Dingli), who have been very kind. I have been to dinner several times . . . There was a court-martial on board this morning on a blue-jacket (sailor) who had struck a ship's corporal. He got two years imprisonment with hard labour and dismissed the service. I had to attend with my dirk (short sword) and tail-coat.

———— ∞ ————

Ned's ship for Mediterranean duty, HMS *Alexandra*, was powered by both sail and steam and carried a Captain, Lord Walter Kerr, as well as the Admiral in charge of the whole fleet, Sir Beauchamp-Seymour.

HMS Alexandra, *Malta, 24 May 1881.*

HMS *Alexandra*, Malta, 4 Apr 1880.

My dear Mother, We are going out tomorrow for a month's cruise. Our food is very good; we have three meals a day with hot meat each time . . . the mess is a shilling a day, and that takes a good lot out of our pay. For instance this month:

Mess money	£1.11.0
Wine bill (average)	10.0
Extra bill (average)	13.0
Papers	2.0
Servant 10/- Man 2/6	12.6
Tailor (average)	1. 5.0
TOTAL	£4.13.6

Sir Adrian gave me his box at the Opera the other night and I took five others. 'Marie de Rohan' was acted but 'Faust' is tomorrow and I hope to get to it; it is all in Italian and I think it is very stupid. Walton must send me my dressing case as I shall want to shave soon.

———— ∞ ————

Ned wrote to his brother:

Sicily, 11 Apr 1880.

Dear Willie, I have bought a small pistol, silverplated, with ammunition for 15/6d. The last time I was in Malta I was

with another fellow called Taylor and I had brought my pistol with me intending to go to the polo-ground and practise shooting. It is about two miles from the town, Valletta, and we had walked about one when a four-wheeler passed and the man said he would take us there for 6d. So we got in; when we were about 300 yards from the polo-ground he stopped and said 'You pay me for de car', but we would not until he got us there. So he took a key out of his pocket, unlocked the box-seat and took out a large iron thing (a handle for a jack). As we would not pay him and he would not go on, we got out and walked away, then he levelled this thing at my head, so I took out my pistol (which was not loaded) and pointed it at his head. This frightened him awfully . . . he jumped on the box and drove off.

I think I will go in for the torpedo course when I am a Sub-Lieutenant as then you know 'The Secret' for which the Government paid Mr Whitehead 25,000 Pounds and you also get 2/6d a day extra. Besides there are no torpedos in small ships so they must put you in a large ship.'

———— ∞ ————

The Gunnery School of the Royal Navy was ancient and famous. The Torpedo School, HMS *Vernon*, was new and little known, having become a school in its own right only in 1876. Ned's decision in 1880 to choose 'torpedoes' as his speciality rather than the better known occupation 'gunnery' was to have a marked effect on his career, as the Torpedo School later became responsible for many major developments in the navy including telephone (demonstrated on board HMS *Vernon* by Alexander Graham Bell), electricity, radio, naval mines, depth-charges, balloons and aviation. Rivalry between the two schools remained intense for a century, the Gunners regarding the Torpedomen as untidy and undisciplined, and the Torpedomen ridiculing the Gunners as 'Gas and Gaiters'.

The word torpedo comes from the torpedo fish, or electric ray, a fish provided with electrical antennae for stunning its prey. The first successful torpedo was used in the American Civil War – 1862 to 1865. It consisted of a metal case containing 45 kg of explosive carried at the end of a spar projecting from a Confederate submarine, running awash, which hit and sank the Federal frigate *Housatonic* and, in the process, also sank itself.

From its invention in 1866, the Whitehead torpedo was the prototype of all subsequent torpedoes except electrically propelled ones. It was accepted by the Austrian Navy in 1868 and was 3.5 metres long and 400 mm in diameter. It ran 600 metres at seven knots. It weighed 300 kg and carried 30 kg of gun-cotton. A compressed-air engine drove a single screw. As it was intended to run straight there was no horizontal steering. Depth was controlled by vertical steering which was accomplished by 'The Secret', a hydrostat which operated mechanical levers and planes to control elevation and depression. It was rapidly adopted by the British and other navies and its speed was increased to twenty-seven knots by 1887. In World War I German torpedoes sank more than 5,700 ships, representing over eleven million tons

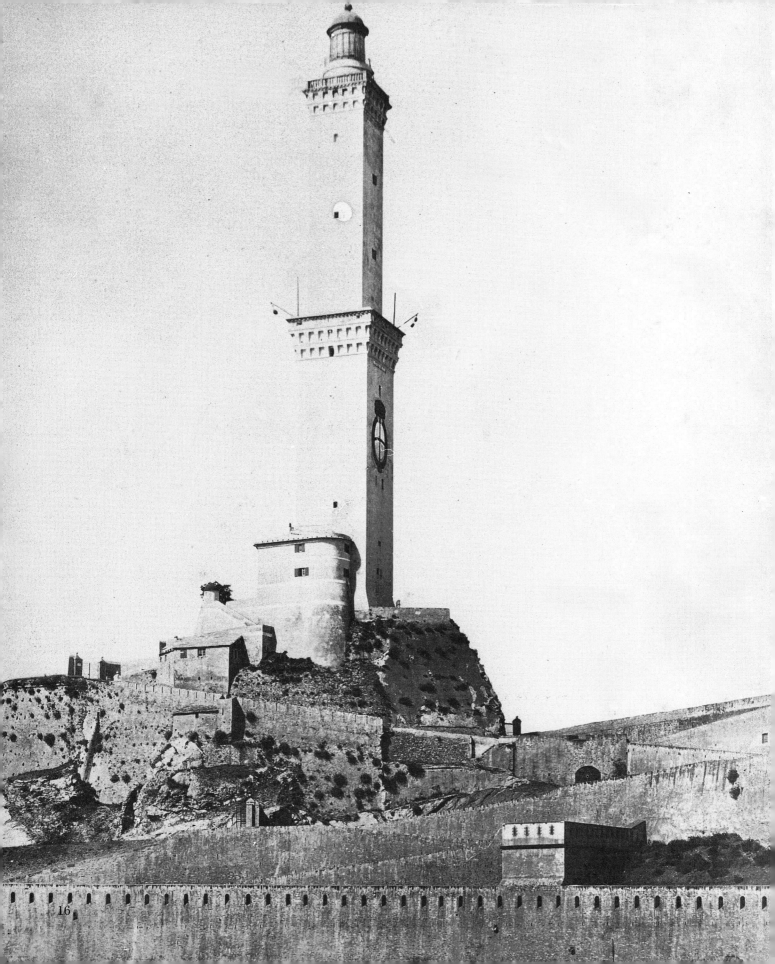

16

Above: Genoa Harbour – 1880.

Left: Lighthouse, Genoa – 1880.

Below: Panorama of Port at Genoa – 1880.

capacity, and came close to starving Britain by blockade. In World War II the Allies lost some twenty-three million tons of shipping, the torpedo again proving itself to be a major maritime menace.

———— ∞ ————

In April 1880 Ned wrote to his sister:

My dear Elise, I do not expect we shall stay out here more than two years and a half as the boilers are in very bad condition, so that if we are not capsized or blown up, or if I do not kick the bucket, you may expect to see me at the end of that time.

———— ∞ ————

Corfu, 25 Apr 1880.

My dear Mother, Lots of Albanians came on board and I bought a knife all covered with blood and three notches on it . . . since we have been in here we have been firing Whitehead torpedoes; we killed about 50 fish.

We went ashore to church this morning and the priest spoke English very well. It is a very nice place and it is easy to see that it once belonged to the English.

You seem to think that this (career) is very little better than being a bank-clerk! Let me tell you, there is about as much resemblance between these two things as there is between plum duff and dubbin.

———— ∞ ————

Civita Vecchia (Rome), 26 June 1880.

We left Naples for Bastia where I did not go ashore. A man came on board with a quantity of things such as trinkets, clothes, socks etc. and spread them out all over the deck; about a hundred blue-jackets and marines collected around him. I saw one marine take up a parcel of socks and stow it away in his breast, and walk off with it.

I sent a corporal down after him and took him before the Officer of the Watch . . . next day he was sentenced to 84 days' imprisonment.

Civita Vecchia, 3 July 1880.

As I had not been to Mass, I went to the church opposite the hotel. After this we saw St Peter's, the Colosseum and St Paul's. This morning I went with a party of officers from each ship to visit the Duilio *(an Italian ship). The most wonderful thing on board her is a tunnel, about 20 feet high and 48 yards long, in which two torpedo boats are kept. If she wants to get these out, she lets enough water in to float them, opens a stern door by hydraulic power and the torpedo boats steam out.*

———— ∞ ————

HMS *Alexandra*, Genoa, 14 July 1880.

Dear Mr Heathcote, You asked me to write to you. We have seen the Italian ironclads and their 100-ton guns; the general opinion in the fleet is that the Duilio *and the* Dandola *will break down as soon as they go to sea. They are trying to do what we have done in five hundred years in half as many months.*

———— ∞ ————

Villa Franca, 23 July 1880.

My dear Mother, We have been having some exams for the last two weeks. We had Steam and French today. I did the latter very well but knew nothing about Steam of which we have only had about two lessons. On Tuesday we fired 6 electric broadsides . . . one of our marines who had been ill for about a week died that night on account of the firing. He was buried the next day at sea; the service is very solemn.

There is a Yankee ship in here. Today one of them came on board and said, 'I guess and calkilate that we are going to show these Britishers how to drill this evening.' We happened to have the same evolution, down upper yards [lowering of the spars which support a square sail], which we did in 30 seconds but they took two minutes.

I send you a list of what will become of this month's pay . . . How can I exist for a whole month on 2/-?!

Lighthouse, Genoa – 1880.

Power Play
in the Adriatic – 1880

In 1876 the Turkish Ottoman Empire still occupied most of the Balkans. The Russians were making headway against the Turks and approaching the Dardanelles. The Western European powers were no more enthusiastic that the Russians should control the Balkans than that the Turks should continue to do so. In fact, Churchill states that Prime Minister Gladstone wanted Turkey 'to clear out from the provinces they have desolated and profaned'. A diplomatic solution was reached at the Congress of Berlin in 1878. Bosnia-Herzegovina was allocated to Austria, Russia kept Bessarabia, Britain received Cyprus, Bulgaria became independent and the Turkish Empire was reduced considerably. In his summary of the events Churchill ends on a laconic note clearly justified by subsequent events: 'No settlement could have been more than a temporary one.' Nevertheless the Congress of Berlin and the menacing power of the international fleet did ensure peace for thirty-six years. In 1880, Dubrovnik was known by its Italian name 'Ragusa'; Port Gravosa and Teodo Bay were nearby.

— ∽ —

Port Gravosa, 7 Sept 1880.

My dear Mother, We found four Austrians and a Russian [ship] here, and since then two Italians and a German have come in. Today we fired 21 guns in honour of the coronation of the Czar of Russia.

— ∽ —

23 Sept 1880.

The Captain left here last Saturday in the Helicon . . . I think he is going to Scutari to see about some Pasha that the Albanians have murdered. If he has been, what a nice little row there will be. All the Admirals came on board last night to hold another conference but, though I tried to listen down the Admiral's skylight, I could not hear much.

On Saturday we had a splendid picnic. There were about twenty of us and four Austrians. We had sausages, mutton chops, chickens and an unlimited supply of the best Hungarian wines from the Archduke's private cellar . . . The Archduke came rather late . . . We did not shove off till about 7 o'clock. We suddenly found one of our fellows was missing and had to lay off for an hour while a search was made. He was at last found asleep under a fig tree.

— ∽ —

Teodo Bay, 29 Oct 1880.

My dear Grandmamma, Thank you very much for the 3 guineas. On Wednesday we had a man killed by the fore-topgallant yard coming down with a run on his head.

— ∽ —

Teodo Bay, 4 Nov 1880.

My dear Willie, There has been a most brutal murder ashore here at a white house just opposite the ship . . . an old woman and her daughter living alone there had 1000 florins left to them. Last night about 8 or 10 brigands came down from the mountains behind the house and broke in the door. Having beaten the old woman and her daughter, they hung them by a rope from the ceiling. They were found soon after by some people passing, but the old woman was dead. The daughter had saved herself by catching hold of the rope with her hands and thus holding herself up. I had passed there a day or two before and asked for a glass of water which the old woman gave me.

On Monday morning one of the cook's mates tried to commit suicide. He jumped overboard; a man went after him and picked him up. This is a very unlucky ship; ten men have died since we have been in commission and five of these we have killed [presumably in accidents].

We are great friends with the Austrian officers who are the best fellows of the whole lot. The Russian midshipmen are great hulking brutes and their ships stink.

— ∽ —

Three letters to his mother from Malta follow:

14 Nov 1880.

On Monday we lit fires in all 12 boilers and had the yearly speed trial. We got up 15 knots but our average was 14½ which is very good for a ship like this. Next day we exercised firing torpedoes. The port aft torpedo, which was the one I was attending, was very nearly lost. It was set to go 240 yards and the air ought to have shut off. However the air leaked . . . we had given up all chance of picking it up and were steaming away when one of the signal men saw it floating quietly past. We found it had gone 2,000 yards.

— ∽ —

8 Dec 1880.

I am very sorry we were not at Teodo when the fleet left there. I will give you an account of it as you cannot believe the newspapers. The English got under way at 2 and wheeled round followed closely by the French; the speed was about 13 knots. The Italians could not get up more than 10; the Russians could not get under way at all. The Germans kept it up for some time, but had to give up in the end.

— ∽ —

20 Dec 1880.

We are having exams now, but we don't excite ourselves about them, as it is always best to get a bad place at first and a better one afterwards so that you are reported as having made progress. I wish I could afford to send you Xmas cards but my expenses, including white gloves for the dances, are too much.

— ∽ —

In 1881, Ned kept a handwritten daily diary:

2 Jan.   Called on Mrs Strickland. Lunched with Lady Dingli. Some very nice young ladies at Mrs Strickland's.

4 Jan.   An earthquake prophesied for tomorrow.
               Got main yard down.

————— ∞ —————

Ned also wrote to his sister from Malta:

Dear Elise, We tried to blow up (upset?) the parson at school with gunpowder; we kept putting it in the candles and blowing them out. He said he would stop our leave for a week, but just then a great explosion blew up several books and knocked a lamp down, so he reported us.

From the diary:
6 Jan.   Had my leave stopped with eight others.

————— ∞ —————

Below: The harbour at Nice, 1880.

Bottom: Austrian, British, French, German, Italian and Russian Fleets preparing for the International Demonstration off Bosnia in 1880.

Alexandra's *Bear*
– 1881

On 28 January 1881 Ned wrote home:

My dear Mother, On Monday we practised with the small guns; the vent piece of one of the Armstrong breech loading 20 pounders split into pieces.

The top part struck the captain of the gun and nearly killed him.

Found the Swedish frigate Vandis *here with the Crown Prince of Sweden on board.*

The Invincible *has got a new captain, Fitzroy. He went down in the double bottom (hull) today and caught a fish there; it was about six inches long . . . he sent for the mates of decks and told them that the ship stank from double bottom upwards; then he sent them on board here to see how we keep things clean.*

Two of our midshipmen had their leave stopped for an indefinite period for stealing brass from a small ship.

On Tuesday all the torpedo boats of the fleet were away firing Whiteheads. One of them went into our steam barge and made a frightful hole.

The bear we got from HMS Rapid *is very friendly. If you want to keep him quiet all you have to do is put your hand in his mouth and let him suck it. He put his nose to the Admiral's voice-tube and blew down; the Admiral whistled up again upon which the bear blew down as hard as he could and astonished the Admiral who had his ear against it.*

HMS Alexandra's bear.

Midshipman Grenville (centre) and the cast of 'HMS Pinafore'.

From the diary:

15 Jan.   The bear swam ashore very riotous and quite drunk. He tore Bacon's trousers to bits.

2 Feb.   Got an invitation from Miss Hill to go for drives on Friday and Saturday but had to refuse.

8 Feb   Went on shore to Bizazzas for egg-flips. Borrowed ten shillings from Michael.

13 Feb.   Lunched with Lady Dingli and Sir Adrian. Called on Capuchin Fathers Mullia and Emanuel. Very nice priests.

———— ∞ ————

Malta, 15 Feb 1881.

My dear Mother, We had very rough weather last week. The Decoy *came in and reported Lieut-Commander von Donop had been washed overboard from the bridge. . . .*

Willie will find the Merchant Service very rough. I had to stand enough knocking about at first and it is much worse in the Merchant Service.

———— ∞ ————

From the diary:

22 Feb.   Up (raise) lower yards and topmasts. *Invincible* first.

23 Feb.   (am) Knocked *Invincible* endways. *Alexandra* 1min 37 sec, *Invincible* 2min 1sec (Admiral looking on). (pm) Down upper yards. *Invincible* first.

———— ∞ ————

HMS *Alexandra*, Malta, 28 Feb 1881.

My dear Mother, There was a splendid performance of 'Pinafore' at the Opera House. It was got up by officers of the Army and Navy and of course plenty of ladies were found in

HMS Alexandra *(centre) and the fleet in Malta Harbour, May 1880.*

The Gun Room Officers, HMS Alexandra *– 1881.*

Malta who did not mind acting. Grenville, our smallest midshipman, was the midship-mite. He had about the best part as he had to chuck some of the ladies under the chin.

This morning we left harbour at 8am in company with Superb, Invincible, Hecla, Thunderer and Falcon. We went round Filfola Island, a rock about 220 feet high and 250 yards long. The Thunderer made the best firing but of course every shot struck. It was a splendid sight; you could see the broadsides of six huge shot rushing along at a frightful rate to the island; then all of a sudden you saw boulders weighing several tons flying through the air. The Superb fired a common shell on the bow [before she was abreast of the island] and this caused it to strike the rock at an angle so it glanced off and fell only 12 feet astern of Thunderer. It is my birthday on the 21st (aged 16).

———— ∞ ————

From the diary of 1881:

13 Mar.	Called on Mrs Strickland. Met Miss d'Amico there.
17 Mar.	Went out by myself for a sail in *Emmie* in the afternoon. Dutch gunboat *Surinam* arrived.
28 Mar.	Went on shore to practise for the athletic sports. Going to enter for the 220 yards and hurdle race.
29 Mar.	All officers were photographed with Admiral in foreground. Had a boil on my chin; I had to keep my hand over it.
30 Mar.	Got my proof photograph. Did not think it a bit like me. Ordered a dozen. Had hot poultices put on my chin.
2 Apr.	Ran in junior officers 220 yards with about 25 other fellows. And of course got the outside billet.
5 Apr.	Went on sailing boat with Allenby.
7 Apr.	*Thunderer* sailed with 2,000 tents, biscuits and some extra doctors for Khios.
11 Apr.	Received telegram saying that Uncle Frank had died in his sleep and telling me to tell Amy. I got leave and hunted Sir Adrian up in a lawcourt in

which he was sitting president and told him about it. He told me not to say a word to Amy. Poor Uncle Frank; I am quite sure he is happy. So ends that generation.

18 Apr.	Slipped and went out of harbour under steam. Made sail going out. Went 8 knots under all plain sail.
22 Apr.	At Naples. Saw Virgil's tomb. Bought some bawdy pictures.
2 May.	Porter went to Monte Carlo. Won 48 Pounds.
4 May.	Porter went to Monte Carlo and lost.

———— ∞ ————

Villa Franca, 5 May 1881.

My dear Mamma, On Thursday I received a letter from Aunt Clara saying that they would be in Genoa. I went to the Captain at once and got leave . . . I ran upstairs and met dear Grandmamma, Aunt Clara and Uncle Edward. Aunt Clara was great fun and told an awful lot of funny stories. She showed me the place in Genoa where Grandmamma first met Grandpapa (which reminded me of the National Gallery). Grannie gave me five Pounds and Aunt Clara a Napoleon. You must excuse the latter part of this letter being badly written as the bear is under the table and has been taking pieces out of my trousers and trying to digest my boots.

———— ∞ ————

Malta, 29 May 1881.

My dear Mother, I write to acknowledge the receipt of five Pounds which I paid to my tailor. Please do not think me extravagant as a suit of uniform costs nearly five Pounds. One of our fellows got a cheque for seventy Pounds the other day; fifty-two went to his tailor.

———— ∞ ————

HMS Hibernia *in Malta Harbour, 1880.*

From the diary of 1881:

24 May.	Queen's Birthday. God save the Queen at age 62. Ships dressed; fired salutes and soldiers fired *feux-de-joie*.
27 May.	Went on shore with de Laski. De Laski confirmed in Bishop's Palace. Lord Walter stood godfather.
3 Jun.	The bear went overboard at 5pm and we had to send the seaboat's crew after him.
4 Jun.	Went to dinner with the Admiral; sat next to Sandy.
7 Jun.	Got a scratch from the bear and had to go on the sick list.

———— ∽ ————

Argostoli, Cephalonia, 12 June 1881.

My dear Elise, I have had a bad leg for the last few days but it is better now. This town is a miserable place with no shops. Our band is going to play on shore. Fruit is very cheap. You can get as many eggs and cherries as you can eat for two pence.

———— ∽ ————

From the diary:14 June. Going through Ithaca Straits we passed the two Greek torpedo boats that came into Malta Harbour.

———— ∽ ————

Avlona, 19 Jun 1881.

My dear Mother, We have just received the dreadful news from the Monarch *that Gunnery-Lieutenant Baker has been killed and nine men injured by the explosion of a hand charge. I knew Lt Baker very well. Uncle Ed must remember him as the Lieutenant who gave us a glass of sherry in the wardroom. Those hand charges are the most dangerous things possible; you hold the pistol in your left hand, throw the gun-cotton with your right, firing it as soon as it is in the water. If you are the slightest bit nervous, you may pull the trigger while the charge is in your hand. Our Torpedo-Lieutenant had a very narrow escape of this, as the pistol went off but luckily there was a defect in the electric lanyard so that the charge did not explode. If it had gone off it would probably have killed the Admiral and the Captain as well as the Prince of Naples in whose honour we were having torpedo experiments.*

The Admiral lost his sword overboard this morning and is furious.

———— ∽ ————

From the diary of 1881:

20 Jun.	Passed the coast [near Albania, Montenegro and Bosnia]; a few brick houses and a cemetery. Why we had to make a

demonstration about such a place as this is inconceivable.

23 Jun.	While attending bathers I ran a man down in the gig. I saw somebody swimming down there when I was abreast of the buoys but I looked again and I suppose he must have dived as I saw nobody. Soon after that I felt his head against the boat.
24 Jun.	No school in afternoon as Mr Kenach felt rather seedy, with a bad cut on the back of his head.

———— ∽ ————

Curzola, 25 Jun 1881.

My dear Willie, I have just been put in the signals again as one of the signal midshipmen is sick and I am the only one they can rely on.

The bathing in Gravosa was splendid, the water being very little colder than our bodies. I hope you have learnt to swim and have conquered your dislike of the water.

You will be sorry to learn the old bear is losing its sight. One eye was put out in the Rapid *by a man painting it, and the other is getting a cataract over it.*

———— ∽ ————

Spalatro, 27 Jun 1881.

Any amount of boats came off to see the fleet as soon as·we anchored, some with very nice young ladies in them; and all the midshipmen got hold of a nice piece of 'gear' and took them round the ship.

I am supposed to be doing algebra. The old parson is walking up and down now just behind me but he does not suspect anything. I have just asked him for some more algebra questions so that he thinks I am working hard.

P.S. Tell Oswin [their younger brother] not to address my letters 'Master' Charlton.

———— ∽ ————

From the diary:

1 Jul.	Austrian Governor-General came on board and we saluted him. Any amount of people came on board and I had to take some awful 'gear' around.
4 Jul.	Maraschino is going fast. Lots of 'gear' came on board asking for it, and wanted us to go ashore with them.

———— ∽ ————

At sea, 5 Jul 1881.

My dear Mother, At Zara we anchored 300 yards from the shore; it is a large town nearly surrounded by water and is a great manufactory of Maraschino. Before we got here we paid 5d for a small liqueur glass full; now we pay only 1d. We bought 12 doz; have been drunk already. It is a very good liqueur; much better than can be got in England.

On Saturday we arrived at Lussin Island. There are two towns, one called Piccolo (small) and the other Grande (large), but Piccolo is the larger!

In the afternoon I went out with two other fellows for a pull (rowing). We landed on an island and employed ourselves in catching some large insects which made a frightful noise like birds chirping. We went back to the boat and I suddenly discovered I had lost my watch. I returned and we hunted for nearly an hour, but as the grass was three feet deep, we could not find it.

At general quarters we fired two broadsides . . . battering charges palliser shell, 2,535 pounds (1,150 kg), and 435 pounds of gunpowder; several shot came out of the racks (due to the vibration).

— ∞ —

From the diary:

7 Jul. At Trieste. Went ashore with Whyte by seven bell boat. Very big streets and lots of cafes. We wanted to find some women, but it was too early and none of them were out. We saw several very nice ones and any amount of bawdy shops.

12 Jul. Got a note from Willie saying he could swim.

Trieste, a painted panorama of the city and harbour.

Top and above: Venice in the eighteen-seventies.

Trieste, 12 Jul 1881.

My dear Willie, The bathing is really beautiful, awfully warm water; the great thing is to take a running jump from the top of the gangway, about 20 feet. I had not been in the water two minutes when I was stung by a large jelly-fish on my arm, and somebody sang out that there was a pilot fish (a sure sign that there is a shark near). The people here say they have often seen sharks since the Egyptian fleet came in here about 16 years ago.

———— ∞ ————

14 July 1881.

We went and watched the ladies bathing; they had a great barricade to keep off the sharks.

Some English ladies and gentlemen have just looked in to see the 'dear little midshipmen' (from 5ft 6in to 6ft 2in).

———— ∞ ————

Venice, 28 Jul 1881.

My dear Mother, Jones and I found a very nice hotel called 'Italia' with gardens on the Grand Canal. There were very few fleas about, but as we left the windows open any amount of mosquitoes came in.

———— ∞ ————

Malamocco, (undated)

My dear Mother, How kind of you to send me another watch; I hope it has got a third hand as it is the one thing necessary for taking time for gun drills.

———— ∞ ————

From the diary:

9 Aug.	Got a new watch from home . . . it seems a very good one.
14 Aug.	Metcalfe died of sunstroke.
15 Aug.	Sent funeral party on shore to inter the remains of the deceased. People on shore behaved very badly to them. Got Able Seaman Johns put in irons for calling me and Annis 'Bloody Irishmen'.
19 Aug.	Went on board *Invincible* to court martial at 9.30am. Mr Johns pleaded guilty so I had to give no evidence. He was sentenced to 12 months' hard labour.

———— ∞ ————

Termini, Sicily, 15 Aug 1881.

My dear Mother, The chief constructor who arranged the ventilation of this ship ought to be made to live down there in the after-flat, where we have to wash and dress; the men in cells have to be taken on deck every hour for air, and the sentry down there is supplied with a fan. I heard a man in cells say the other day that h *** was a trifle to it.

———— ∞ ————

At sea off Sicily, 21 Aug 1881.

Dear Willie, I will describe a scene on the quarter-deck last Friday afternoon; people are allowed on board without any distinction of class; three of the lowest class of women sitting around the capstan each with a naked baby; five other women, two dirty children and an ancient man sitting down on the port side just before the gangway and yelling across to two other people on the starboard side who are putting their dirty hands on the paintwork. Above all the beautiful odour peculiar to the nation. It is my afternoon watch, so I get hold of the bear, make him savage with a broom on the forecastle and then drive him aft on the quarterdeck. In about two minutes they have all made tracks, except one old lady, whom the bear caught by the petticoats which he was making short work of until rescued by a gallant marine.

These abominations of teetotallers have stopped our rum at last; the Admiralty has issued an order that all officers' rum is to be stopped at the end of this month. I should not have drawn my rum until I am eighteen.

———— ∞ ————

From the diary:

22 Aug.	*Superb* exercised her electric light in the evening; about the best I have seen out here.
24 Aug.	There was a row in the middle watch about my making cocoa in the gunroom, and the Commander gave orders that the gunroom was to be kept locked at night.

———— ∞ ————

HMS *Alexandra* at sea, 12 September 1881.

My dear Mother, We left Cagliari on the 1st. The next day was a very bad day for us as we lost our bear overboard. It was my first watch 8pm to 12. I was on the battery and the bear was in the first launch; the starboard side of the launch overhangs the ship's side about a foot. The bear was asleep in the bows and there were three midshipmen in the stern sheets smoking. The bear got up very sleepy and tried to get over the wrong side. When we saw her go to the wrong side we walked forward to haul her up again, but she let go and fell in the water. There was a cry of 'the bear's overboard sir' . . . If we had only stopped the ship she would have swum alongside; as for myself and the boat's crew we were quite willing to go away and ready too; but I think the Admiral thought there was some danger of the ship's screw going through the bottom of the launch. She was watched swimming in our wake until close by the Thunderer's bows . . .

(At Palma, Majorca) we had the regatta for the Admiral's Cup which was won by our barge. Our blue-jackets are very poetical:

> *The Alex's bear fell overboard,*
> *with all the fleet behind her,*
> *But none did care*
> *For the Alex's bear*
> *So we thrashed them for a reminder.'*

There was to have been a grand bull-fight in the arena on Sunday. I paid six shillings for my ticket . . . it came on to rain very heavily at about 1 o'clock. However we all left the ship at half past with oilskins etc. and made for the arena. When we got there we were told there was no bull-fight as it was too wet. It was an awful swindle . . . everybody was very sorry we missed it as, although it is a very cruel sport and not at all suited to English ideas, we wanted to see what was the Spaniards' idea of pleasure.

I got a letter from Elise; can't you manage to make her spell a little better, though her writing is very nice.

— ∞ —

At sea, 17 Sept 1881.

My dear Willie, I suppose you have already heard about the bull-fight where we were so awfully 'sold'. It was nearly as bad as the West Country 'sell' of Signor Soldino; it is always a great joke on board against West Countrymen. A Lieutenant RN had a bet that he would decoy over 30,000 people down to Plymouth under false pretences, so he advertised all over the west of England that Signor Soldino would fly across the harbour at Plymouth on a certain day. When the day came the railway companies had special trains running to Plymouth from all the big towns, even as far north as Bristol, and crowds of people assembled around the harbour to see him fly. They waited about four hours in drizzling rain and then someone passed the word around that it was a 'sell'. By the railway tickets alone they had 60,000 people so the Lieutenant won his bet but nobody knew who it was for several years after. Ask a West Countryman who Signor Soldino ('Sold' I know) is! Alexandra and Superb are East Country ships, but the Monarch and Invincible are West Country, so there are always great fights when the men are on leave.

We had a little excitement yesterday. When we got outside we set port studding sails (extension sails used in light winds). Just as they gave the order 'hoist away' a man was knocked overboard into the water; the Captain got awfully excited, three men went overboard after the man and they hove him round one of the life-buoys. After about two minutes the Captain seemed to realise that he was under sail. Then he made an awful mess of it for he braced up the headyards instead of letting go . . . However in about ten minutes the men were picked up.

— ∞ —

Gibraltar, 4 Oct 1881.

My dear Elise, Vice-Admiral Sir Beauchamp-Seymour GCB will probably be promoted to full Admiral at the beginning of next year and we shall probably go home about next July.

(Captain) Lord Walker asked me and another midshipman out riding with him yesterday. We rode along the beach for a long way, about seven miles, then forded a river and struck into a thick wood; after about four miles of this . . . a man told us to take the left-hand road over a bridge . . . after another four miles we were told we were utterly wrong . . . had a splendid feed under the trees: ducks, chickens, shellfish, beef and some very good country wine to wash it all down . . . We had a grand race along the beach coming back but, just as my horse was passing the first one, he suddenly stopped and began to groan. I had smashed my whip over him before so there was nothing for it but to walk him for a bit. I don't wonder that the horse dealers object to letting out their horses to Naval Officers . . . I cannot tell you how stiff I am today; we must have ridden about forty miles.

There is an awful difference between the English and Spanish sentries. The Spaniard has a dirty bayonet, filthy dress, lolls about anyhow, never salutes officers and is allowed to smoke while on duty.

— ∞ —

Port Mahon, 13 Oct 1881.

My dear Mother, The Navy temperance man, Mr Trevelyan, is coming on board here for a cruise when we go to Malta . . . he is going to be made to work from midnight to 4am in the stoke-hole, and then we are going to give him his own oatmeal drink [that he recommends in place of rum] for the stokers.

— ∞ —

From the diary:

20 Oct.   We are going to give a grand ball when we get back to Malta. Lord Walter has offered fifty Pounds and all of us are to give a Sovereign each.

— ∞ —

Syracuse [Sicily], 25 Oct 1881.

My dear Mother, I shall try for a small ship next time, as you learn more about seamanship in a bugtrap than in a flagship.

— ∞ —

From the diary of 1881:

3 Nov.   Saw Aunt Barbara and Veva.
5 Nov.   Portuguese gunboat *Rio Duoro* arrived.

HMS Minotaur, *Port Mahon.*

8 Nov.   Called on Fathers Emanuel and Costa. Fr Costa told me that Veva was engaged to be married to a Marquis de Sien. I asked her about it and she seemed rather vexed about it, although I told her it was only a yarn amongst old monks.

12 Nov.   I hear that Willie has got effusion of the knee-joint from an accident on the (Merchant Navy Training Ship) *Conway.*

14 Nov.   I wish I could hear something from Willie.

15 Nov.   Got a letter from Willie . . . his leg is not serious.

21 Nov.   Went on the range and fired 102 which just makes me a first class shot. An improvement on last year's 72.

—— ∞ ——

Ned and his brother Willie obviously enjoyed questioning each other about their knowledge of seamanship:

Malta, 22 Nov 1881.

My dear Willie, Answers to your seamanship questions:
(1) Clew of topsail gone. Take the bowline up through a block on the topsail yard and haul up the leech of the sail to the yard . . .
I send you questions in return:
(1) What lights does a 'broken adrift lightship' hoist? . . .

From the diary:

1 Dec.   Grenfell made 124 at the range.
2 Dec.   Went to bazaar for Wesleyan Chapel. Called on Aunt Barbara who said it was wrong to go to this bazaar and we had a great argument about it. Had a fine flirt with Veva.
8 Dec.   Danish gunboat *St Thomas* arrived.

—— ∞ ——

Malta, 10 Dec 1881.

My dear Elise, Our ball was a splendid affair and the decorations were beautiful. The ballroom was hung with flags and trophies of officers' swords and midshipmen's dirks. There were 750 invitations accepted; about 300 ladies and 400 gentlemen came. Lots of gentlemen however were non-dancers so that nearly everybody who wanted a dance could get one. Sir Adrian and Lady Dingli and Veva were there, but I could not dance with anybody, as I am always afraid of treading on the ladies' toes or dresses with my delicate hooves. Supper began shortly after twelve and I took a lady in. Afterwards we went into one of the most sheltered nooks for four dances although she was engaged to somebody else for each one.

—— ∞ ——

From the diary:

10 Dec. My bad head has gradually worked off.

———— ∞ ————

Ned gives a breakdown of costs for the ball:

RECEIPTS		EXPENSES	
By subscription £250.12. 6		Decorations, flowers	£20. 2 . 3
		Banners, rosettes	10.18 . 7
		Stationery, programmes	21.18 . 4
		Cloak rooms	2. 8 . 4
		Wines, etc.	69. 6.11
		Supper	95. 0 . 0
		Ballroom hire, crockery	
		breaks, club servants	39. 7 . 0
Balance deficit	23. 2. 9	Workmen, band	14.13.10
TOTAL	£273.15. 3	TOTAL	£273. 15. 3

The above deficit has been made up by supplementary subscriptions.

———— ∞ ————

Malta, 12 Dec 1881.

My dear Mother, The wardroom gave a farewell dinner for Lord Walter last night. He told me he had a letter from you lately, and asked me for your address.

———— ∞ ————

Lord Walter wrote to Ned's mother:

Malta, 11 Dec 1881.

Dear Mrs Charlton, I am very sorry to leave Alexandra, *but as the move is an upward one for me I could not refuse the offer.*

I am glad to give you a very good account of your boy. He has never given me any anxiety and does all he has to do enthusiastically and well. (sgd) Walter (Lord Walter Kerr).

———— ∞ ————

From the diary:

19 Dec.   We had Lord Walter's Certificates given us today. I got 'much', the majority got 'to my satisfaction'. Powley got 'he has always done as he was told'.

CERTIFICATE: Mr Edward Francis B. Charlton has served on HMS *Alexandra* from 18 Jun 1880 to 16 Dec 1881 with sobriety and much to my satisfaction. Signed Walter T. Kerr.

———— ∞ ————

Malta, 21 Dec 1881.

My dear Mother, I don't go in for dancing at all. I don't care for it. I suppose you will say I am shy; never mind, I prefer

sitting the dances out to dancing; but of course I don't sit out with ugly girls.

We make dark holes at all the dances with a cushion in the corner and a curtain hung in front, so that people outside can only see the feet of the couple inside. Aunt Barbara said it was very wicked to make these places, and Veva said she thought so too, but unfortunately I had seen her in the darkest one of all, so when Aunt Barbara went out, I made her acknowledge it.

You will be interested to know I have to shave twice a week.

———— ∞ ————

From the diary:

21 Dec.   Dance on *Temeraire* from 2 to 6pm but could not go. Hear Veva was looking very well there.

22 Dec.   Went on shore in afternoon and saw Aunt Barbara and Veva, who was very done up.

24 Dec.   Went on shore to confession at the Jesuit Church.

25 Dec.   Went to Monsigneur Vertu's chapel with my cousins and dined with them afterwards.

26 Dec.   Sent Veva a Christmas card.

———— ∞ ————

At sea, 8 Jan 1882.

My dear Willie, This is the roughest weather we have had since we left England. A tremendous sea came into some of our midshipmen's hammocks. The parson was so sick that he could not take us to school. I put on my oilskin to go rounds this morning and I was coming aft with a fair wind when the oilskin got round the foresheet and was instantly torn to pieces . . . don't you envy me. All this for 1/6d a day.

———— ∞ ————

Corfu, 30 Jan 1882.

The Admiralty has issued an order that ships are not to shift topmasts for drill, as there is generally someone killed. But old Sir Beauchamp does not care a bit.

———— ∞ ————

Corfu, 5 Feb 1882.

On Wednesday afternoon the First Lieutenant always takes us for seamanship for an hour and he said we were to go out sailing in the pinnace. There was a strong breeze blowing with a nasty choppy sea and as the pinnace is a very nasty sea boat, we asked him for the launch instead but he said we had to have some practical seamanship, and by Jove, it was practical with a vengeance. There were six mids, six blue-jackets and the 1st Lt. A sudden squall struck us, the water rushed in over the lee gunwale and over she went. I tried to get my coat off but could not; at first I

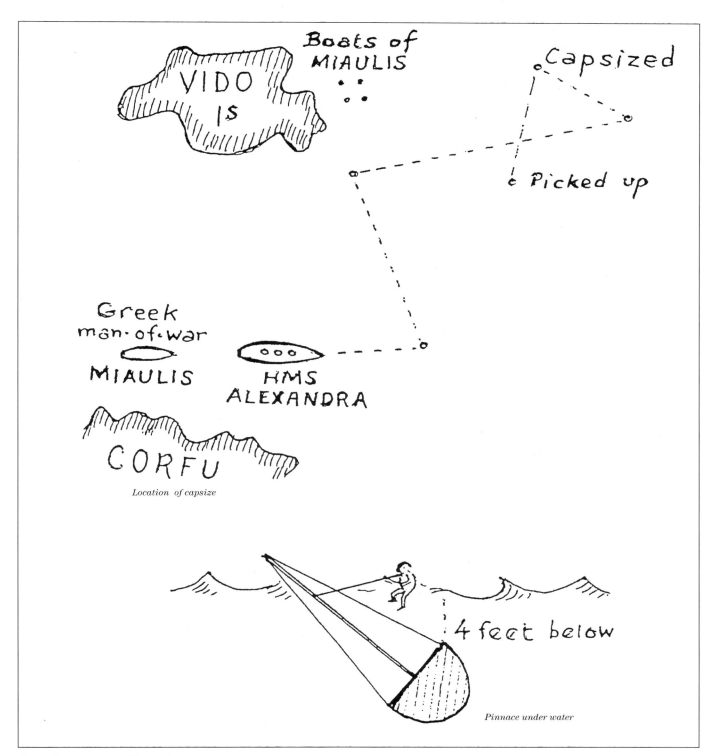

Ned made some sketches of the capsize.

thought it rather a joke but when I saw our distance from the ship it was no joke at all. In about five minutes one man called Phipps began struggling but he was kept up by some of us. Gradually several men began to strike out, and it was becoming serious. At last somebody sang out that there were some Greek boats quite close to us and everybody bucked up. The first two boats picked nearly everybody up but I hung on, with Phipps by me, for the third boat. Suddenly the pinnace came to the top near us and I made for it, but before I could get there Phipps dragged me under twice. Luckily I found a rope's end and lashed him on securely to the gunwale and kept his head above the waves breaking over us. He was quite insensible when he was dragged in by the Greeks. It was lucky the Greek boats were out exercising and were near us. We went on board the Miaulis *next day and thanked the Greek midshipmen for picking us up.*

———— ∞ ————

Malta, 18 Feb 1882.

My dear Mother, I find I must send you my tailor's bill as I cannot afford to pay it off now as there have been so many subscriptions, dances, balls etc.

———— ∞ ————

Malta, 4 Mar 1882.

I received the bank note for 20 Pounds today and I paid the tailor's bill at once. I thought you would be very angry, but how kind you are, dear Mother.

Naples, 31 Mar 1882.

My dear Elise, We saw all over Pompeii. I was rather disappointed until I saw statues and pillars being brought to light after eighteen centuries.

———— ∞ ————

Malta, 15 Apr 1882.

The Undine *and the* Harrier, *two schooner yachts bought by the Admiralty for stopping the slave trade in the Mozambique Channel, have just arrived from Portsmouth. They have experienced seven gales. The* Undine *had all her bulwarks smashed in; this is the kind of ship I would like to be in when I am Sub-Lieutenant.*

I am Midshipman on the 1st Cutter now, and have got charge of a field-gun and a Gatling gun when we land a battalion.

———— ∞ ————

The Bombardment of Alexandria – 1882

The ancient Egyptians built a boat canal linking the Mediterranean and the Red Sea in 1300 BC. This was abandoned in the eighth century. In 1854 the French Consul obtained permission from Said, the Turkish Governor of Egypt, to build the Suez Canal. The necessary capital was subscribed by the French, the Turks and Said. In 1875 the British bought Said's forty-four per cent from Said's successor, the Khedive Ismail, and an Anglo-French alliance gained effective control not only of the canal but also of the Egyptian Government. The Khedive retained nominal control. Access by all nations to the Canal, which reduces the distance from Britain to India by 5,000 miles, was guaranteed by the Constantinople Convention. In 1881 Colonel Arabi led a popular nationalist revolt against the Khedive and a consortium of nations went to the Khedive's rescue. A report is given in 'The King's Ships': 'In July 1882 *Alexandra*, commanded by Captain Charles Hotham, and flying the flag of Admiral Sir Beauchamp-Seymour, lay at Alexandria at the head of 14 ships. On 11 July the *Alexandra* fired the first shot, the Egyptians having refused to surrender. The *Alexandra* received a 10 inch shell through an unarmoured portion of her side, which lodged on the main deck with the fuse burning. Gunner Israel Harding picked up the shell and immersed it in a tub of water. For this act he received the Victoria Cross.' Britain retained troops at the Suez Canal until 1956.

HMS *Alexandra*, at sea 35 miles from Corfu, 15 May 1882.

My dear Willie, On the war-trail again. Just as I was going ashore with the Catholics, the Admiral comes on deck and says, 'Make a signal: Prepare for sea immediately. Steam up for 8 knots.' The yarn is that Arabi has corpsed the Khedive, there is an awful row in Egypt and we are to support the Egyptian Government. We took 1 hour 24 minutes from the time we got the telegram till we were ready for weighing the second anchor. Wait till I land with the field-guns; perhaps we shall all get medals yet. We expect to get to Suda Bay at 10 o'clock tomorrow morning and we only hope the Turkish Fort will open fire on us.

Khania, Suda Bay, Crete, 16 May 1882.

We have just got in here. It is a very deep harbour surrounded by high hills. We all bathed this evening.

HMS Alexandra *after the bombardment; shot-hole through the funnel.*

Suda Bay, 20 May 1882.

My dear Mother, I must tell you about our paper chase here. (a game in which a few horsemen called hares spread a paper trail and many other horsemen, starting later, follow the trail and try to catch the hares). All morning we were tearing up paper until we had about four mail-bags full. We all got horses and for an extra 6d I got one belonging to one of the officers of the Turkish ship Insha Allah. *Our hares got away about 1.45pm. and we gave them twenty minutes' start. After about an hour's hard riding we sighted the hares and they separated. I followed one of them with two other fellows, but for some reason I thought the other would be easier to catch . . . I found that everybody was out of sight. I went across country in the direction I thought they had gone . . . I got in a deep gully and thought I would make a rush and get up the other side. I got up all right but both stirrup leathers went and, as I was close by a house, I went in. There was an old Pasha (high-ranking Turk) there and he gave my horse to an attendant, made me squat down and gave me cigarettes and some kind of liqueur. As soon as the leathers were all right he took me round his gardens, gave me a bouquet of splendid roses and showed me the way to Khania . . . I left him with many courteous acknowledgements and as I went past a house I saw some of the ladies of his harem walking in the garden. They looked very astonished and covered up their faces with a kind of thick white veil . . . I came across one of the hares soon after and caught him and we rode into Khania.*

The Cygnet *came in with the sad news of the death in Malta of one of our Lieutenants, Mr Lake, from fever. The* Bacchante *arrived with Prince Edward and Prince George.*

— ∞ —

Suda Bay, 28 May 1882.

My dear Elise, We had the regatta last Thursday and this ship won a lot of prizes. There were two races with the Turkish man-of-war . . . they splashed and pulled a very quick stroke while our men took a good long stroke, making their boats move about twice as fast. The Superb *beat us;* Bacchante *came third with Prince George steering. Prince Albert is as big a gawk as ever, but Prince George has improved awfully. (Prince Albert, elder son, always frail, died when only 27.)*

— ∞ —

Off Alexandria, Egypt, 2 Jul 1882.

My dear Mother, All the ships are dressed in honour of the Sultan's birthday. I was sent into Alexandria harbour in my cutter yesterday with delicate machinery and 2,000 Pounds in gold.

(Colonel) Arabi's guns on shore are loaded and trained on us, but we (in turn) could smash up the whole place (with the ship's guns). I hope this row comes to something, as we shall be so frightfully jeered at when we get home if we don't

do something. Our old Admiral is now called 'Demonstration Beechie'. We all feel so war-like here and they won't let us blaze at them.

— ∞ —

The diary gives the following list of ships off Alexandria:

British:	*Invincible, Monarch, Beacon, Condor, Bittern, Helicon, Cygnet, Decoy, Alexandra, Temeraire, Iris, Superb, Sultan, Inflexible, Penelope.*
French:	*La Galissonnière, Alma, Thetis, Bisson, Hirondelle, Forbin, Aspic.*
American:	*Galena, Lancaster, Quinnibeg.*
Egyptian:	*Mahroussa, Mehemet Ali* and two troop ships.
Greek:	*Hellas, King George.*
Russian:	*Asie, Zabiaca.*
Dutch:	*Marnise.*
Turkish:	*Idzeddin.*
Austrian:	*Laudon.*
Italian:	*Castelfidardo*
Spanish:	*Saragossa*

No doubt Ned would have been well aware that at the Battle of the Nile in 1798 – just off Alexandria – Admiral Sir Horatio Nelson engaged in the most successful naval victory ever achieved by a British fleet. With his twelve battleships, including one called *Alexander*, he destroyed almost the whole of a thirteen battleship French fleet by attacking them at nightfall and, in a tactic then unprecedented, fighting on through the night.

— ∞ —

Off Alexandria, 7 Jul 1882.

My dear Willie, This is the strongest fleet of all nations I have ever seen together. There is a boat's passage in between the lighthouse [under Arabi's control] and the breakwater. It is very narrow and you have to be very careful going through it when there is any swell. I have been in there nearly every day this week and can shoot the passage splendidly under sail now. I have to go in for mails and despatches. Last Wednesday I left the ship under sail in my boat with the Commander and Torpedo-Lieutenant to reconnoitre the works. We stood through the passage, and then ran her up in the wind, so as to stop her way and went aground under the lighthouse battery. This was only a feint, and while we were getting her off we had a good look at the fort. The Admiral told Arabi that if anything more was done to the fortifications he would take it as an insult and would let them have it.

— ∞ —

10 Jul 1882.

Hurrah, we bombard the forts at 5am. The common shell for the first round are labelled. My round has 'Cough mixture for Arabi Bey'.

13 Jul 1882.

At 6.40 we fired the challenging shot; just after heard their first shot drop astern of us. As we are not allowed to cheer there was tremendous clapping and we let rip with our broadside of 2,535 pounds. I was in the main battery. At 7.30 the lighthouse battery was silenced, at 8.30 Fort Pharos was silenced, at 9.00 a small magazine blew up, at 11.00 Fort Ada blew up. The only one left was the Montcrief. My guns burst two common shells over this battery one after the other and each time new men came but our third shot went into the embrasure and dismounted the gun and, by Jove, in ten minutes I am blowed if they were not seen trying to mount it again but our Nordenfelt soon stopped their little game.

About 12 o'clock, as our broadside was not firing, I was sent up the main top to have a few rounds out of the Gatling. When I was about half way up I heard a 'whish' but I knew it was no good trying to get out of the way so I continued running up aloft; just after I felt a kind of blow on my legs and I looked down and saw that a round shot had just cut away the shroud about two feet below where I was; very lucky I did not stop and try and get out of the way.

A 9 inch Palliser shell came through the fore part of the foremost funnel and blew up the steam launch killing one man.

Captain Fisher's ironclad train, Alexandria, July–August 1882.

Ras-el-Tin Palace, Alexandria, 27 Jul 1882.

My dear Mother, On the 13th we landed marines and the next day I went ashore with the blue-jackets. Every Arab we saw carried a flag of truce. When I was going round at 2am we saw three men climbing over the wall with loot of some kind. When they saw us they dropped it and ran. We rushed after them, caught two, but the other one was getting away so we brought him down with a shot in the leg. One of these men has since been shot and the other two got four dozen (lashes).

In the morning Arabi sent twenty (railway) engines into the station to get provisions and coals. I was sent with a torpedo party down to the lines and when we saw the engines coming with a flag of truce up (Arabi's little game) we blew up the line with gun-cotton so Arabi lost 20 engines.

On Monday we were sent down to this Palace as a bodyguard for the Khedive. They say that the enemy had from 1,800 to 2,000 killed or wounded.

My dear Willie, Last Friday our two companies were suddenly ordered away from the Palace of Ras-el-Tin. We marched to the principal railway station when we got into what is called the 'ironclad train'. It consists of two empty trucks in front to blow up any mines there may be on the line; then comes an engine covered with sand bags; then a truck covered in boiler plates with a Nordenfelt and two Gatlings mounted on it; next comes our three carriages. We went about 2,000 yards past our lines. Arabi fired three rockets which went over the train and two shells which fell short and then sent out a thousand cavalry and infantry. Our forts fired the forty pounders at them and the first shell burst amongst the cavalry and stopped them. Next day de Chair, the other Midshipman of my company, disappeared and search parties were sent out but nothing was heard.

Landing troops at the Khedive's palace after the bombardment of Alexandria.

Alexandria, 13 Aug 1882.

My dear Mother, Our prisoner messmate de Chair is getting on all right at Cairo. He wrote to us last week but his letter (nearly all about what a good fellow Arabi was) had evidently been coached. They are pretty certain to give us all a medal for this action as there is a Royal Duke out here now.

An [Egyptian] gentleman wrote to Captain Thomas the other day: 'Sir, I beg to inform you that one of the Inflexible's shells with a live fuse in it is in my drawing room and I would be much obliged if you would have it removed.' The shell weighs 15cwt and stands 4ft 3in high.

∞

29 Aug 1882.

I had a letter from dear Grandmamma on Sunday. She calls this the dark side of my profession but nobody seems to consider it so and I think myself very lucky in coming in for it.

Just heard we had 120 killed and wounded yesterday.

∞

On 9 September 1882 Midshipman Charlton transferred from HMS *Alexandra* to a sailing ship, HMS *Cruiser.*

Midshipman de Chair was released. He, Allenby and Charlton were among only six officers from HMS *Alexandra* who attended the fiftieth anniversary dinner commemorating the Bombardment of Alexandria held at the United Services Club, Pall Mall, London on 11 July 1932.

CERTIFICATE: Mr Edward B. Charlton served as a Midshipman on HMS *Alexandra* from 17 Dec 1881 to 8 Sept 1882 with sobriety and to my satisfaction. Mr Charlton was present at the Bombardment of Alexandria and landed with Naval Brigade. Promising young officer. Signed Captain Chas Hotham.

∞

HMS *Cruiser*, Malta,
21 Sept 1882.

My dear Mother, Don't write any more to get me out of this ship; now that everything is over I am only too glad to be here and learn a little seamanship. Captain Darwin is a very good man to have for a Captain although rather rough in his language to us occasionally. Our 1st Lieut Farquharson is an awfully smart little fellow; most men say that if it were not for him the ship would have gone down long ago. She was once a steamer and fired the first shot in the Chinese war, thirty years ago . . . Her armament is now reduced . . . One great advantage is there is no coaling, smell of oil or rattling of engines on board.

Interior of the lighthouse fort at Alexandria after the bombardment.

HMS Cruiser, *a sailing ship, Malta.*

Corfu, 15 Oct 1882.

We left Malta on Friday. I never had such an enjoyable passage in my life; no row of engines.

I went ashore to church this morning with the Catholics. The Greek priest read an English sermon but we did not find out it was English until he had nearly finished.

———— ∞ ————

Corfu, 19 Nov 1882.

My dear Elise, We were at Butrinto last week and I went out shooting with Martin. It was raining hard but we got 15 couple of snipe and two plovers between us.

———— ∞ ————

Corfu, 31 Dec 1882.

Dear Grandmamma, I got your present for which I must thank you. We spent a very pleasant Christmas Day here and had the lower deck beautifully done up with effigies of Arabi.

Admiral Lord Alcester, formerly Sir Beauchamp-Seymour, is here taking a rest after the fatigues of the Egyptian war. He has a fine house on shore and has his band play in the square every evening. He has asked me to dinner tonight as I belong to his own ship. I must say I would much rather not go as I don't fancy dining with these great nobs.

Corfu, 1 Jan 1883.

My dear Mother, I dined on shore last night with Lord Alcester and he told me that I was going home with the Alexandra's old crew. The Admiral gave us a very good dinner.

The average amount of duff made on Xmas day for each man was 3½ pounds and next day any amount of them went to the doctor.

Although Ned's only surviving handwritten diary is for 1881, there are occasional typewritten extracts from a diary in his folio for 1883. There are very few letters home in 1883 when he was on duty in Britain or the North Atlantic.

———— ∞ ————

Extract from diary:

5 Jan.	I got my leave stopped for a month because the foretopmast would not get upright; all through No. 1's pig-headedness.
8 Jan.	Had to go twice in the pinnace with officers. Awful shame, I think, to drag 13 men and a Midshipman away in the rain and keep them waiting just because two officers want to go mashing (drinking).

Opposite: HMS Neptune, *alongside at Gibraltar.*

Corfu, 10 Jan 1883.

My dear Mother, I never mention my own health to you because I have never had a day's sickness since I have been out on this station. I have only once been in the sick-list and that was from a dig in the leg by a marlin spike which came down from aloft.

— ∞ —

Extract from diary:

22 Jan.   Called on Mrs Strickland. She gave me four boxes of oranges for different people and a kiss for her son at Windsor.

CERTIFICATE: Mr Edward F. B. Charlton served as a Midshipman on HMS *Cruiser* from 9 Sept 1882 to 27 Jan 1883 with sobriety and attention and entirely to my satisfaction. Signed Commander Se. Darwin.

— ∞ —

At home on leave in England. Extracts from 1883 diary notes:

1 Mar.   Had my first experience of hunting the wily fox and enjoyed it immensely. Had two horses and came off first in about two minutes. Found [the fox] close by here but lost after 25 minutes' run. Lots of jumps; only came off once more.
5 Mar.   Assisted at Uncle Henry's first Mass.
8 Mar.   Lancaster. Got my medal.
21 Mar.   Tynemouth. Willie arrived at 7am. I rushed down from the bath-room to the front door to open it for him and put my fist and fore-arm right through the glass. Bad gash; the doctor stitched me up beautifully.

21 Mar.   Oswin and Frankie had to be licked for smoking on the sly.

From March 1883 to June 1884 Ned served on HMS *Neptune*, a full rigged barque with engines and two funnels placed side by side. The ship had formerly been the *Independencia* of the Brazilian Navy.

— ∞ —

Below: Channel 2 Squadron at target and lower boom torpedo practice, 1883. HMS Neptune *firing.*

Main Picture: HMS Neptune, *HMS* Sultan *and HMS* Agincourt *alongside at Gibraltar 1883.*

CERTIFICATE: Edward F. B. Charlton served as a Midshipman on HMS *Neptune* from 28 Mar 1883 to 17 June 1884 and conducted himself with sobriety, zeal and attention to his duties – a personable young officer. Sgd M.T. Maxwell.

Ned also spent time at the Royal Naval College, Greenwich, in the same class as the future King George V.

———— ⟨∞⟩ ————

Extracts from 1883 diary notes:

17 Apr.	Portsmouth. Her Majesty passed in the *Alberta*. Had a good view of the old lady.
14 May.	Plymouth. Went on shore; found a letter from Mother to say she would be here today and on coming back who should I see on the poop but my dear Mother herself.
2 Jun.	Vigo (Spain). Fine long bay with islands at the mouth.
18 Jun.	Arosa Bay. Went in with stewards in the morning. A d*** swab called McDonald got drunk in the forenoon and the Commander makes out that the liquor came on board in my boat. No proof whatever and not likely to be.
2 Aug.	Queenstown (Ireland; now Cobh, Eire) very pretty, fine harbour and river.

———— ⟨∞⟩ ————

The next four months were spent on a further voyage to Ireland, Spain and Gibraltar. In February 1884 Ned's brother William married Teresa Walmsley.

In December 1883 Ned took an examination in arithmetic, algebra, geometry, trigonometry, mechanics, theory of steam, practical and theoretical navigation, charts, and French. He obtained only 986 marks out of a possible 2,400.

The previous year he had explained to his mother: 'How we pass for Sub-Lieutenant: After we have served four years as Midshipmen we have to pass in seamanship; it is a *viva-voce* exam before a Captain and two Commanders. Full marks are 1,000, 900 is 1st Class, 750 second class and 600 marks must be obtained to pass. Besides this our logs, certificates and papers are examined and we have to take about 100 sights in the last six months. After we have passed we go home and have to be in Greenwich on the 13th of the month after we reach England. We remain there for nearly a year and pass out in navigation which includes all mathematics and pilotage. Then we go to the gunnery ship HMS *Excellent* and pass in gunnery and torpedoes. After that we are full-blown Sub-Lieutenants and have to wait for promotion which depends principally on how we pass.' In June 1884 Ned took the final exam for Sub-Lieutenant.

CERTIFICATE: Mr Edward Charlton has served on the *Britannia* for 182 days and on the *Q. Adelaide*, *Inconstant* and *Alexandra* for 182 days as a Naval Cadet, and on *Alexandra*, *Cruiser* and *Neptune* for 4 yrs and 1 day as a Midshipman. We have strictly enquired into his professional knowledge and all details of an Officer's and Seaman's duty and state our opinion of his proficiency:

	Full No	Nos obtained
State of his Log Book from the date of his first appointment and if it contains Tracts, Charts etc.	75	70
Aquaintance with Stowage in Ship's Holds.	75	70
Knowledge of Masting Ships, Fitting Rigging and Sails, Laying out Anchors Sheers and practical knowledge of a Seaman's duty	400	385
As Officer of a Watch, Working and Manoeuvring Ships under all circumstances of Wind and Weather	300	270
Knowledge of Flags and Signals, Manner of performing Evolutions of a Fleet, including Semaphore and Morse Code	100	100
Knowledge of Regulations for avoiding Collisions at Sea	50	50
TOTALS	1,000	945

and are of the opinion that he is able to perform the duties of Officer of a Watch on any of Her Majesty's Ships and is entitled to a First Class Certificate.

Sgd dated	Rich E. Tracey	Captain	HMS *Sultan*
18 Jun 1884	G.H.S. Boyes	Commander	HMS *Achilles*
	A.E. Curson-Hone	Commander	HMS *Sultan*

Having obtained the rare honour of five first-class passes, Ned was promoted at age twenty to Acting Sub-Lieutenant. For the next eighteen months he continued training on HMS *Excellent* and HMS *Vernon*. In April 1885 he was awarded a First Class Certificate with the following results:

Subject	Full Marks	Result
Algebra	125	114
Geometry	125	115
Trigonometry	125	111
Mechanics	125	87
Physics	100	57
Steam Engine	100	74
French	200	169
Winds, Currents	100	98
Prac Navigation	200	194
Naut Astronomy	200	179
Naut Surveying	100	97
Observations	100	95
TOTAL	1,600	1,390

On 10 November 1885 Ned obtained a First Class Certificate in Pilotage with these results:

	Full Marks	Mark obtained
General Navigation	300	273
General Pilotage	200	190
Compasses	200	190
Pilotage of the English Channel	300	289
TOTAL	1,000	942.

Right: Sub-Lieutenant Edward Charlton.
Below: Neptune's *Cutter Racing crew 1884.*
Bottom: HMS Neptune, *alongside at Gibraltar; formerly the* Independencia *of the Brazilian Navy.*

A Lieutenant in Africa – 1886

Lieutenant Charlton took passage in RMS *Pretoria* from Plymouth via Madeira and St Helena to Cape Town. During the passage he wrote to his brother Willie, who farewelled him, and to an uncle, Father Frank, to thank him for his kindness to him in the old country. On arrival at the Cape he commenced two years' service on HMS *Rapid* under Captain A.W. Musgrave. During this tour of duty he wrote home regularly.

———— ∽ ————

HMS *Rapid*, Simon's Bay, 9 Feb 1886.

My dear Mother, The whole Colony seems in a very poor state and suffers from depression in trade, disease of vines and cheapness of diamonds. [Simonstown] would be nothing but for the Naval station. It stands on the side of a hill and consists of one long street in which are the Club, Admiral's and Chief Magistrate's houses.

The Wardroom [of HMS Rapid*] is on the main deck 25ft x 15 ft with cabins on each side. My cabin is abaft it and well under the counter. This is a great advantage as the scuttle can be kept open in almost any weather. The ship is a regular box of guns, on the upper deck 5.5in each side, a 6in astern and 6in bow chasers. I have charge of the port battery and stern gun. Mighty few ships now-a-days have six guns in a battery. Complement of men and officers about 180 and a good lot they are too. The skipper is very much liked. His only relatives in England are the Musgraves in Cumberland. Mrs Musgrave is a very nice woman, lots of go in her. She met the*

Nottingham Charltons last year; I disclaimed any knowledge of them. Furlong, our No. 1, is a married man but his wife is at home. I get along very well with him, although he is a bit of a blusterer. Gale and Steel are both capital fellows. Wilkin, our Sub, is also a good sort. Now we come to the peculiar people. Our Senior Surgeon, Dr Spencer, is a teetotaller, non-smoker and worst of all non-speaker. He has never been known to speak to anyone except the Chief Engineer.

———— ∽ ————

23 Feb 1886.

This is letter writing under difficulties, as a gale blows freely along the table and everything has to be weighted down. My cabin is too dark without candles and I cannot afford them all day.

———— ∽ ————

Simon's Bay, 16 Mar 1886.

My dear Elise, There had been various dances and picnics ashore to which we had been hospitably invited and for some time we could not make up our minds what to do in return. At last we decided on a picnic on a large scale on an outlying farm; a meeting was called and I was elected chief bottle-washer and floor-scrubber. I scoured the country for a couple of days and we decided on the de Stadler's farm, about seven miles off. Transport was the next problem; all persons with own carts or horses were to use them. We

Some of the picnickers at de Stadler's Farm, Simonstown, 1886.

engaged all the mokes and ramshackle traps in Simon's Bay. Another job was the invitations. Our secretary was continually being pestered by Mrs So-and-So wanting to know if the What-do-you-call-'ems were coming as she wouldn't come. This is the consequence of cliques in a small town. However, we got over it by asking everyone. Six carts were hired to hold four or five each according to size of occupants. At the last moment we found so many old Dutch Mammas were coming, none of whom weigh less than 16 stone, that transport officer Wilkin was sent round to delicately hint to them the heat of the day, dangers of the road etc. Only one, Mrs Smellekamp, fetched out and she boasted she never stirred out of the cart the whole way; poor horses.

We had the front of the farm house, three capital rooms, one as a ladies' cloak room and the other two for dancing. I got up a capital floor with chalk and we adorned the walls with foreign ensigns. The lunch was laid in a lovely avenue of oak trees, and we had any amount of swings, Aunt Sally [a game in which a figure of a woman's head with a pipe in its mouth is set up, and the player, throwing sticks, tries to break it] etc. to amuse the crowd. All was ready by noon as we anxiously awaited the guests. Riding bachelors kept coming in about every ten minutes or so reporting progress of the caravan, about twenty carts and carriages were toiling along over the sandy track, the gentlemen all shoving at the stern. Then the ladies had to get out and shove too.

At last Wilkin came in and said refreshment was wanted instantly, so we formed a life-saving party and met the cavalcade about a mile off with two jugs of claret for the ladies. Everyone had a gigantic thirst and very soon made short work of our liquor. Old Lady Hunt Grubb, the Admiral's wife, led the way most pluckily. If it hadn't been for her, some of them would never have fetched. Everything went off beautifully and you can imagine what a success it was when a one-legged man was seen dancing the Sir Roger. One fellow managed to photograph a couple spooning and there has been an awful lot of humbug about it. There must have been about 80 people there. We now feel quits with the people ashore.

My 21st birthday is next Sunday and I am to give a bit of a dinner to celebrate it.

A report on the picnic appeared in the press and states: 'Dr Coulthurst RN exhibited his famous performing horse "Diamond" to the admiring spectators, and was succeeded by Captain Savage, Lieutenant Brooker R.E. and other highly-accomplished equestrians, who speedily converted the open space into a "Ménage", put up leaps and knocked them down again, and finally so terrified the onlookers by the ardour of their performances, that dancing was again resumed. The "Naval Bachelors" are to be congratulated upon the excellent manner in which they carried the whole affair through. It is now a matter of speculation how long these gentlemen will be permitted to remain "Bachelors".'

Simon's Bay, 28 Mar 1886.

My dear Mother, The Raleigh is in and we are to get to sea as soon as possible to stop the German pranks in the Cameroons.

———— ∽ ————

At sea, 9 May 1886.

Dear Father Frank, Here we are at last on our awful Gold Coast. No time on board like Sunday after Church for writing letters. We have about 20 Catholics on board, nearly all Irish, and I have just finished reading prayers to them. Our Captain does not force all the men to be either Church of England or Roman Catholic like some do. In consequence I sometimes get about 40 instead of 20. I am afraid this is principally because my prayers are short and sweet. Leaving on the 16th we rounded the Cape and got a fair wind. Engines were stopped and fires put out, all plain and studding-sails set and so we rattled up 1,000 miles. Mossamedes [Angola] is the capital of the province and belongs to the Portuguese. We saluted, and saw one white man in the fort loading all the guns to return it; the niggers fired the guns and then ran away. Sugar and cotton are grown in small quantities. The plough is unknown, all the work being done by 'Liberados' as the Portuguese call them, but it appears to me to be the worst form of slavery. A white swab stood over each gang with a whip of rhinoceros hide (sjambok) with which he belaboured the men and women alike, especially the latter if the babies slung over their backs started crying. We felt very much inclined to knock him down. They do not seem unhappy however.

At Esquimina is a large plantation kept by a Senhor Pinia (commonly called Peanuts) who is always hospitable. Peanuts employs 500 niggers who are very well kept and no sjambok is allowed.

On Cape St Mary is a stone pillar erected by one of the early navigators in AD 1460. [Shortly after the death of Prince Henry the Navigator in 1460 his Captain, Diogo Cao, discovered the Congo River and Cape St Mary in Angola. In 1487 Bartolomeu Dias, his successor, first rounded the southern end of Africa.]

———— ∽ ————

St Paul de Luanda (Angola), 12 May 1886.

The Racer, one of our sloops, is here and we first see the effects of a few months on the Coast. Captain is very bad with fever, two Lieutenants and a doctor more or less ill, a Sub-Lieutenant bad, First Lieutenant just able to dodder around; we have sent them off to St Helena at once.

Nothing has ever flourished here since the suppression (so called) of the slave trade. All the streets have been paved but are now run to grass . . . The weather being damp, thermometer steady day and night at 80°F, my cockroaches are coming out beautifully. I am cultivating spiders in my cabin against them.

Fernando Po, 28 May 1886.

My dear Mother, We left Luanda on the 18th and steamed up to Cabinda. There is only one English factory and a native village. The first object seen on landing is a cemetery where are the graves of Naval officers who have died of fever. King Jack owns the village conditionally under the Portuguese. He was dressed in a Post Captain's frock coat and on seeing us asked us what we were going to 'dash him'. We dashed His Majesty a small amount of baccy and he produced a bottle of Trade gin and insisted on us helping him polish it off. The Cabinda people are about the thriftiest and best made on the Coast. Their cemetery was placed in an almost impenetrable thicket and the graves ornamented with empty gin bottles, in number according to the standing of the deceased nigger. Thus a boss man would have eight or ten gin bottles planted over him.

Fernando Po island is covered with most marvellous tropical vegetation. The Spanish send all their Cuban refugees here as an easy method of getting rid of them; a few weeks on this island is enough to finish off most white people. What makes the coast so bad is the awful dampness.

— ∽ —

Accra (Gold Coast, now Ghana),
8 Jun 1886.

Some fellows always take quinine on their return from shore but I don't believe in physicking myself unless there is actual necessity. Up the Bonny River [Nigeria] we had a grand palaver of native Chiefs on the poop. [British] Consul Hewitt had just deposed King Oko Jumbo. The chiefs came to consult how they were to break the news to the old scoundrel without breaking the peace at the same time. It was a curious and amusing sight to see each Chief come alongside in his war canoe with about 40 paddles, with tom-toms beating. Their canoe names were peculiar: Dublin Green, Manilla Pepple, Squeeze Balla-Gel and Tom Halliday.

— ∽ —

At sea off Cape Palmas (Liberia),
19 Jun 1886.

Our last mail at Cape Coast Castle brought me your letter of 17 Apr. The Gold Coast jewellery made here is unique, and we get it for its weight against our sovereign gold and about 5% for cash to the nigger. Education is rapidly progressing among them as proved by the Master-at-Arms having sold to him a 22 carat gold ring that when put in acid had nothing left but the brass inside.

— ∽ —

Sierra Leone, 28 Jun 1886.

There are two telegraph steamers in here now, completing the cable from England, and we have just received the first wire ever sent to Sierra Leone.

The educated nigger out here is a beast, and actually won't get out of your way in the street unless you hustle him. They call themselves 'men and brudders'. One of them asked me if I was 'partaking of my consitootional perambulations'.

We dined with the 1st West Indian Regiment; they stay out here one year which counts as two years' service and then they get a year's leave on full pay.

— ∽ —

At sea 70 miles ENE of St Helena,
28 Jul 1886.

You know I told you how healthy we are all keeping; we were scarcely out of harbour when fever made its appearance and before nightfall there were eight cases. Everyone pulled through however.

HMS Rapid proceeded via St Helena, Tristan da Cunha and Simon's Bay to Australia.

Partial Protector in the Antipodes – 1887

For no fewer than 40,000 years Australia was settled by Aborigines, hunter-gatherers who invented the boomerang and produced the world's oldest known cave paintings.

In voyages between 1606 and 1680 Dutch explorers charted the west and south coasts of Australia. They declared the land to be flat and unproductive and did not settle. Captain James Cook charted the east coast of Australia in 1770. It has recently come to light that Portuguese explorer Cristoval de Mendonca may have charted the east coast as early as 1522 but kept the charts secret as he was 'trespassing' into that half of the new world which had been awarded to Spain by Pope Alexander VI in 1493 (the world divided by Longitudes 51°W and 129°E).

When the British Colonies in the United States gained their independence, the British Government selected Botany Bay as a convict colony. The First Fleet reached Sydney in January 1788, the Government having declared the Continent 'Terra Nullius', i.e. owned by no one. The transportation of convicts to the Eastern Colonies of Australia continued until 1851; to the Western until 1868. Research over the five-year period to 1837 indicates that the crime rate among the 'descendants of convicts' had dropped to 1.0 per 1,000 compared with 3.0 for 'freed convicts' and 1.3 for 'free immigrants'. About one third of the convicts were Irish. The attitudes of British and non-British new arrivals did not always correspond. The first Australian Cardinal, Patrick Moran, landed in Sydney in 1884 stating, 'From this day I become an Australian.' In 1899 the last British Governor of New South Wales Colony, Earl Beauchamp, stated with good intent, but with the opposite effect, that Australia had 'turned her birth stains to good'. This led to a popular pseudo-advertisement: 'For birth stains, try Beauchamp's Pills.'

When Ned arrived there were six British Colonies; these were governed by British Government-appointed legislators and local landowners, the Crown having ultimate control. In 1901 the six Colonies federated into the Commonwealth of Australia, a member of the British Commonwealth.

HMS *Rapid*, Albany, Western Australia,
11 Oct 1886.

My dear Mother, This craft has kept up to her name well, though Willie will jeer at our runs compared to a clipper ship like the Wanganui, *but they are mighty good for a man-of-war built to sail and steam as well. We ran along between 39 and 42 degrees South and took one or two enormous seas.*

On Sunday, just as our prayers were over, a regular 'green un' came over washing away our 7 pound gun, lifting the wardroom skylight and pouring down on our devoted heads. The water came right onto my bunk which could not be dried for a week. Our tom-cat fell overboard and we rounded to pick him up with our whaler; just in time as the albatrosses were swooping around him. The cat was saved but the whaler was stove in while hoisting.

The town of Albany, 1,300 inhabitants, strikes me as being remarkably well built; also the absence of slums. We landed to taste the draught ale and found the Sunday Closing Act in force but (travellers were permitted a drink, and) we certainly were travellers. Afterwards they told us that Naval Officers were always allowed in. One of our fellows made a bit of a mistake. He had bought a book called Botany Bay, True Tales of Clever Criminals in Early Australia. *This book he exhibited in the hotel asking some of the best people in the town if they had ever seen it. N.B. Albany was once a convict station. The faces of those people were a study.*

Albany on King George's Sound, Western Australiia, 1886.

Ship's Company HMS *Rapid*, Brisbane, May 1887.

Adelaide (South Australia), 21 Oct 1886.

Dear Grannie, In a book I have just been reading a young counter-jumper soliloquises thus: 'How I should like to be a sailor, feel the briny spray dash against my face . . .' Yes, and trickle down the back of your neck during the first few minutes of your four hour watch, until in a short time you have not a dry rag on you, to find your servant has capsized your bath into your sea-boots, and then be told the Captain wants you to take two reefs in the topsail, an evolution which will keep you facing the wind and hail for two hours . . .

The scenery of Australia from a ship is disappointing; there is none. We are now painted black with red ports and look much more war-like.

Gold was found for the first time in this Colony during the last week. From 400 to 700 people leave the town daily.

— ∞ —

27 Oct 1886.

Unfortunately the gold fever is so strong that we could not safely give our men leave. Imagine the temptation to our tars when they got a couple of glasses inside them, and the

fellow standing them, wanting a mate to dig with. I should have liked to visit the diggings but could manage only one day on the line when I got a view of the Adelaide plain.

— ∞ —

Sydney (New South Wales), 9 Nov 1886.

My dear Mother, The lovely electric light on South Head, the most powerful one in the world at 6,000,000 candle power, was seen 50 miles off. The harbour is certainly the finest in the world, with numerous bays. On the points with the finest views you see the splendid mansions of the wealthy Kangaroos, and behind them the masts of the biggest congregation of merchant vessels in the world just show over the tops of the gum trees. We lie in Farm Cove with the Governor's Palace above us and Botanical Gardens right down to the water's edge; so close that we can smell the flowers. About sunset all the beauty and fashion come down to look at the ships and are well criticised through our glasses. I know very few heiresses as yet . . .

The steam trams are neither more nor less than street railways and a disgrace to civilisation. You have to buy tickets for them, there are regular stopping places, and three or four cars on at a time, fitted with Westinghouse brakes, and two storeys in height, smoking cars etc. They get up a speed of quite 30 miles per hour, a whirl of movement if possible worse than London City.

Old Tooth, who has done well in beer, has asked me up the river in his yacht to the Parramatta races.

———— ∞ ————

At Sydney, 20 Nov 1886.

Dear old boy, We are getting used to the noise and bustle which almost drove us wild at first. The people are very good to us, in return. I suppose, for our defending them?

Last week I received an invitation to a sale of land at Katoomba in the Blue Mountains. Champagne and other dainties were provided by the Auctioneer. The advertisements were full of the Katoomba Lake of which there was a picture with splendid walks, esplanades and terraces. [Katoomba, a mountain top, is not an ideal site for a lake.] Land sold at 10/- to 25/- per foot of frontage of the lots which ran back 120 feet. In George Street, Sydney it is 2,000 Pounds per foot. I heard one man doing a growl as he had bought land at 11/- per foot. When he boasted of the house he would build there we suggested he ought to look at it. His lingo, when he found it marked out down the side of a precipice with 20 tons of pebbles on it, was strong. He missed the train going back.

We went down the great Zig-Zag; when first constructed it was the finest piece of engineering in the world. The train runs down in three shunts and a fall of 1,200 feet. At the bottom we found the village of Esk Bank [now Lithgow]. Esk Bank was laid out by Government who first placed a Race-course, then a brewery and a Church, then an Hotel. The houses come last.

Last night the 'Mikado' was played. Lord Carrington, the Governor, sent us off several tickets so I collared one. We were among the toffs. I had a mighty lord on each side of me, about the biggest looking idiots in the house. I didn't care for the play; perhaps the company of the two idiotic hereditary legislators was the explanation.

———— ∞ ————

24 Nov 1886.

We have had a jolly tea-party on board and my opinion of Australian beauty has gone up.

———— ∞ ————

At Sydney, 24 Nov 1886.

Dear Father Frank, Admiral Tryon is at Melbourne in the Nelson; the flagship always wants docking about the time of the Melbourne races, curiously enough, and has to go down there for it. As for myself, I am not anxious to meet the old Admiral; I remember jamming his fingers in a Nordenfelt some years back and he may not have forgotten it. The labourers' wages are enormous, 12/- and 10/- a day; they won't work under 10/-. All the lazy men join the great unemployed whom the New South Wales Government give three meals a day. At one time they used to get 6d a day as well as their chop, but the taxpayers couldn't stand that. All the great unemployed have votes; hence their power to refuse 5/- a day wages.

Noumea, New Caledonia, 13 Dec 1886.

My dear Mother, We leave in a day or two for the New Hebrides which people at home are making a row about. The French have annexed them, much to their Naval Officers' disgust, and are sending their 'Récidivistes' (convicts) there.

———— ∞ ————

New Caledonia,

My dear Oswin, I should have written to you before but you were not worth 6d; it is 2½d from here, so I can afford it! We were not sorry to leave Sydney as our whole time was taken up with returning calls to all the bosses and people with unmarried and ugly daughters who thought us good catches? The length of the Coast line of the harbour is about 200 miles and as these people live on all sides of the bays and coves it was no slight job returning about 150 calls amongst eight of us. There are ten in our Mess but old 'Mortality' Staff-Surgeon and Craddock, our oily boy, are dead letters. They belong to the Salvation Army, and will not speak to anyone who is not 'saved'.

I had a 6d dinner on shore one day; there were ten courses to choose from and when I chose beef-steak and kidney pie I got a plateful more than I could eat piled with potatoes and greens. After that came a sweet, a fine cup of tea and bread ad lib.

This island is by a coral barrier reef. Some of the pale blue tints are magnificent. The Catholic Church put up by the Government is a miserable affair and everyone was astonished when I took my men there. Here French-men never go to Mass; it is derogatory to their dignity; they send their women and children. There is a very good Club and an excellent brass band of about sixty convicts. One was Mayor of Paris during the Commune and shot the Archbishop. You can shoot anyone loafing about after 10pm. The French will never make Colonists as they have no enterprise.

———— ∞ ————

Noumea, New Caledonia, 22 Dec 1886.

My dear George and Frank [his younger brothers], We had a 'grand chasse' last Sunday; our skipper shot a stag. We kept it on board for two days, temperature 85°F, until it got too high so our skipper sent it as a present to the Captain of the French man-of-war who immediately asked him to 'déjeuner' and made him eat some of the rotten carcase.

Yesterday it was my day on board and we spotted a man swimming from the [convict] island to the mainland; as the place is crammed with sharks we sent a boat after him and found he was a burly convict with heavy irons on his legs, enough to sink any ordinary man. We returned him to the prison and found he was one of three who got away in a dinghy last year to Brisbane 900 miles away.

HMS *Rapid*, Noumea, 31 Dec 1886.

My dear Elise, Thank you so much for your photo; my cabin is a regular gallery now but the worst of it is I never go out without finding my messmates wrapped in admiration and have to kick them out.

The harbour is very healthy; we have an empty sick-list and two doctors kicking their heels; the younger sawbones has taken to writing a treatise on mosquitoes and is catching and bottling them all day for examination, but they are are numerous as ever. [Handwritten note later inserted by Ned: 'he would have been ultra-famous had he continued this line and found "anopheles".']

——— ∞ ———

Port Sandwich, Mallicolo, New Hebrides, 18 Jan 1887.

My dear Mother, Our next visit was to Havannah Harbour in the same island [as Vila]. This is the 'great' French Port, about which you are making such a noise in the papers, 3 Officers (two sick) and fifty soldiers (26 sick). They are encamped in miserable huts made of mud. The island has not been annexed, so these soldiers are in the absurd position of living on a plot of land bought from an English trader. We don't recognise their authority.

There was a missionary at Havannah, a Scotchman of course. He was about 6ft 6in tall and we at once understood why the Natives call white man chop 'long pig'. All the sea coast is held by him in trust for the Natives so the French won't get much if they do annex.

Last Saturday we had a fine picnic in the whaler and saw our first genuine cannibals. They were preparing a feast and out hunting for delicacies. By their filed teeth we could see what one of these might be and kept our arms pretty handy. Lucky the dead man was not a great chief or the death of another (and the eating also) would become necessary.

——— ∞ ———

Havannah Harbour (New Hebrides), 29 Jan 1887.

There is a law out here that no English trader can sell arms to the Natives and we are supposed to stop them but as Morgan, an English trader, said, it was much better policy to sell rifles to them which blew up their owners when fired, than to let them use their poisoned arrows. These latter are poisoned by being left in the face of a dead man whilst the body is mortifying. The French Doctor has assured us this is a fact as he has seen the corpse hanging up with arrows in it, but it has been denied by many writers.

The row at Ambrym was because one of Morgan's Natives had murdered a bush nigger and the tribe of the latter, being short of a skull, were not particular whose they got. Trade was stopped and Morgan's tribe could not go after copra. These latter are all men from other islands, for a

nigger won't work for a white man in his own home where he can get enough to live on for the picking. From the ship we could see the fighting tribes and a very fine set of men they were, all armed with guns and rifles supplied by Morgan in spite of the Pacific Law. We got the chief on board, fired a shell for him, and blew off the siren until the poor man was terrified nearly out of his life. He promised to give up the murderer.

——— ∞ ———

Noumea, 2 Feb 1887.

We left Havannah and found ourselves at Erromango where they ate four missionaries about ten years ago.

——— ∞ ———

HMS *Rapid*, 20 Feb 1887

The Admiral is in New Zealand and the longer he stays there, or in Jericho, the better we shall be pleased. He has treated us very badly so far by not allowing us into Melbourne when we were passing on Cup Day.

——— ∞ ———

Sydney, 31 March 1887.

Admiral Tryon asked me to dinner last night and was awfully kind; he is an excellent host and we got talking over the old Mediterranean days. I had to put off a pleasant invitation in order to accept the dinner, but to be asked by an Admiral is as good as an order.

——— ∞ ———

Moreton Bay, Brisbane, Queensland, 24 Apr 1887.

Our presence is required here in order to hold a Court-Martial on Lieutenant Hesketh of the Queensland gun-vessel Gayundah for misappropriation of Government money. This vessel flies the white ensign but does not belong to our service and we can't think how her officers come under the Naval Discipline Act. Admiral Tryon refused to try him but received an order from the Admiralty to do so as a test case.

——— ∞ ———

Sydney, 11 May 1887.

Dear old boy, Hesketh was sentenced to be dismissed HM Service. The trial was most uninteresting and the poor devil was doing no worse than most of the people up there who live entirely on credit; will borrow a hat and mortgage it for a pair of boots.

Our navigator was away on leave and I had to run the difficult job of getting out of Moreton Bay. The Rapid draws 15 feet and the Opal, astern of us, draws 19ft 6in. There is only 20 feet on the bar, however she got along all right. I felt as pleased as possible when my first job as pilot of a fleet was over.

We are ordered to try all sorts of Courts-Martial. The most important is the Tyne and Myrmidon collision in Bass Strait at 2.30pm on a fine clear day. The latter was a wooden ship and was struck fair amidships by the iron bows of HMS Tyne and yet scarcely received any damage whilst the bows of the Tyne are all smashed in. Apparently they closed to chinwag to each other. Capt Hoskyn of the Myrmidon came on deck suddenly, and put the helm over, causing the collision. H.V. Simpson, Officer-of-the-Watch on the Tyne when she collided, is also to be tried. He was at the Britannia with me and passed out first when I was second.

———— ∞ ————

At sea, 27 May 1887.

My dear Mother, I told Willie all about the Courts-Martial. The Tyne and Myrmidon case lasted five days and there was some hard swearing on both sides. The Court seems to have held that as the Tyne was the overtaking vessel she should have kept clear; this point is left unsettled by the rule of the Road. Capt Hoskyn of the Myrmidon lost one year's time for hazarding his ship, i.e. not reducing speed before striking, and Lieut Simpson lost all his time as Lieutenant and was dismissed his ship. [A few years after this unfortunate event H.V. Simpson resigned from the navy; he was recalled for duty as Commodore 2nd Class in World War I.]

———— ∞ ————

Port Moresby, New Guinea,
26 Jun 1887.

Dear Elise, . . . We visited a black colony just on top of the hill half a mile outside Cooktown; you must remember that the advance of civilisation has driven the Aborigines nearly all the way up into the York Peninsula and it is the rarest thing in the world to see one of them on the coast down south. Up here they are gradually being exterminated. These people will only work just to get enough for them to live on; then they stop and consequently their position never improves. However the black trackers and police shoot them on the slightest provocation up country. This black colony had come in for their annual supply of blankets, given by idiots at home, for clothes of any kind are not worn by either sex and they all go about perfectly in Nature's garb. The blankets are at once changed for tobacco. Their huts are made of branches laid across boulders and I never saw such coal-black skins in my life. One old man was very sick, apparently rheumatic fever; he was lying in the dirt with nowt on, and a charcoal fire laid along his back from one to two inches off. Altogether they are the most degraded type of human creatures I have yet encountered.

We passed out of the great barrier into the South East Trades; no wonder Captain Cook was glad to get clear as the navigation is bad enough now with steam, and charts laying down almost every shoal.

No sooner had we anchored in Port Moresby than Romilly

(Deputy High Commissioner, 1,300 Pounds a year and nowt to do for it) told us of the massacre of a native teacher and eight men at Motu-Motu. We sailed the same evening and anchored off the bar of the Heath River. It appears the Motu-Motuans were out fishing and, on rounding an Island, were suddenly surprised by the Mori-Avi tribe located about twelve miles up river. The party was slaughtered before they knew where they were; only the teacher's wife, badly wounded, escaped to tell the tale. As we were getting the anchor up next morning the whole Motu-Motu tribe came off in canoes to visit us. They are said to be the finest set of men in New Guinea and were mostly six foot of good physique and pungent odour, but no stamina, as a couple of turns round the capstan put them quite out of breath.

We went to Yule Island that day where there is a large Catholic Mission; French priests and brothers and a house building for six nuns. Their situation is capital, ground well cultivated and there can be no comparison between the actual effect of these people and the London Church Missionary Society; even our own officers acknowledge it but cannot account for it.

Our Doctor visited the wife of the teacher who was killed and found she had six arrow wounds, but the worst wound she had was cut in her stomach to let the pain out, and of this she will die. Poor woman, she is a Tahitian and is thus left to die amongst strangers.

———— ∞ ————

At sea off Basilaki, 21 July 1887.

My dear Mother, We have been fighting the Basilakians (between the easternmost point of New Guinea and the Conflict group of islands). About three months ago these Islanders, who are the terror of the more peaceable Islanders all around them, had the luck to find a schooner – manned by six Chinamen with a Chinese Captain, Ah Gym by name – wrecked on their shore; they were sailing under British colours, and had been bêche-de-mer [sea slug] fishing. The natives induced the group to come ashore with them where they treated them well, fed them up for several days, then killed them and ate them, Ah Gym alone escaping. As he holds a Master's certificate under our colours we were told off to avenge their death.

Last Monday, with six Hayti Island natives on board, we manned and armed boats, and having sent the natives flying into the bush with half a dozen shell round their huts, advanced to the shore . . . found the place deserted . . . burnt three villages.

On Tuesday we sent the Hayti boys ashore, to our surprise they returned with three Chinamen's skulls. [The next day] our boys were again sent ashore but did not care about leaving the beach; about noon I had just caught a 7 pound Kingfish when out thundered a broadside from the ship. We hurried on board, and found that a 'boy' had been speared in the thigh and wrist . . . we bombarded all the houses and I landed with a party of 40 men and completed the destruction, burning all and ringbarking the coconut trees near the beach; also destroying a lot of valuable *outriggers. I very nearly fell into a pit covered with bush in which were numerous spear heads placed pointing upwards but, thank God, just saw it in time. It was rather interesting to see Ah Gym recognising his old crew by their skulls; he did not seem a bit affected, simply said, 'This is my Mate', 'That is Ah Gee', and so on . . . We are going to present each boy with an axe and a knife tomorrow on account of the excellent way in which they did their work.*

— ∞ —

Samarai, New Guinea, 6 Aug 1887.

Dear Father Frank, Romilly came back from Milne Bay in the Hygeia *last Saturday where, as Deputy High Commissioner, he had been investigating a case. It appears that three weeks ago a large Slade Island canoe went to Milne Bay to trade, and the natives there, being short of grub, captured the canoe and killed and ate eight of the crew. A small boy escaped as the women hid him under their grass petticoats, and the ninth man got clear into the bush where he remained for six days until starved. He was forced to go down to the beach and was of course collared at once. They tied him to a coconut tree, and proceeded to fatten him. He was fed on yams and bananas, and made to drink salt water to make him sick. On the fourth day he managed to get a message through to Killerton Island, where there is a native Mission-teacher. This man had only a musket and no ammunition, but he went over by himself and found them just going to kill the poor man. Three ovens were ready for the poor devil, and fresh banana leaves had been laid out on which to cut him up. His hair was twisted into the barbs of a man-catcher spear which pulled his head well down so that he could receive a clean tomahawk blow. The teacher went up and threatened them with the musket, and they let him go. These small islands round here all have*

different races and languages, they all distrust each other, and consequently are continually at war. We have only a protectorate over New Guinea and so have nothing to do with native quarrels and cannibalism.

— ∞ —

At sea 100 miles of South Cape, New Guinea,
13 Aug 1887.

A good bag is most important to us after 70 days on salt grub – as we stow 90 only – and I have become quite a good hand at catching fish. We gave a dinner to the trader and Government Agent at Dinner Island from our own catching in New Guinea:

SOUP	*Bêche-de-mer*
FISH	*Broiled Kingfish*
ENTRÉES	*Salmis of pigeon, clams fixed up somehow*
JOINTS	*Parrot pie with a white cockatoo chucked in*
VEGETABLES and	*Boiled yams, fried bananas paw-paws*
SWEETS	*Sago and coconut pudding.*

— ∞ —

Cooktown, Queensland,
26 Aug 1887.

Dear Mother, Your letters of July arrived this morning and the papers are full of the Jubilee of the Queen; we have utterly refused to subscribe any more money. We gave a silver model of a typical war ship of 1837 and one of 1887. The Colonists don't care about it and say it is only putting money in the pockets of the Kensington gang.

Cooktown Harbour, Queensland, 1887.

The people here are getting up all kinds of entertainment for us; also on account of Race week. All the gold, silver and tin miners are coming in and they are a mighty rough lot too. The Harrier has come in so I have my friend Powley to chum with. We made the ascent of Mount Cook, 1,500 feet, the other day, leaving the ship at 3am and being on board before sunset. We could see the 'Barrier Reef' out to seaward and the windings of the Endeavour river just like a silver thread for miles to the westward.

I got up a rifle match with the Cooktown Defence Corps and we beat them by 14 points. They were a most friendly lot but I am glad that we beat them, as no Naval team has done so for 9 years, and they had been backing themselves 3 to 1.

New Guinea is to be declared a Sovereignty so we may be kept here for some time. It is no good to us but it would never do to let anybody else have it.

We are going to lay the foundation stone for old Cook's monument and I am to be in charge of the Brigade of Seamen from Rapid, the Harrier Marines and the Defence Corps when we shall fire a feu-de-joie.

11 Sept 1887.

Cooktown is a spreadout little town with a population of over 2,000, one third of which is Chinese. Some of our fellows tried to break the Chinamen at gambling and of course were well cleaned out. Tuesday and Wednesday were the Race days. We hired a buggy and drove out to the course with a white ensign and jack flying, and the bugler playing astern. A colonial custom is selling by auction the right to sell liquors at the Grand Stand during the week; also the sale of licences for so many gambling booths by auction. The former right was bought for 240 Pounds. On Wednesday the Chinese had won, in the miner's opinion, too much money so their booths were stuck up, two had their pigtails cut off and were flogged round the course. The police looked on approvingly and only arrested one man for knocking a Chinese senseless with a billet of wood. I asked the Magistrate what he gave this man, 'Oh! 10/- fine; it don't do to encourage John Chinaman.' As far as I could see they were a most peaceable lot; the white man would get no vegetables were it not for John and his terrific patience.

People of the Motu-Motu tribe, New Guinea, 1887.

At sea off the south coast of New Guinea,
8 Nov 1887.

I think I told you how we had been punishing the Natives of Orangerie Bay for killing a couple of German traders under our flag. The temptation for them must have been enormous. Take a similar case; imagine a New Guinea canoe arriving off Tynemouth, poorly manned and with a couple of million Pounds on board. One hundred and forty Pounds of trade gear was equal to that in the eyes of the Natives.
HMS Rapid *joined HMS* Nelson, Diamond *and* Calliope *visiting New Zealand ports.*

———— ∞ ————

Auckland, New Zealand, 29 Dec 1887.

My dear Mother, There is a splendid harbour fitted with beacons and lighthouse, piers and wharves, and a dock just completed big enough to hold any vessel but the Great Eastern, *yet there is comparatively no traffic, and only one big steamer has come in since we came. It is a pretty town and has a magnificent free library. We have been having such a time here in every way. The kindness of the people is sometimes overwhelming, so different are they to the Queensland inhabitants and so much more like the old folks at home with rosy cheeks and healthy complexions; chubby children too, instead of the poor weak little ones up in Cooktown.*

———— ∞ ————

Auckland, Dec 1887.

My dear Oswin, This is a capital place and the people are chucking everything at us, club passes, tennis courts, races, railway passes, oratorios, concerts and even Turkish bath tickets. Such living I never saw before, even at Greenwich College, but a small ship like this is quite lost in such a big place, and we would sooner have stopped a bit longer at Russell which is now quite a small place. Before the War there used to be over 1,000 inhabitants but there are now under 200. The place has never recovered from its burning down by the Maoris.
Our Admiral has had experience of the cattle laws in these parts; he brought two horses down from Sydney in the Nelson. *An order came from Wellington to send the animals away into quarantine and to have the Admiral fined 300 Pounds. Not because there was anything wrong with the horses but simply because the Government Vet had been too lazy to examine them. The Admiral wired back, 'Unless my horses are released immediately and the fine withdrawn I shall leave with the Squadron for Australia'. Consequent profuse apology of New Zealand Ministers, for the Squadron puts at least 500 Pounds per day into their pockets.*
On 5 January 1888 the Squadron left Wellington for Sydney.

HMS *Rapid*, Sydney, 2 Feb 1888.

My dear Teresa (William's wife), The people here have just finished celebrating the Centenary of the Colonisation of New South Wales, and the whole place has been en fête for the last ten days. The weather has been simply perfect, and even seemed to shape itself to assist whatever was going on, for instance on the sailing day of the Regatta there was a splendid breeze and on the pulling day a dead calm. Banquets, feasts, openings of halls, unveiling of statues, agricultural shows, races and cricket matches have been following each other in continuous run, ending up last night with a grand illumination of the harbour; all our men-of-war lighting up with coloured lights at all yard-arms every now and then. There was a strong breeze to carry off the smoke, and just when it was all over up came the old moon and showed the harbour to us crammed with every conceivable sort of craft. Everything here is six times as flourishing as when we went away, and even the sharks have increased in size and voracity. One was caught yesterday, with a gold watch and part of a waistcoat inside.

———— ∞ ————

Sydney, 20 Feb 1888.

My dear George, Great fun goes on in the Parliament House here, and they never hesitate at calling each other any names under the sun; last week two members had it out in three rounds. Sir Henry Parkes in the Assembly told a member last year that he was not even as good as guano. Although he is the Premier he is as bad as any of them.

———— ∞ ————

HMS *Rapid*, at Sydney, 8 April 1888.

Dear old boy (Willie), Our relief has just come in on the Thalia *which has made fast to her buoy close to us, after a 'marvellous' passage of 132 days from Plymouth; a merchant vessel came in at the same time 76 days from London. We are ordered home through the Canal luckily, instead of the Horn.*

CERTIFICATE: Edward F. B. Charlton served as a Lieutenant on HMS *Rapid* from 12 Dec 1885 to 11 Apr 1888 and conducted himself with sobriety; he is a good sailor in every respect and is a most promising officer. Sgd Archer W. Musgrave.

———— ∞ ————

In addition to the letters Ned wrote to his family in England, which were typed and bound in his folios, this unbound handwritten letter to a namesake was found loose:

HMS *Thalia*, at sea, 24 April 1888.

Dear Uncle Ned, As we get into Townsville tonight, I must have a line ready for you. You can't imagine how disappointed I was at not seeing you again to thank you for

HMS Dart *and HMS* Rapid *in Farm Cove, Sydney dressed to celebrate Century Day (first centenary of European settlement), 30 Jan 1888.*

your unceasing goodness to me during the few happy months of our stay in Sydney. I look back to it now and shall always do so as the happiest period in my existence and at a time when I had everything man could possibly wish for at my age in my grasp. We got away half an hour earlier than I expected and Ina was the only one I saw before we shot out of view of the pier.

Ina will tell you how I felt at leaving Miss Popsy and you at College Street last Sunday. Do not forget to send a couple of our group photographs to Aden; if you give them to Ina, she will look out for them. I will be careful not to forget your messages for home and hope you will settle your property soon and we shall see you up north; though I like to think of Ina under your care.

With love to Popsy, I remain your aff' cousin (nephew), Edward Charlton.

Audrey Urban said that Ned 'broke the heart' of at least one young lady in Sydney and recollects that an Australian woman, a Mrs McHugh, visited Ned and his family many years later and told a story how, as a youth, she came into the drawing room of their home in Sydney to find Ned and her very pretty sister standing close together at a piano. She remembered Ned saying as she entered the room and disturbed them, 'Here comes the southerly buster.' Perhaps the younger sister was Miss Popsy and the sisters stayed in the home of Ned's namesake?

———— ∞ ————

HMS *Thalia*, Thursday Island (North Queensland), 2 May 1888.

My Dear Mother, 'Homeward Bound' after knocking about for 2½ years; the very sound of the word fills me with joy at the thought of your welcome faces.

We are now coaling 230 tons for the next trip of 4,000 miles. This means nearly 80 tons on deck. This place consists of about 100 houses made of corrugated iron with no attempt at comfort or cleanliness. 'Make a pile and clear out' is their motto. The only church in the place is a Sacre Coeur Convent connected with the New Guinea Mission. I called on the French Priest today.

A French Convict ship is ashore outside and we are to go and assist her. The convicts are stowed in cages like wild beasts.

At sea 700 miles ESE of Seychelles,
1 June 1888.

Dear old boy (Willie), The 22 May dawned clear enough and we were cracking along with every stitch of canvas set, though the old tub will never get up more than 8 knots. About noon old Gillett, who was on watch, told the Captain it looked a bit black to windward and a few minutes after he put the helm up to keep away. The Captain said it was naught and told him to bring her back to her course. Just then the squall struck, creating one of the finest scenes of confusion I ever saw. Three top-masts and the same number of topgallant studsail booms went off crack, the sails splitting in every direction; one lower boom going under the bows and the other up and down the fore rigging. To add to the medley they let go all the upper sheets, and upper sails immediately flying into ribbons . . . By degrees we got the wreckage in and have now managed to patch up most of the sails again.

The same night poor Gale, one of our Lieutenants, died at midnight, death being accelerated by the heat. It is a sad thing to lose a messmate after being with him for three years especially when 'homeward bound'. He was only 35, the eldest son of a West Country Rector, and has half a dozen sisters.

2 Jun 1888.

Gale's effects were sold last week and fetched 38 Pounds, a much greater price than would have been obtained ashore. I purchased his binoculars for two guineas and gave 4 Pd 10/- for a fine oak chest. Only his books, sword and private papers were kept for his people.

———— ∞ ————

Aden, 16 Jun 1888.

Dear Grannie, This is an awful hole; mountains of lava and not a speck of vegetation. I must tell you about a sad catastrophe that occurred to a button orchid from New Guinea that I was bringing home for you. It was a pretty plant on a dead branch and lived very well on condensed water. In an evil hour I thought it would improve on deck. To my horror I found our old goat had had a rare feed off the juicy berries. the worst of it is you can't thrash a goat and I owe him several grudges now, for eating my leather braces,

Slave dhow from Persian Gulf, Aden, 1888.

bootlaces and half my Chinese grass mat. Give him a lighted cigar and he will lick the end till it goes out and then swallow the whole.

———— ∞ ————

Somewhere in the Red Sea,
23 Jun 1888.

My dear George, I always sleep on deck on a rug and grass mat, wearing a night shirt with a red cummerbund, a fez and Turkish slippers, in fact looking like a respectable Turk.

The Captain bought a donkey at Aden; a nice little beast about 9 hands and a great chum of the goats, and between them they have established a league against the dogs, whom the donkey kicks on the head while the goat butts them in the stern.

———— ∞ ————

Port Said,

My dear Mother, We passed an immigrant ship, crowded, and bound for Brisbane. Any amount of girls on board, and the people will be delighted to get them for servants, at what you would think most exorbitant wages: 30 to 40 Pounds [per annum] and everything found.

———— ∞ ————

The Thalia arrived in Plymouth on 18 July 1888 and Ned wired home: 'ARRIVED. DEO GRATIAS', only to be sent to join a major fleet exercise in the Irish Channel. Though disappointed at not being given leave, Ned wrote:

SS Xema, at sea off Milford,
19 Jul 1888.

My dear Mother, I intend to make the best of this bad job and to enter heart and soul into the work, whichever fleet they may turn me into.

———— ∞ ————

HMS Iris, 22 Jul 1888.

I had my choice of the Hercules without a cabin, or coming here with one, as both are short of lieutenants; naturally I chose this and have fallen in good hands. The wardroom is a regular palace on the upper deck with electric light everywhere.

———— ∞ ————

For some unrecorded reason Ned transferred from HMS Iris to HMS Hercules after four days. For the next three weeks the two mighty fleets – 'British' and 'enemy' – each with more than a dozen ships fought mock battles and then 'the enemy' tried to blockade Admiral Tryon's fleet from

reaching Merseyside. Ned admired eccentric Admiral Sir George Tryon, commander of the 'Enemy' fleet, and respected hardworking Rear-Admiral Markham, commander of the 'British' fleet. At the start of the 'War' Tryon stated that he would 'lie comfortably in harbour, take his own time, create false alarms, worry and harass without serious intent, and, finally, when the blockaders were worn out and sick of the cry, Wolf! Wolf!, his forces would attempt to break the blockade'. It was, as The Torpedomen states, a golden moment for any officer who was seized with ambition.

———— ∞ ————

HMS Hercules, just entering the Mersey,
9 Aug 1888.

Really capital fun, and old Tryon seems to have laid his plans very well with the result that we are steaming into Liverpool with five ironclads while 'the enemy' is looking for us somewhere. It does seem hard luck after coming 12,000 miles to get within 80 of home, and go away again.

The notes typed from Ned's logbook indicate that he considered that he had learnt two lessons from the exercise:

1. Aug 12.   Took in 400 tons of coal. Average (loading rate) 32 tons per hour. Fleet delayed 5 days taking coal after being only 4 days at sea at moderate speed. (Loading) appliances are so bad.
2. Aug 16.   The British Public receives most, if not all, their information from the newspaper reporters who, although some of them scarcely know one end of a ship from the other, constitute themselves critics. Abolish them on men-of-war except for pictorial papers.

———— ∞ ————

HMS Hercules, Lough Swilly,
14 Aug 1888.

Dear old boy, They have made me Censor of The Standard Correspondent's reports, as he put in a lot of nonsense, so you may hope to see an improvement in the twaddle he writes.

Torpedo Trials and Triumphs – 1889

From 29 September 1888 to 30 June 1889 Ned studied at the Royal Naval College at Greenwich, London 'with sobriety and in accordance with College Regulations'. He wrote occasionally to his brother Willie who had left the Merchant Navy and was farming in Northumberland.

———— ∞ ————

Royal Naval College, Greenwich, 13 Oct 1888.

Dear old boy, Work is mighty hard and I am fairly bunged up with X and Y but cannot resist football. We torpedo-men are justly indignant at having to dig trenches with the gunners!

———— ∞ ————

5 May 1889.

We had a very gentlemanly exam at Easter in Fortification, Chemistry, Physics and Electric Lighting but only know the marks in the former as yet. I was second, 435 out of 500, but Aynsley beat me with 440. However I showed them the way to dig and build bridges in the practical exams. These blasted mathematics flatten me out though. After four months of differential and integral calculus we arrived at something useful yesterday – the distance a horse in a [leaking] watercart would go if he started with a cart full and his speed varied inversely as the amount of water in the cart.

From July 1889 Ned's base was again the torpedo training ship HMS *Vernon* at Portsmouth. *The Torpedomen* explains that HMS *Vernon* was in fact made up of several venerable hulks connected by gangways – the old wooden *Donegal* known as *Vernon I*, a three-decker *Marlborough* known as *Vernon II*, a pioneer ironclad *Warrior* used for wireless

telegraphy and known as *Vernon III*, and the *Actaeon* used as a workshop and called *Vernon IV*. While based on *Vernon* Ned served on Her Majesty's Torpedo Boat No. 77 at the same time that Prince George, later King George V, commanded HMTB 79. Neither suffered the embarrassment of the commander of HMTB 76: stuck in the mud with a gash in its side in Portsmouth Harbour in full view of enthusiastic photographers. In July 1990 Ned became commanding officer of HMTB 82.

———— ∞ ————

HMS *Vernon*, Portsmouth, 6 Oct 1889.

Dear old boy, I find torpedo work is much better than X and Y at Greenwich. I wouldn't go through that show again for double pay.

We got through a fortnight's diving in the Portsmouth mud and have added that to our other accomplishments.

I saw the British Association has been up your way and the 'Charlton Spur' is in this week's Graphic.

———— ∞ ————

HMS *Vernon*, Portsmouth, 15 Oct 1889.

My dear Mother, Just received your letter and Lord Walter's. I am surprised at the latter saying it would affect my interests as I don't think Frank [his brother] being a Royal Navy Engineer would make the slightest difference to me; anyhow I am not in the least bit afraid of that. If you understand perfectly what position you are putting him into at Keyham [the Royal Naval Engineering College] and the sort of lads he will have to associate with, and then do not think it will be hindrance enough, or that he will do better anywhere else, by all means put him in. It is his own choice so he ought to do

HMTB No 75 at sea.

well. I have no objection to his going.

Keyham may be a magnificent place and a splendid education; I simply judge by what I see produced there, after six years' study, and a more offensive lot of bounders than those at Greenwich last year I never came across. The class entering now may be better as I know the Admiralty are very anxious to raise the social standing of the Branch. They were going to abolish nominations for the Navy when I was in the Britannia *but have not yet done so. It will be a bad day for the Service when this does happen as we have job enough now making stokers out of men of their own class. Take for instance our two messmates in the* Neptune *'G' and Slade (or 'Sloide' as he was called by 'G'). 'G's' brother is a shoemaker at Weymouth, brother-in-law a baker; as you can imagine we don't care much about having his friends to tea. Slade, now lecturer on Applied Mechanics at Greenwich to Engineers, is a very clever man but his English is of the strangest. The pay in the Constructive Department is the best and some very clever men are turned out.*

CERTIFICATE: Lieutenant Edward F. B. Charlton attended the Special Full Pay Gunnery Class on board HMS *Excellent* from 3 Jan 1890 to 28 Feb 1890. Sgd Compton Domile.

———— ∞ ————

HMS *Vernon*, Portsmouth, 6 May 1890.

Dear old boy, Many happy returns of the day. What old fellows we two are now; 23 and 25. The work here is pretty stiff and we are kept hard at teaching dear old captains, some old enough to be our grandfathers.

———— ∞ ————

Royal Navy and Army Club, Piccadilly, 16 July 1890.

I have been a week in town at Admiralty expense and naturally have been enjoying myself. Two hours a day is not very arduous after our slavery for the Vernon *exams. We finished them all a fortnight ago and I was lucky enough to get first place. Now I am a fully qualified torpedo-man and entitled to examine people myself, and worry them too.*

My boat this year, No 82, suits me well as she is the Vernon's *own pet and lies alongside the wall within 30 yards of my cabin. I think another year in England on the* Vernon's *staff is a sound idea, as it counts 'ship of war at sea' time, full pay etc. The only drawback to the Naval profession is, as I am beginning to discover, THE SEA.*

———— ∞ ————

HMTB 82, Alderney, 7 Aug 1890.

Your letter has just reached me at this den of pirates and I wired my acceptance of the awful responsibility at once. I suppose I will be godmother if it is a girl.

The three pirates Nos 82, 86 and 87 are on the warpath and as nothing can beat us in the Channel, 23 knots, we are likely to lead 'the Britisher' a lively time.

In May 1891, riding his motorbike, Ned visited his brothers Oswin and George near Cambridge, toured the Lake District, and met his sister-in-law Teresa and brother Willie near Bellingham in the Tyne Valley. Ned made a note: '510 miles from Portsmouth in seven riding days which speaks well for my machine. The Quadrant Company has always been noted for good material and workmanship.

After his vacation Ned returned to the torpedo training ship HMS *Vernon* where one of the officers, Jackson, was studying the first use of 'Hertzian waves' (radio) for signalling from torpedo boats including attempts to distinguish between friendly and enemy craft.

———— ∞ ————

HMS *Vernon*, 20 July 1891.

My dear Elise, I am here all alone; the Captain is the only other executive officer not mobilised and he is away on leave. A Doctor, two paymasters and an engineer complete our complement but two of them are married and generally I have both ships all to myself of an evening and with only 150 men to look after. However there is a lot of work and now I have a brand-new torpedo-cruiser, the Vulcan, *to play with. [HMS* Vulcan *was a 6,600-ton torpedo-boat-carrying cruiser used for the testing and improvement of torpedoes. Experiments led to the introduction of gyro control of steering and consequent greater accuracy.]*

On Saturday I had to go and do guard duty to the Queen and got a capital view of the old lady as my torpedo-boat had to lay about ten yards off the [Royal] yacht, the creek being so narrow. She walked on board without much trouble and took a chair on the quarter deck. A tribe of babies and nursemaids interrupted my view of her but it was still amusing to watch all the people bowing and scraping to each other.

CERTIFICATE: Edward F. B. Charlton has served as Lieutenant on HMS *Vernon* from 1 Jan 1889 to 4 Feb 1892 and conducted himself with sobriety and in all respects to my satisfaction. Sgd A.K. Wilson [Arthur Knyvet Wilson, later Admiral of the Fleet]

On 5 February 1892 Ned sailed in the SS *Arcadia* for a second tour of duty in the Mediterranean. After encountering bedbugs on HMS *Hibernia* and rats on HMS *Humber*, he boarded the battleship HMS *Colossus* for Alexandria. In comparison with HMS *Rapid*, which had ten officers, and HMTB 82, which had only two, the *Colossus*, with thirty-seven, must have seemed a giant indeed.

———— ∞ ————

HMS *Colossus*, Alexandria, 21 Mar 1892.

My dear Mother, I could not be on a more comfortable ship or with a nicer lot of messmates. My cabin has just been painted and, as Torpedo-lieut, I have charge of the electric light, I very soon installed three lights in it. The new cabin furniture is very good; well worth 1d a day. A fine port and lots of air.

Since the loss of the Serpent *an assistant navigator takes sights every day. I was curious to see how my observations*

Above and below: HMTB 76 holed and aground on a mudbank in Portsmouth harbour and later in dry-dock.

Convict labour working in Portsmouth dockyard in 1891.

would come out after not having used a sextant for nearly four
years. With a Fleet-at-Sea every ship signals their latitude and
longitude at noon and, although we were not 20 hours away
from land, there was no less a difference than 30 miles in
longitude and 9 miles in latitude. Mine was as correct as any
of them although I differed entirely from our navigator.

We anchored and ran a torpedo or two. By a great fluke I hit
the target first time at 400 yards and that goes a long way
towards giving people an idea of your powers. As a matter of
fact the torpedo was quite new to me and could have curved
anywhere.

We are anchored in the same old billets as before the
bombardment. The old familiar forts still show the external
marks of their hammering 10 years ago, but the guns are gone
and the whole town practically rebuilt. Everyone blesses the
bombardment for getting rid of a lot of filthy streets and dens.

I spent all my money quail shooting at Abou Hommos with
another fellow. Capital sport, 100 first day, 110 second and
146 third – when our parson joined us. All in standing corn.
The poor 'fellah' has a rough time. After tramping an
indignant Arab's corn for some time we gave him a piastre
(2½d) as a sort of peace offering. Our guide and boys rushed at
him and would have taken it away if we had allowed them,

'What for you give him backsheesh?' We explained we were
only trying to compensate him for injuring his corn. 'Nevarr
mind him b****y fool'. The advice was sound as in ten
minutes we had a hundred owners demanding backsheesh
around us and had to charge them and hit them over the head.

———— ∞ ————

Alexandria, 3 Apr 1892.

Lord Walter Kerr left us on Wednesday for Malta and was
heartily cheered as he passed through the Fleet; he was
immensely popular as the Admiral. His successor
Markham, the Arctic explorer, is a bit of a nugget.

———— ∞ ————

Malta, 24 Apr 1892.

Poor Wasey [F. Hammond?] died in hospital here over a
month ago; a capital fellow who was on the Britannia with me
and came through the torpedo course on the Vernon last Sept
with me; it was Malta fever. De Chair is now in hospital and
pretty bad. I looked him up, he seemed much pulled down
poor fellow. He is supposed to have got it running about at

60

the canteen on torpedo work, but it is so common now that it is impossible to say where it was picked up.

Ned then goes on to report on a 'curious case of carelessness' one afternoon when HMS *Colossus* was to bury a Catholic seaman and HMS *Tamar* was to bury a Protestant stoker. A signal from shore requested Father Barton to take both funerals. The two ships sent their respective burial parties to their respective cemeteries, three miles apart, at the same time, and only then did the poor padre learn that the two deceased were of different faiths. He managed to resolve the dilemma when he found that yet another ship, HMS *Amphion*, was burying a Protestant at the same time and had a parson available. Malta fever, first isolated in 1896 and now known as Brucellosis, was clearly a major health hazard.

———— ∽ ————

Vourlah Bay (Asia Minor), 23 Jun 1892.

My dear Mother, I am in excellent health at present, having recovered from a severe attack of 'curried prawns' last Saturday which seized most of us. I am qualifying for 'The Lord High Executioner' in 'The Mikado' as I am now carrying on as Commander, First Lt, Gunnery-lt, Torpedo-lt, Naval Instructor and, yesterday, Officer-of-the-Guard. Our Naval Instructor has gone to hospital in Malta and, as the Midshipmen's half yearly exams were on, I have had to examine them all, correct papers and send results home to the Admiralty. It has taught me a power of mathematics.

Pharlerum Bay (Greece) 28 Jul 1892.

The Country was on the verge of bankruptcy and it is thought that our (fleet's) money – roughly 1,000 Pounds per diem – will probably pull the country through. I made friends with an ancient Greek, M. Psicha, who runs the railways. He entertained us at the Cafe Minerva and gave us the very best dinner I have had since leaving England. The Minister for the Interior came in and I was much amused to hear that his pay was 700 Drachmas – 20 Pounds – per month which is less than I myself am getting. The Prime Minister only gets 1,000 per month and works 19 hours per diem. He was brought up in England and is in fact half an Englishman which is probably the reason our Government supports him.

———— ∽ ————

14 Aug 1892.

My dear Oswin, (Admiral) Markham inspected the men and ship and then we prepared for battle in every way, splinter nets up between the guns, deck sanded to prevent us slipping in 'blood' etc. The torpedo boats were hoisted out with war torpedoes in them, as I did not want to fire live torpedoes. The only people we could spare for the boats (due to the large number on the sick list) were quite unable to do anything beyond pulling the string. When the Admiral told me to fire a torpedo from the boat, I said, 'Aye, Aye, Sir; but I think it right to tell you that they are fitted for action, will run 800

Officers of HMS Colossus, *1892. Ned is second from the left, third row from the front.*

yards and sink if they don't explode against any of the Greek men-of-war in the harbour first', so he belayed the order, but had the laugh on me afterwards when he said, 'Fire one for exercise from the ship at the torpedo boat steaming around.' I got off an excellent shot which passed under her but then sunk in 13 fathoms to my intense disgust. It took us 30 hours' hard work to find it. It had had 77 practice runs and never shown any signs of going down. It is rather curious that no torpedo had sunk from this ship since last inspection 13 months ago.

———— ∞ ————

Rhodes, 24 Aug 1892.

My dear Elise, We stopped at Suda Bay, Crete, for a week. The place has not changed much in 10 years, but the island still remains in a state of anarchy, and agrarian and religious outrage, very much like Ireland. The Christians seem much more to blame than the Musselmen.

It is a grand sight to see half a dozen battleships racing. We left Suda Bay and ran at full speed to Rhodes doing 323 miles in 24 hours, beating all the others except the Trafalgar.

———— ∞ ————

Samos (Aegean Islands), 3 Sept 1892.

My dear Mother, We went over to Rhodes by ourselves for a couple of days. It is a curious place under Turkish rule, no Christians or Jews are now allowed inside the walls after 9pm although these same walls are covered with coats-of-arms from the old Crusaders and Knights of St John. The houses of the Grandmasters are now the harems of the fat, lazy and unspeakable Turk.

We had great fun ashore with a large camera endeavouring to elude the Turkish officials who have very strict rules and will not allow any photography whatever. We had just fixed up the camera to photograph a curious old street when a Turkish patrol with a very stout officer came up and told us we mustn't. We packed up and moved on, the armed guard following us, then 'happy thought' just as we turned a corner we whipped the camera out of the box and put it under my coat, another fellow collared the legs, and the lens and slide fell to another's share. When the guard came around the corner we had separated and were strolling away in different directions. The Turks started after the party with the empty box and tripod, leaving us alone. We soon came to a grand old church, used as a mosque, and by placing the camera on a wall, got a very good shot. After another two miles tramping we stopped at a cafe and asked the tired and surly old officer to have a cup of coffee. He was soon quite restored and we parted the best of friends.

———— ∞ ————

At Thasos (Greek Island), 2 Oct 1892.

Dear Frank, There have been so many changes owing to fever. Jackson has gone to HMS Jamaica and Karslake is our new Captain, both good sorts, though two more opposite men could not be imagined. Jackson said the ship was cold and painted all upper works black. Karslake says the heat is fearful and we are going to paint them white immediately.

I have been shooting with Lord C. Beresford; big party for four days. Lord C is an excellent host and brought up all his cooks and stewards and any amount of whiskey and a cask of beer. Blue-jackets are curious beggars. One, an Irishman, was left in the cutter to sleep, and during the night, the dinghy bumped into her stern. He got up, loaded his rifle, saying, 'Begorrah! the rebels are upon us', and had to be soothed by his mates. Next day he went shooting with the same rifle and got a crow in the head at 400 yards. I was lying in the reeds watching for duck about dusk and was very nearly shot by him, as he took me for a pig on seeing the rushes moving.

Have had a live shell jammed in a 46-ton gun all day and only just got it out.

———— ∞ ————

Salonika (Thessaloniki), 27 Oct 1892.

My dear Mother, The sequel to the jammed shell was amusing and instructive. Our guns are only 12 inches in diameter and as they are 27 feet long we could not find anyone small enough to get down the bore and unscrew the fuse without a fair chance of suffocation. I got into the powder chamber in the rear easily, 16 inches in diameter, and measured the position of the shell, etc. and was in about ten minutes. Then the captain-of-the-gun went in and was there about half an hour putting strops on it.

I felt my head twirling a bit after, but thought nothing of it until I saw him come out with a red bald patch, 4 inches across, on his scalp, the fresh fouling having removed all his hair. I went and washed my head mighty smart, but was rather late. It came off mine to a small extent, blistered up, but has nearly grown again. I had no idea saltpetre and muggins was so powerful.

We spent one day at Marathon Bay where Xerxes fought his great battle and I wandered all over the plain after snipe and could sympathise with Xerxes. On Sunday I made up a big picnic of Mids etc. for a walk to Thermopolae. The cutter had some difficulty getting in and we all had to 'off breeks' and wade ashore, carrying our breeks round our necks and trudging two miles through a marsh. After walking 6 miles and thinking we had another four to go I heard a hail from a neighbouring mound. 'Hi! you fellows. this is where Leonidas stood', and found Rear-Admiral Markham calling us. The place where the 300 Spartans made their stand was once 50 feet only from the sea, but the Bay has so silted up that it is now five miles of well cultivated plain and marsh.

CERTIFICATE: Edward F. B. Charlton served on HMS Colossus as Lieutenant (T) from 7 Mar 1892 to 21 Sept 1892 with sobriety and attention to his duty. Sgd I.S. Jackson.

———— ∞ ————

Malta, 22 Nov 1892.

My dear Mother, We have just got a new engineer out from Keyham and you will be glad to hear he says Frank is one of the most popular youngsters they have there.

Malta, 19 Jan 1893.

An awful row is brewing here over the appointment of another Maltese Catholic Chaplain. Admiral Tryon knew well the wishes of Lord Walter and everyone else on the station, but unfortunately Lord Walter happened to mention that an English Jesuit would probably come out. Tryon thought the name Jesuit quite enough, the flames of the Inquisition rose up before him; he already felt his portly frame writhing on the rack. He hied away to the Maltese Archbishop and at once got a Maltese appointed. The man appointed, Canon Cassar, is as good a Maltese as can be found but he can never gain the confidence of the blue-jackets.

———— ∞ ————

Salonika, 12 Feb 1893.

My dear Elise, My letters are a bit erratic as I never feel any inclination to write until the postman has gone ashore, and then I have to console myself with a gin cocktail; it occurs all too often I am afraid. As you have been numbering your letters so must I, but plead ignorance to any number over MDCCCLXXXXIII.

———— ∞ ————

5 Mar 1893.

As we left Salonika the sun set over Mount Olympus, 10,000 feet and with clouds 2/3rds of the way up, and clear summits. It was simply a dream of beauty, the snow turning red and reflecting downwards into the sea.

———— ∞ ————

Milo, 19 Mar 1893.

My dear Mother, I collected 8 Pounds 10/- for the sisters at Canae, in aid of their orphanage. They brought on board several pieces of work including a Berlin wool parrot with a green head and yellow tail. I raffled them with 1/- tickets for the officers and 6d for the men. Nearly everyone went, including the parson; rather different to the bigoted ass on the Inflexible *who got the Captain to stop their lottery.*

You know the Venus de Milo was found here. Whether the Venus was built here or not, the women are very pretty, with charming voices and good manners.

———— ∞ ————

Piraeus, 31 Mar 1893.

We gave the Gunroom a picnic at a place called Devil's Bridge. There are several great hoof-marks about – pointed out by the natives as the work of 'The Father of All Evil'. I think they took me and my bicycle for him too, especially as I rode into the village with a kitten on my shoulders. It came about like this: coming up a gully I saw a lot of boys heaving stones and heard a cat squall. On approaching I saw the poor beast was hanging from a branch by its hindquarters and all the devilment of the village was stoning it. I went for those boys with my dogwhip, cleared them out, put the kitten on my shoulders with its mouth bleeding and rode to the village. The kitten jumped out of the basket as we were taking it home.

The entrance here is very narrow. Last time this ship was here, in going out, the second anchor caught on a Greek gunboat's anchor and they heard a fearful row astern and found the Greeko was being forcibly towed out when they had no intention of going to sea.

CERTIFICATE: Edward F. B. Charlton served as Lieutenant (T) on HMS *Colossus* from 22 Sept 1892 to 12 Apr 1893 and conducted himself with sobriety and attention to his duties which he has conducted with zeal and to my entire satisfaction. Sgd N. V. Karslake.

Construction of Corinth Canal, Greece, completed 1893.

Navigator
on HMS Hood –1893

On 1 June 1893 Lieutenant Charlton joined HMS *Hood*, the Royal Navy's largest battleship. He gives a description of one of the most bizarre and tragic collisions ever to occur in naval history.

———— ∞ ————

Union Club, Malta, 4 July 1893.

My dear Mother, The dear old Colossus is close to us and I think every soul was on deck to see their relief, their band playing 'All very fine and large'. The Hood does seem a thumper being the largest that has ever been inside by 3,000 tons. They are doomed to disappointment; having left the fleet two days before the disaster only to get the order: 'Detain Colossus'.

(right-hand column) alter course in succession 16 points, i.e. 180 degrees to port, and Port line alter course in succession 16 points to starboard'. Had they turned within two cables this would have been the track (see Fig. 2). (The Rear-Admiral in charge of the left-hand column) Markham thought it too risky and would not until directed to by Tryon. His confidence was so great in the Admiral that he answered thinking the starboard line was intended to circle outside him on a much smaller degree of helm (see Fig. 3). He obeyed the order and put his helm hard down as also did Tryon, resulting thus (see Fig. 4) [A collision being imminent, Markham in] Camperdown with engines at full speed astern and going at five knots struck (Victoria amidships).

It was a fine afternoon and, being Thursday, the men were making and mending clothes, or asleep in their

HMS Victoria, *on the occasion of the Queen's Birthday, Valetta Harbour, Malta, 24 May 1892.*

We were very anxious to get details of the loss of the Victoria. The survivors got in here on Friday. Loring [later Rear-Admiral E. K. Loring] dined with me last night and I managed to get a certain amount of information. Poor Bourke has come out of it completely white-haired. It happened like this and there can be no doubt about the reason. Columns of division line ahead six cables apart (1,200 yards), the correct distance when ships are in columns (See Fig. 1). (Aboard HMS Victoria at the head of the right-hand column the overall commander of the whole fleet Admiral) Tryon had always said that ships can turn in two cables, and twice before, in manoeuvres at home he made a similar signal to this disastrous one, but the Rear-Admiral (in charge of the left-hand column) would not answer it (believing that ships could not turn 180 degrees in as little as two cables). No doubt Tryon was obstinate. The signal made was: 'Starboard line

messes, and a great number on deck. The Camperdown struck the Victoria on the steel deck just about the submerged torpedo flat, the ram entering at least 20 feet, as the Victoria's steel deck has cut into the Camperdown's bow for 15 feet. The hole in the Victoria was 12 feet horizontal.

After the collision, boats were immediately manned on board all ships but Tryon made: 'Annul sending boats but have them ready'. Luckily the Dreadnaught's were already in the water and remained down, the ship towing them.

The Victoria heeled over about 10 degrees for 6 minutes or so quite steadily and then went to about 25 degrees. Perfect order on board, the men aft all fallen in, the men forward getting out a collision mat and the bows slowly sinking, vessel's head turning inshore and slowly steaming for it. The bows got deeper until the water came over the forecastle and washed the men and mat about when they were called

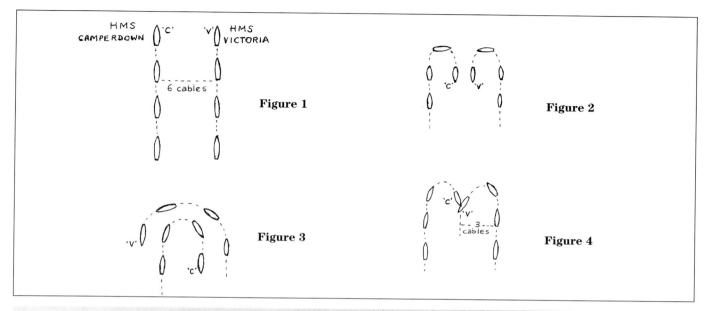

HMS Victoria *passing under the high-level bridge at Newcastle-upon-Tyne, where she was built.*

aft, the two Lieutenants Collins and Munro coming aft by different routes; Collins over (the deck), Munro through the battery and so drowned. Thus ten minutes elapsed. Accounts differ as to the time before she went down. They had no time to realise they were going down; some say it was a minute, some 45 seconds and the Staff Commander, Smith, who was standing beside the Admiral, heard the latter remark about 45 seconds before she went. 'I believe she's going, Captain Smith.' He replied, 'I think she is, Sir.' When the foremost bulkhead in the fore stokehold must have given way she rolled smartly over, keel up and went down nose foremost, the screws racing around in the air and doing some havoc amongst the poor unfortunates on her bottom. One survivor actually had his stomach ripped open by a blade.

The account in The Times last Wednesday is untrue and has caused much annoyance; there was no fighting with knives in the water and the men were all fallen in till she lurched over when everyone had to do the best they could for

themselves. As she went down the suction carried hundreds down to various depths – 10 to 12 fathoms – and they all came shooting up again with probably the decks below bursting up and killing several who thought they were well out of the screw. Coming up from the depths like that and amid such awful surroundings the men then lost their heads. Nearly all the survivors state they were clutched, often by expert swimmers, and having to fight for it. This is the only way one can account for so many Midshipmen being drowned, as they were nearly all on the bridge; they were not powerful enough to keep people off. One poor Mid who went over to the leeward was seen to go down the funnel as the funnel took the water, and there are hundreds of equally horrible cases. The Admiral and all those around him were washed off the top of the charthouse and all those around him were saved but Tryon's cap and telescope were all that came to the surface of him.

The Hood makes the station stronger than before the Victoria went down as regards ships, but Tryon cannot be

HMS Nile *standing by to assist survivors from HMS* Victoria *as she sinks off Syria.*

The damaged bows of HMS Camperdown *after her collision with HMS* Victoria.

replaced. It is an awful slap in the face for the Vice-Admirals having Seymour, a full Admiral, sent out because none of the former are up to standard. The Duke of Edinburgh would make the best, but he is, unfortunately, out of the question. We shall have the Court-Martial on board.

Let me relieve my mind with a yarn. The Mids had a grand dinner on the last night [before the fleet sailed]. At midnight one called Robbins, a chubby faced boy from the Victoria, could not be found so they went away without him. At 2.30am the Mid of the middle watch found him in a certain house of accommodation; as they could not get at him they awoke him by squirting cocoa at him through the 'jalousie' [Venetian blind] with an engine-room squirt.

Of the 600 men on Victoria, 359 lost their lives. The Court-Martial was held in Malta: 'with the deepest sorrow and regret the Court finds that this collision was due to an order given by the then Commander-in-Chief, the late Vice-Admiral Sir George Tryon.'

— ∞ —

Malta, 6 Aug 1893.

My dear Elise, Did you see about my being wrecked on Ricasoli Point a fortnight ago in one of our Torpedo Boats when going to the rescue of the Colossus's launch which had been hove right up on the rocks? Our craft I knew to be unreliable and I only went away in her as I thought life might be in danger. At the critical moment our engines refused to move and in two minutes we were also high and dry on the rocks. Our Mids, who were all with me, enjoyed it immensely and stuck to her although one or two were washed overboard, and no wonder as there was only a red hot funnel to hang on to. We were dragged off by a steam tug, very little the worse, the damage very slight considering. Coming back we met the Triumph in the entrance going home with the Victoria's survivors.

— ∞ —

Phalerum Bay, 20 Aug 1893.

The new Admiral was determined to brace up our nerves after the Victoria and kept the ten ships in a double quarter line [diamond-shaped formation] at a cable (200 yards) apart steaming ten knots and the officer of the watch to carry on – i.e. no one else being allowed to interfere. At this speed you cover a cable in 35 seconds. There is not much room to spare, especially as we are 3⅔rds cables long. We astonished everyone by our station-keeping. She turns out to be a wonderful craft at manoeuvring, though bigger than any of them.

As being Navigator of the biggest [naval] craft in the world only gives me 2/6d per diem extra, I shall be very glad when our new Navigator comes out, as the extra responsibility is not worth the recompense and interferes with my own job.

— ∞ —

HMS Hood, Santorini, 25 Oct 1893.

Dear Mother, We are to start coaling at Porus again next Sunday; this coaling on Sunday in peace-time is a most

senseless job and quite unnecessary, but it has been the rule out here for the past three years. It comes hard on the men after a week's routine that on their only day of rest they should have to turn to and work harder than ever; the only reason for it is to save 20 Pounds or so in demurrage of the collier.

This ship does not go to Italy with the Admiral; our skipper volunteered for these parts on account of the shooting on which he is very keen; carrying about five dogs and a Greek ruffian as a keeper.

— ∞ —

17 Dec 1893.

The Alphonse Club had great doings at Kalamouti; we got over 100 head of game in two days. There is nothing like having a skipper who is very keen on shooting as we can generally get steam boats to take us about and no obstacles are raised to getting up many jolly expeditions; ours savour more of 'la picnic' than of 'la chasse'.

— ∞ —

Malta, 25 Feb 1894.

Dear old boy, Your epistle of 17th was seriously delayed by a most fearful 'gregale' which lasted five days. The 'gregale', or NE wind, is the only one that can blow into the harbour and cause inconvenience. The Bishop generally works up prayers and has bells rung on the second day, but this time he was properly sold as, on the third day, it redoubled in violence. Things were fairly quiet until a Swede, the Freya, and a Russian, the Pamiat Azova, came in, the latter requiring to be docked. The Russians were disgusted at having to get all their powder and explosives out before we would allow them to dock. Now we have all these under our care and find them very interesting and primitive. She is a hulking great beast in appearance but a fraud as a fighting ship.

Last Monday we gave the foreigners a dinner at the Club and did them well. I had to go and our young soldier Oldfield. As the gregale had commenced we asked to sleep ashore; the skipper said 'They'd be d****d fools if they come off. Tell them to stop till they're sober', and so we did. It was very well done and after numerous 'healths' we saw them all under the table. The Russians and the Swedes hate each other like poison but we sandwiched them well apart. The Swedes are capital fellows but the Russkys are lousy swines and generally unhealthy. Their Torpedo-Lieutenant tried to embrace me repeatedly offering to show me all his 'torpilles' but I evaded his advances and got him to kiss two Cameron Highlanders who were taken unawares. We didn't want any of their French customs. It was a fearsome and gruesome night and my recollections are queer; no doubt I had a sparkle on. I recollect well seeing a Naval Lieutenant at a cab stand with a cab full of Russians and half a dozen of us trying to move them off against the police. The cab wouldn't budge, so we went 'full speed astern' just as she got away on 'full speed ahead'. The old horse, assisted by his jockey, went off at a gallop and the Russians fell out either side. Then a

Officers of HMS Hood, 1894. Ned is eighth from left back row.

cove told us he was a policeman in plain clothes so we said, 'Why the **** aren't you in uniform', and knocked him in the gutter. Then there was a glorious heav'o and the police retired for reinforcements. Lord knows how anyone got on board that night. The last thing I remember was laying in the door of a bawdy house in the street and placing a policeman's head through it when he expostulated. Then I had a small altercation with some flower pots which had got across the gangway at the hotel. After ascending many miles of stairs I found our young soldier just turned in. We had a large two-bedded room at the top of the hotel and a door in it opened into another room. Hearing a baby crying he soliloquised, 'A baby next door; where baby, there nursemaid, there nursemaid next door,' opened the door to find an old lady pacing about in her chemise with a baby in her arms and the expected nursemaid in bed. He offered to assist the old dame who was not a bit surprised to see a boozy article in his nightshirt and only recommended that he go to bed.

The weather was so bad I did not get aboard till 4pm and now they want me to go for a return dinner but I sturdily refuse.

— ∞ —

Malta, 26 Mar 1894.

My dear Mother, I have just paid 21 Pounds entrance to the United Services Club for old fogies, but the best in London.

The Stations put up for Holy Week are life-size statues made about fifty years ago but frequently repainted and too ghastly for words. The Scourging is nothing but a mess of gore. These are all carried through the streets on Good Friday and I rode out to Citta Vecchia to see the procession. It started at 7.30pm. and finished at 1.30am. I visited the Church where the people taking part were gathering and it was amusing to see all the performers arguing with one another just like behind the scenes at a Newcastle pantomime. Simon of Cyrene and a Roman centurion had a struggle for a helmet on the floor, and a small boy who was carrying Peter's ear on a sword cried because he could not carry the bag of money as well.

— ∞ —

Talanta (near Argos and Mycenae, Greece),
12 May 1894.

We have come here to stop the earthquakes which have been going on for the last fortnight. On 24 Apr we arrived at Nauplia and found ourselves in for a second round of Easter festivities, our Easter having been very early, the Greeks missed that moon altogether and got their Easter excessively late. On Good Friday they had their first earthquake. We came round here at 12 knots not knowing how we should find things. I had made great preparations to land with 100 men. I never saw any place in such absolute ruin; all the coastal villages built of stone and mud are level. Every village lost a few killed, some as many as 60. Talanta itself looks all right from the sea but nothing could be more deceptive. The reason why it is not level is that the mortar stood better than the mud. I went into one man's house and congratulated him on the strength of his foundations, the house being apparently uninjured. With tears in his eyes he took me upstairs and showed me all four cornices just on the point of falling outwards.

Not a life was lost here and they tell a curious tale; the first shock was not very severe and little damage was done but, being Good Friday, 'at the hour Jesus Christ was dead' as they expressed it, as usual all the people left the Church in procession. (They were in the open) when the big shock came, throwing them off their legs, wrecking every house and opening chasms kilometres long in the hills behind. The Church itself, a beautiful structure, is a hopeless ruin, the dome lying in the middle.

— ∞ —

Thaso, 27 May 1894.

My dear Elise, Our work consisted mainly in landing all the timber for [rebuilding] the numerous villages; about 100,000 baulks and 80,000 planks, and in building a village for the inhabitants of Scala.

HMS Hood.

HMS Hood, Gibraltar, 1 Jul 1894.

My dear Mother, I have now to look after the canteen accounts which is no small job as they turn over 4,000 Pounds a year and I was pitchforked into it in April when D (Dundas) went sick before he had made out the usual quarterly statement. He was too ill to question. What with gear bought in Turkey and Greece, okes, Pounds Maltese and English, cantars and rottos, kilos and centimetres, casks of pickles and boots, bags of sardines and bathing drawers, and bottles of flour and raisins, it was no slight job and my language has turned the white paint of my cabin to emerald green. To add to it all the Maltese tradesmen are the greatest scoundrels unhung, any one of them being quits for two Greeks and a Jew; luckily I weighed everything or I would have been seriously done. The trick was to send up goods to the Levant, the invoice showing no weights; then after we had consumed them the weights would appear on their bills. Such small errors as making 20 cheeses average 87 lb instead of 78 lb is an example.

The Captain read to us the thanks of the Greeks to our Foreign Office and the Admiralty, 'for our services in repairing earthquakes'.

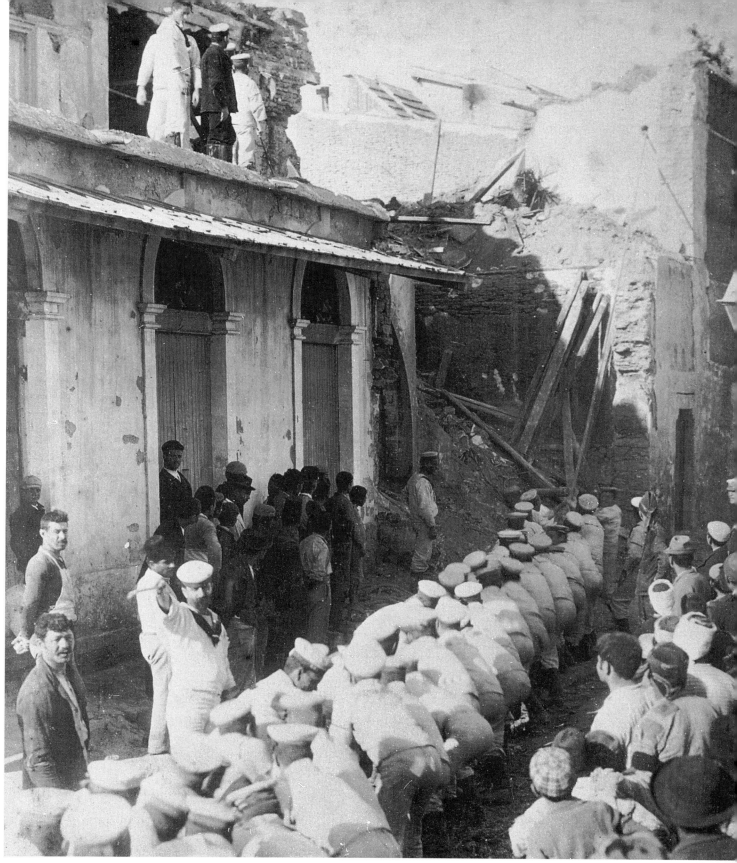

Sailors of the Royal Navy help restore a Cretan town after the earthquake of 1894.

Gibraltar, 8 Jul 1894.

Dear old boy, We came in in slashing style under old Mike Seymour, altering course 8 points at 1½ cables at 12 knots. The anchoring however came very near a fiasco. The Admiral gave the order (to the whole fleet) to stop and haul down (signal) cones – the 'intelligent' signalman hauled down the anchoring cone as well. We let go the anchor doing 8 knots and the cable went past me in a sheet of flame. I didn't attempt to check it until about 10 cables had gone out when we put the brake on and dragged it taut, smashing the bow torpedo booms to pancakes. It pulled up at 1¼ cables. We only had 16 (in total). Two ships parted (lost their anchors) but none had 15,000 tons to bring up (to a halt).

———— ∽ ————

Tenedos (now Bozca Ada, Turkey), 9 Sept 1894.

Oswin's address I do not know though no doubt the police would find him as he must be well known up there by this time. He has not let me congratulate him on clearing out of Cambridge with such a brilliant flourish.

Rejoice with me now as I am the First Lieut (Lieutenant-Commander) of the finest battleship afloat bar none, and known as Appy Oods in marine circles. Dundas was invalided and the Captain applied for me to be First Lieut.

We have just gone through the yearly ordeal of Admiral's inspection and expect an A1 report as I am up to all the tricks of these inspecting Admirals. Thus Admiral says while down in the depths, 'Dynamo disabled.' The electric lights disappear for a second and come on again. 'What's up?' says the Admiral, 'didn't I say "dynamo disabled"?' 'Yes, Sir, but another one has been put on' – for we keep two running for the occasion. The Admiral grunts at being done and roars, 'Damme, I mean lights shot away.' 'Aye aye, Sir', followed by total darkness till the faint glimmer of Coulomb's candles become visible and which were all alight beforehand. More grunts until the Admiral falls over a magazine hatch and finds it expedient to repair the lights again.

Just before leaving Malta I had the finest fight I have had yet with four Maltese blades who were evidently out at night giving their bulldog a little cat practice. Naturally I caught the bulldog a h*** of a smite with my stick and he cleared out howling. The blades surrounded me and one of them caught hold of my coat and said, 'What for you hit that dorg?' I replied, 'I'd hit you the same if I found you bullying a cat.' Backed meanwhile towards the gate where I knew there was a sentry. Then one of the swines ran at me from behind and hit me in the face with one of his clenched fists. I immediately plugged the fellow in front who had hold of my coat and he went down like a log and was last seen with his head in his hands moaning. At first I was in a devil of a funk and thought they would smash me into jelly, or knife me, as they attacked me together. But in a short time I realised they were useless with their fists. I got more and more buckish but the sentry turned out the guard. The last I heard from my opponents was, 'Now we go for

police', and no doubt, had I given them time to do so, I should have been carried off to the station. As it was I was none the worse, my collar having saved me from a rock held in the hand.

———— ∽ ————

Kalamuti, 20 Jan 1895.

Dear Richard, I saw in the Globe *yesterday the death of one of my greatest friends in the Service, Doctor McKay, killed by a lion on Lake Nyasa where he was stationed in the* Pioneer. *Poor fellow, he finished off the lion but died three days later. McKay was a grand fellow. I owed my life to him more than once when experimenting with unknown chemicals in the* Vernon's *laboratory and his death I feel exceedingly. RIP.*

———— ∽ ————

Sigri (Greece), 19 Feb 1895

My dear Oswin, We ended up at Salonika by giving a dance at which everyone enjoyed themselves. Blunt, the British Consul-General, is virtually Governor of the place and has the Turks entirely under his thumb.

I had an enjoyable three days shooting up country with our skipper. The party consisted of our skipper, flag-captain and myself, all of different persuasions though Christians, a Spanish Jew and his nephew, and the Bey and his Cavass, Musselmen, who were our hosts and spoke only Turk, Greek and Bulgar. A fine mixture. We commenced the shoot on Friday, which is the Turkish Sunday, shot over the Jewish Sabbath into our own Sunday.

———— ∽ ————

Malta, 5 May 1895.

There is a namesake of ours here; a surgeon on the Anson *and a good fellow. He is an Irishman and an ugly bounder and I won't claim him as a connection.*

———— ∽ ————

Beirut, 8 Jun 1895.

The Alexandria week was a very gay one. I dined with the Khedive at the Palace, one of the best dinners I have ever attended. Poor fellow, he detests us English and must feel himself in rather a poor position as the uncrowned King of Egypt. Lord Cromer keeps a very taut hand over him and he is little more than a puppet well provided with a harem.

Tell Frank he is to be congratulated on the success of his conspiracy for the abolition of the Senior Mess at Greenwich though he won't reap much benefit from it himself.

———— ∽ ————

HMS *Hood* at Boudrum, 8 Jul 1895.

My dear Elise, Our summer cruise so far has been a weary one, heat increasing and the places getting more desolate.

Poor old Crusaders! How glad they must have been when the Turks kicked them out.

We went off from Beirut to Tripoli and passed over the exact spot where the Victoria lies but that was no reason for the Admiral going to tactics at night. Even old George Tryon used to fight a bit shy of night tactics.

— ∞ —

At sea 200 miles east of Malta, 9 Aug 1895.

My dear Frank, I should not think there is any chance of you getting the Terrible yet and may the Lord preserve me from ever being in a ship with 48 boilers.

I lost a torpedo at Kos just before we left, but it didn't worry me as he was a centenarian – 100 runs – and on the previous run, three months before, he had a collision with another torpedo in the water, damaged his internals, and had to be sent home for repair.

— ∞ —

Thaso, 8 Sept 1895.

My dear Elise, My dark room is a very good one and well fitted up and, though well supplied with air, at 102°F, I do not care about spending much longer there than I can help. This is due to Admiralty economy in giving us an air shaft to the upper deck that is divided down the middle – one side being uptake from the boilers. I give up photography when I have to use ice in the developer.

HMS Hood *buries her bows whilst steaming at high speed.*

Dear Father Frank, The whole squadron, 21 ships, has been gathered for our annual regatta. We lost the race in the pulling, where our seamen, well known to be the best in the fleet, were beaten by the Hawke's *stokers. What is the British sailor coming to when the stoker can beat him at pulling an oar.*

CERTIFICATE: Edward F. B. Charlton has served as Lieutenant on HMS *Hood* from 1 Jun 1893 – done duty as Senior Lieut since 6 Apr 1894 – to 28 Oct 1895 and conducted himself with sobriety and entirely to my satisfaction both as Senior and Torpedo Lieutenant. He is well worthy of advancement being an able and zealous officer. Sgd Edm F. Jeffrey.

— ∞ —

HMS *Hood* at Salonika (then Turkish, now Greek),
8 Nov 1895.

My dear Mother, The Admiral got permission to come here on the plea of getting the washing done and giving the men leave but was told to keep the fact secret from the Turks. He told Consul-General Blunt that 20 ships would arrive on the 6th but that the information was to be kept secret. Just after Blunt received this he met Vali, the Turkish Governor, who asked him when the fleet was expected; Blunt told the diplomatic lie and knew nothing about it. 'Curious,' said Vali, 'but Mrs White of the Collingwood Arms just told me the Fleet was expected on the 6th' – and sure enough on the 6th the fleet arrived. [It turned out that] the Admiral made a [visual] signal to the fleet saying we should anchor here next week and this was immediately telegraphed by the bumboatman to Mrs White, a well known character here who keeps a shanty called the Collingwood Arms, supplying sailors with all their desires ashore. She is said to make 500 Pounds per week.

— ∞ —

HMS *Hood*, Salonika, 24 Dec 1895.

Dear Father Frank, Here's to you in a glass of the best. Tonight we have every officer in the ship dining in the Wardroom, 35 in all, so I thought I would drop you a line before dinner as after my remarks may not be so intelligible.

They have got a Midnight Mass on here at the Convent, and tomorrow I am running a picnic about thirty miles towards Mount Olympus in charming country. All saddle and game bags and canteens and luncheon baskets have been requisitioned.

Xmas day on board is a terrible affair and I shall be glad to get away. The wintry weather has disappeared and the snow line is daily mounting up Olympus.

— ∞ —

Salonika.

Dear Elise, We spent Christmas about 40 miles up the line at Karaferia taking our guns, an enormous lunch and plum pudding. It was a lovely day and the six members of the Alphonse Club – motto 'Aut Vincere Aut Mentiri' (If you're

not successful, at least make up a story about it!) – had our Xmas dinner on the edge of a babbling stream under the shadow of Mount Olympus. The shooting in the forenoon was good and we disposed of several woodcock.

The promotions to Commander are beginning to interest me. One of my term on the Britannia, *by name Calthorpe, got it last time over 268 heads and after being only nine years Lieutenant. I am over eleven, however Calthorpe's is for war service and one cannot grudge a fellow his luck; he has been employed on all the East and West African expeditions.*

— ∞ —

HMS *Hood*, Alexandretta (now Iskenderun, Turkey),
28 Mar 1896.

My dear Grannie, The Levant squadron of six great ships is still here helping to bolster up the Turks by putting money into the place, doing no earthly good to the Armenians, and being laughed at by the Moslems. We are prepared to bring off all Europeans, about 30 all told, at a moment's notice, but in case of a massacre we have strict orders not to interfere between the Turks and their subjects, i.e. Armenians. On the 25th a massacre was carried out at Killis and was assisted by soldiery who slaughtered about 200. Today large flocks of vultures have been passing over in the direction of Killis. It seems absurd to demonstrate when you have no intention of doing anything.

— ∞ —

Off the mouth of the Orontes.

Dear Elise, We arrived yesterday and are within 13 miles of the famous town of Antioch, now said to be surrounded by 3,000 Turkish troops, only waiting the word to start off one of their massacres, for they are the same regiments who were employed on this work lately at Marash and Zeitoun. The Porte has suddenly ordered them into this district where the natives are perfectly quiet and peaceful.

— ∞ —

At sea off the coast of Syria,
12 Apr 1896.

My dear Mother, I got a few days' leave at Beirut and saw some of the country in the extreme north of Palestine, including Damascus [now Syria] and Baalbek [now Lebanon]. Messrs Cook rather piled it on – 7 Pounds to see both places. I gather I could have done it cheaper but it paid well to use Cook's – no bother about railway tickets, hotel backsheesh, dragomen or the eternal beating down of prices one has to endure in the East.

In the printed notice in each hotel room in Damascus we observed: 'The Narghileh is Prohibited'. Our Midshipmen asked me what it was and I told them it was a certain useful article generally found under the beds. They did an awful growl, could not make out why it is supplied if it is not intended for use. They did not find out the jest until the last day and would have liked to have slain me for having caused them to wander about the cold passages at night. The 'narghileh' is a hubble-bubble smoking pipe!

On entering Baalbek, the scout of a rival inn told us that they had 'un maladie dangereuse at Cook's Hotel'. We told our proprietor of the calumny. He was furious and went out armed with an enormous blunderbuss and a Crusader's sword to search for the other fellow . . . fortunately for the district he did not fire the blunderbuss and the other fellow left by the back door.

The ruins beat anything, they are incomparable; Phoenician below date 3000 BC; the Roman about AD 100 and Arabic fortifications on top. Nothing I know approaches the beauty of the Temple of Jupiter; no one yet knows how the big stones were got into place 20 feet up the wall, each as long as a cricket pitch, 66 feet, and weighing 1,109 tons apiece.

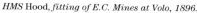

Canea, Crete, 12 Jun 1896.

My last letter from Athens told you we were just off here as the Turks have commenced their 'Armenian Games'. I found 300 refugees in a small courtyard of the French Mission under the care of my old friend Sister Joseph; poor thing, she was glad we were able to make better arrangements for her people. Last Saturday and Sunday 15 villages in a most fertile part of the country were burnt in

sight of the ship by about 3,000 (Turkish) troops. Laying waste to a country like this may be a legitimate act of war of the mediaeval type but we have no business to allow Mahommedans to carry on this way with Christians.

Two old monks came off from the monastery and said they had 1,000 women and children there and the Turks were only two miles off and advancing, so we boarded the Turkish gunboat and asked the captain, in the name of humanity (to desist). No harm was done to them; perhaps there was a suspicion of a threat in our request. On Tuesday the Turks retreated along the beach; they say with a loss of 100. I followed as close as I could get in my launch and watched their flanking parties burning the Christian villages on the way.

Most of the Consuls seem to favour the Turks but it is a difficult position to interfere in. The Christians came off best at Vamos, 10 miles away, where they had shut up 1,300 Turks who were starving. A relief party of 4,000 Turks got within a half mile when they were fallen on and ran away. The beleaguered garrison, seeing their only chance of saving their lives going, made a sortie and some got through, but about 400 were killed.

The ship is filling up with pets, two gazelle, an ibex, a red-legged partridge, three rabbits and a hedgehog, my possession, full of life, who lives on cockroaches, and refuses to be rolled up into a ball unless provoked by our big retriever.

HMS Hood, *fitting of E.C. Mines at Volo, 1896.*

HMS Hood, *in dry dock, Malta.*

On 7 September 1896 the crew of HMS *Hood* were replaced by a fresh crew except for a small number, including Ned, who stayed for a further few months to settle down the new arrivals.

—∞—

Piraeus, 29 Nov 1896.

My dear Mother, I went up to Trikala and we stopped with the station-master, a Greek from Trebizond who spoke four languages. These people on the line are most obliging, provide us with dinner and give us a room where we can spread our stretchers and sleep the peace of the Just after a hard day with duck, cock or snipe. I should like to see the faces of the station-master at Bath if a party of Greek Naval Officers suddenly turned up with all shooting accessories and expected to be treated in like manner.

—∞—

HMS *Hood*, Volo, 3 Jan 1897.

My dear Elise, We had a jolly time at Christmas. The Alphonse Club camped out. We managed to bag 14 couple of snipe *and a duck for the Xmas dinner. It poured for 45 consecutive hours until Sunday. Luckily our tent was a good one; there was a good stout olive tree at each corner and one inside for our Xmas tree decorated with guns and wet clothes.*

—∞—

Union Club, Malta, 13 Feb 1897.

My dear Mother, Finished with Hood *– I was conveyed ashore in a cutter pulled by a party, in various stages of **********, well excitement, numbering 12 officers and it was not without a pang that I bid adieu to the old tank. I am lucky getting a passage home on a Chinese P&O as the Indian steamers are not allowed to call on account of the plague.*

CERTIFICATE: Edward F.B. Charlton served at Lieutenant (T) on HMS *Hood* from 29 Oct 1895 to 12 Feb 1897 with sobriety and to my entire satisfaction. Lt Charlton is an officer that well deserves advancement. Sgd Chas Drury.

Five further Certificates follow Captain Drury's, each being very commendatory; on Torpedo Training Ship HMS *Vernon* from 16 April to 29 May 1897; on HMS *Pembroke* from 30 May

HMS *Victorious* 1897.

to 7 June 1897; on HMS *Victorious* from 8 June 1897 to 27 January 1898; and on HMS *President* under two different Captains from 20 January 1898 to 15 February 1899 where he was 'borne for duty at Admiralty'.

———∞———

Ned's folio includes an invitation to his brother to lunch, the lunch apparently arranged at short notice:

HMS *Victorious*, 22 June 1897.

Dear Frank, You are to lunch here on Sunday at 1.30. I have asked Mother, Elise, Oswin, George, Willie, Willie D-B, Dollie D, Edith, Charlie B, Mary Teresa, Robin Dalglish and H. Weld-Blundell, some of whom will no doubt turn up and I hope all. I will send a skiff over for you and Willie if you want it. I called on you forgetting you had gone up to town. Boat waits an answer, E. Charlton.

Frank replied, 'Thanks for note. Charlie B yesterday had no invitation so I asked him, but your invitation is worth 10 of mine so please carry it out. Thanks for offer of skiff, Yrs FJC.'

Ned's papers also include a letter from a washerwoman soliciting his assistance in recovering money:

HMS Victorious *steaming against heavy seas, 1897.*

Palma de Malloreas, 12 Oct 1897.

To Luit Charlton, Dear Sir i am greatly obliged to you for your kindnefs in writing to me to Barcelona. i received your letter and God blefs you now i am taken in the liberty to ask you the favour if you will kindly speak to the officer of your ship who i have done washing for and ask them if they will pay me if not all what they think proper it is not my fault the washing is missed if they had not sent their servants Drunk on shore. i am a poor woman with seven children. Your bumboat man wanted to pay me in Barcelona but i would not take it until i knew he got everything on board. sgd E. Hunter.

After serving on HMS *Victorious* Ned joined HMS *President* as Assistant to Director of Naval Ordnance for one year and 27 days. The Public Record Office in London preserves the handwritten record of the full list of Ned's appointments, together with the number of days on each ship. His postings over 46 years fill not only the folio sheet reserved for his activities but also a second sheet assigned to one of his fellow 1878 cadets recorded only in a single line as: 'Discharged the Service 6 Jan 1880; unable to pass out.'

In January 1899 Ned's only sister and consistent correspondent, Elise, married Edward Doran-Webb.

HMS Orlando *and the* Boxer Rebellion – 1898-1901

As second in command of HMS *Orlando*, Ned's next tour of duty was to the Far East. His folio commences with cuttings from a news journal which gives details of the ship. Launched in 1886, HMS *Orlando* was initially flagship of the Australia Station and was fitted with two 9.2-inch guns, ten 6.0-inch, and ten three-pounders. She was armoured with sixteen-inch bulkheads and protective steel, two to three inches thick, on the decks. Her top speed was 'a bare 18 knots as compared with the indispensable 22 knots of 1899.' The journal included photos of the seamen, stokers, marines and twenty-nine officers who made up the ship's complement as well as a photo showing Captain Burke, Commander Charlton and Lieutenant Mackenzie described as 'The Cabinet of the *Orlando*'. After a few months Mr Mackenzie was given command of a destroyer and Lieutenant P.N. Wright replaced him.

HMS Orlando, *Commissioned at Portsmouth, 16 February 1899.*

HMS *Orlando*, Aden, 29 Mar 1899.

My dear Mother, We arrived here this morning right up to program and I feel rather proud of having hit the dates so well, the Captain having left it entirely to me, only specifying what speed we had to go.

—∞—

Singapore, 28 Apr 1899.

Tigers have been shot recently within 3 miles and we hear that the islands around contain baboons and alligators; we can't bathe. The Captain was sick, laid up with 'Curried Prawns', so I took the ship out for a few days' firing and exercise. Colombo [in Ceylon, now Sri Lanka] is a great place for diving boys who assemble off the ship in little

HMS Orlando *entering Portsmouth Harbour after 10 years as Flagship on Australian Station.*

canoes and shout for coppers: 'I dive, I dive, heave, I dive, ta-ra-ra-boom-de-ay.' Our Midshipmen were every bit as clever, so what do the young devils do but get into a bit of a dugout and appear off the big Australian mail steamer with similar shouts, much to the joy of the passengers.

Last night we went on a regular wild goose chase after a supposed ship on fire; the officer-of-the-watch, who is a bit of a visionary, sent down to say there was a ship ablaze on the starboard beam and the Captain altered course towards her. I was rather sceptical myself and made enquiries as to the position of Krakatoa [the Indonesian volcano that erupted in 1883 blowing four cubic km of rock into the sky]. There certainly was a blaze and it was only when I realised the direction in which we were steering that I knew that my shot at Krakatoa was not too far off the mark, for indeed it was nothing but a bush fire leading us to destruction.

I had to take to the typewriter as it is so unpleasant to have the paper sticking to your hands and it is certainly the best way of writing in hot weather.

———— ∞ ————

Penang (Malaya), 16 June 1899.

I think I told you we attempted a full speed trial but had to give it up; the stoke-hold in the tropics is no place for a white man. Several men came up saying it was too hot but they were all right; I put them in cell-irons. Five minutes later five

men collapsed and were carried up, so we had to ease down the trial; discipline was not affected by the release of the prisoners which I was delighted to order at once. The question is: which is the finer seaman? The one who sticks to it till he collapses, thereby injuring his health, perhaps permanently, or the one who falls just short of this and bursts the bonds of discipline. There is no limit to endurance; unfortunately we have no gauge to indicate the critical point.

I have two alligator's eggs hatching in my cabin so I expect to wake up one morning minus an arm or a leg.

———— ∞ ————

Ned's folio includes a letter addressed to him:

No.1 Bishop Str, Penang, 2 Jul 1899.

To the Commander of HMS Oroalando *Penang Harbour. Sir; I want to go in your ship to Singapore. Not a single ship won't carry passengers. If we won't go with this ship plenty trouble in my business. In Singapore there is no my agent at all and all my servant in bum-boat. Hoping you will pity me. I have the honour Sir (signature illegible).*

———— ∞ ————

Singapore, 5 Jul 1899.

My dear Elise, Penang proved disastrous to our pets. (My dog) Jim, who came with me to attend a Scotch Christening;

A news journal photo entitled 'The Cabinet of the Orlando'. Commander E.F.B. Charlton, Captain J.H.T. Burke, Lt C. Mackenzie.

perhaps the sight of so much 'whusky' made him think this world too sinful. He had a fit, attacked his friends and dashed over the sea wall. I rescued him and he careered through a Tennis Party fetching up in a Police Station which the police evacuated. At last I had him shot and interred under a palm tree with the inscription 'Here Lies Nelson'.

⧟

HMS *Orlando*, Manila (Philippines),
24 July 1899.

My dear Mother, In a heavy sea one of our people fell overboard from a cutter; he was jerked out of the boat on which he was boatkeeper. All the crew were at the time trying to get into the boat; I saw the whole thing and that the ass, though only two yards away from the cutter, could not get there; also that the sentry on the forebridge with a lifebuoy beside him only gaped in spite of my yells. So as the man was actually drowning below me I had to go in and, with some difficulty, pulled him out. As he had his mouth open, yelling the whole time he was in the water, his back teeth were awash with salt water and he was mighty near gone. On looking at his certificate I found he was said to be able to swim, so I asked him why he didn't, and he replied, 'Please Sir, I can swim but no one told me I was going overboard'.

⧟

Manila, 24 July 1899.

Poor Yanks; how they are enjoying themselves as a colonial power. Their main idea seems to be to get us to take the Philippines and give them our West India islands in exchange. They have their hands full here and it is costing them a mint of money for their methods are extraordinarily extravagant and there seems to be no check on waste. Our steward comes off daily with frozen meat, potatoes etc. all marked 'U.S. Army' though how he buys these things in the open market it is not my job to enquire.

Yankee officers are not allowed spirits unless they have to entertain, hence they never lose an opportunity of seeing strangers, of the right sort, and all at Uncle Sam's expense.

⧟

10 Aug 1899.

The Captain has recommended me for the Albert Medal for Muda River.

The official citation for the award of the Albert Medal states:

Commander E.F.B. Charlton and Lieut Richard Hyde.
At 5pm on 29 June 1899, the steam cutter belonging to HMS *Orlando grounded on a sandbank in the Muda River near Penang. The river is some eighty yards wide, with a depth of twelve to sixteen feet, and flows with a strong current. In order to get the cutter afloat, Commander Charlton, Lieut Hyde and Edward C. Holloway, petty officer, carried out an anchor as far as the depth of water would allow, when on*

dropping the anchor all three were swept off their feet by the current. Lieut Hyde succeeded in reaching the stranded boat, but Mr Holloway was unable to do this, and was directed by Commander Charlton to try and gain the opposite bank, about fifty yards distant, he himself accompanying him. When about five yards from the bank Holloway suddenly threw up his arms and sank. Commander Charlton at once dived and caught him by the hair, but this being short it slipped from his grasp, and although the Commander again dived several times he did not succeed in finding him and he was drowned. Meanwhile Lieut Hyde left the cutter and swam to the place, but was too late to render any assistance, although he remained by Commander Charlton till a landing was effected about fifty yards lower down. Great risk was incurred, the river being infested with crocodiles. **The Silver medal was voted to Commander Charlton, and Testimonial on Vellum to Lieut Hyde.**

⧟

Hong Kong, 21 Aug 1899.

My dear Mother, At present I rather enjoy the Chinaman; this floating population with a family on board each cockle-shell is quite a new experience. I could sit and watch the old ladies in their sampans with their crowds of small children for hours; they have such a queer life and eat such impossible things, and make such quaint smells that at present the novelty delights me.

⧟

25 Aug 1899.

The plague still goes on. Captain Fisher had some great fun out of four of his men on Grafton. *They were found out of bounds visiting the plague-stricken portion of the town. He kept them in the submerged flat, squirted carbolic over them every half-hour and burnt their clothes. The ship being in dry-dock, whenever they had to go outside [for a call of nature] they were preceded and followed by men carrying yellow flags.*

A splendid terrier swam on board this morning. I am putting an advertisement in the China Mail *saying we have a stray dog.*

⧟

8 May 1899.

A Midshipman shot himself on Sat with a beast of a magazine pistol presented to him by his fond relatives before he left home. He was buried in Happy Valley and I have sent his people some photos.

⧟

Nagasaki (Japan), 16 Sept 1899.

We left Hong Kong last Sunday so Frank and I met for 48 hours. It was pleasant to meet him; it had been a bad week for me with three burials, an attempted suicide, courts of

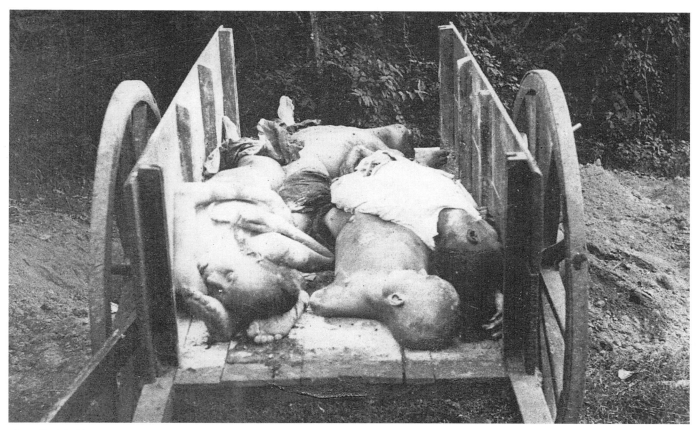

Above: Burial of Chinese dying of the plague, Penang 1899.

Below: Kowloon side, Hong Kong.

enquiry and an inquest, and culminated in the absconding of Ah Ping, the messman who was so strongly recommended by all those with whom he had been. He has let us in for 230 Pounds in England. It is bad enough to have to pay twice over for six months' grub but the situation is intensified when one realises that the whole brunt falls on the wardroom, while one knows that the Captain, gunroom and warrant officers – and Mids who lived off chocolate creams – were all fed off our stores on the way out. I am going to pay up half as President of the Mess and not being married. I think the man took to gambling and opium on the way out, for he was looking a wreck in Manila, but said it would be all right for him when he got to Hong Kong. So it was from his point of view. He got away by the 6pm steamer to Canton.

On arrival here a Jap Official turned up, a pernicious little brute covered with gold lace, who told us to anchor 'behind' the Russian flagship. We translated 'behind' as 'beyond' whereas he meant 'astern of'. When we got beyond we found a shoal-patch and had to go full speed astern. The official is a beast but I like his country-mates the more after a long ride into the country on unfrequented roads.

———— ∽ ————

Kobe (Japan), 18 Nov 1899.

There is every probability of Russia and Japan coming to blows in the near future as the Japs wish to precipitate a row before the Trans-Siberian railways are completed. They would get a hammering, but are very tough and thick-skinned.

———— ∽ ————

Hong Kong, 9 Dec 1899.

Interrupted by fearful yells outside my cabin. A Chinese mother is admonishing her offspring, a little girl aged four. The small one is at present being held over the side by her legs, and as she yells, her head is dipped in the water; the mother tiring of this, as the child only cries worse each time she comes out, has hoisted the small creature on board, and proceeds to ram a rolling-pin, or a piece of wood about the size of one, into its mouth. The child is dropped down to the bottom of the boat and there is peace once more.

———— ∽ ————

Hong Kong.

My dear George, I had a terrible New Year's Eve dining with a gunner at the Peak and then, after walking down, I got to the Royal Artillery Mess and played Rugby till 2am. My remains were up at 6am as, after dinner, a salute was ordered by the Rear-Admiral under the mistaken impression that 1st Jan 1900 began a new century.

HMS Orlando *football team, with Commander Charlton.*

Hong Kong, 5 Jan 1900.

My dear Mother, Christmas passed very soberly and I think most people wondered how Ladysmith and Mafeking were enjoying themselves (under siege by Boer soldiers in South Africa).

I find it rather difficult to write as I barked my right elbow at football. We have been having international rugby matches in favour of the (Boer) War Fund. We had over 2,000 spectators at $1 a head.

10 Feb 1900.

Our sailing orders for Manila arrived and the Commander-in-Chief has given me the acting vacancy until Captain Burke returns [from sick leave] so that I shall find myself Senior Naval Officer in the Philippines with a first class cruiser and two gunboats. $9 extra per diem is not to be despised.

Manila, 8 Mar 1900.

The Americans are beginning to make the place hum; some of them are charming people when one gets to know them. The country around Subic Bay abounds in game, deer and pig mostly, but at present one is liable to be mistaken for an American, and Americans still remain desirable for the Philippine game-bag.

17 Mar 1900.

My dear Dorothy, You know the Americans are at war with the insurgents and have 65,000 troops on the island trying to squash the Philippinos, but the latter have got too wily now and won't wait for the Yankees to get them, but always run immediately they see him coming. Then the Philippinos climb trees and wait till they see a solitary sentinel coming and, when he gets close, they shoot him from the trees and hack him to pieces with their bolos, sort of double-edged bread knives. They will sometimes wait weeks in the trees to get a single American; this is called 'Guerrilla warfare' and is very annoying to the Yankee who lose 20 or 30 men a week in this way alone.

Our terrier, Mike, swam aboard in Hong Kong and made himself quite at home. Mike hates Chinamen; last week one of our Chinese cooks threw some boiling water over Mike, scalding him badly. The man was brought up before me charged with cruelty. I said in my best Chinese: 'Chinaman makee boil doggee belong me, me make boil Chinaman.' He

HMS Orlando *at Amoy, 24 May 1900, Queen Victoria's last birthday.*

was then seized by two lusty seamen and stretched over a coil of rope without his shirt, and a tub of boiling water appeared from below. His yowls at this sight were delicious and the other Chinese were delighted at the prospect of punishment so much after their own heart. Then another tub of cold water was suddenly dashed over him and for some minutes he believed he had been scalded to death.

In spite of the heat we go over to Cavite frequently to play hockey or football in the old Spanish dockyard. On the way we pass the wrecks of all the Spanish ships sunk by Admiral Dewey in May 1898.

———— ∞ ————

Manila, 4 Apr 1900.

My dear Mother, April and May are the two hottest months and even now my cabin occasionally gets up to 96°F but I have got an electric fan from the U.S. Government. It appears they sent out a lot of direct-current fans forgetting that Manila is the only place with current (alternating) and that in most other spots even candles are unknown. As they work well off our dynamo we have been buying them at about half price.

Last month about 150 'Bolomen' charged a squad of 20 Americans armed with rifles over an open space of 150 yards. Over 100 were killed during the advance but the others got in and cut the Americans to pieces.

On 21 Mar, my birthday, two Archbishops and three Bishops came on board to call on me; of course it was quite an accident them coming that day.

———— ∞ ————

In the heyday of the Roman Empire, Britain and all countries adjoining the Mediterranean were united under a single government. Since then, until the recent formation of the European Economic Union, the numerous nations that lie within the former Roman Empire – and their even more numerous races, languages, units of measure and philosophies – have been characterised as much by diversity as by unity. In contrast to Europe, China had one nation, one race (Han 94%), one written language, a common system of measurement and one basic philosophy for over 2,000 years until the start of the twentieth century. In 221 BC Emperor Chin united seven states, built the Great Wall, adopted Confucianism, the Chinese script, a standard wheelbase for all carts, and constructed a tomb with some 8,000 life-size statues of soldiers and horses at Xian. While there were occasional partitions of China as well as foreign invasions, such as that by Mongol Emperor Yuan in AD 1260, these interruptions were largely absorbed without affecting the central structure.

China has long recognised five zones of influence: at the heart (1) the Imperial Capital, surrounded by (2) Tribute-paying Princes, (3) the Zone of Pacification, (4) the Barbarians allied to China and, finally, (5) Outer Darkness. On average the great Chinese inventions – gunpowder, porcelain, printing, and the compass – took 1,000 years to reach the West. In addition to enjoying considerable stability,

citizens accepted the Confucian philosophy which places man at the top of the tree. It is not surprising that the Chinese saw themselves at the centre of the world, all-powerful and self-sufficient. Emperor Ch'ien-lung wrote to King George III: 'We possess all things. I set no value on objects, strange and ingenious, and have no use for your country's manufactures.' Nevertheless Arab and Indian merchants had been trading with China and had been paying tribute to the emperor for many years by the time the first Western traders arrived in 1601. The Westerners regarded trading and the teaching of Christianity as a right; they considered the payment of tribute to be an imposition and from their success in colonising Africa, America and India, they regarded themselves, under God, as being at the top of the tree. The classic irresistible missile had met the immovable object.

But even if these factors were not enough to ensure a clash, others were also manifest: excessive rigidity within China which discouraged change, considerable corruption on the part of Chinese officials, and an iniquitous trade conducted by Western merchants which would not have been tolerated back in Europe, viz. the growing of opium in India and the selling of it in China. The Chinese traded silver or tea in exchange. In 1800 Emperor Chia-ch'ing prohibited the import of opium but the trade continued to expand for many decades, from 0.2 million kg in 1790 to 1.8 million kg in 1839. This made it the most profitable merchandise Britain had ever found in the Orient. In a crackdown on the illegal trade, the Chinese destroyed 2.6 million pounds of forbidden opium in 1839. In retaliation Britain attacked China, the British guns completely overpowering the Chinese junks. The victors imposed a penalty of $6 million on the vanquished; China had to cede Hong Kong and grant immunity in future to foreign criminals who broke Chinese law.

In 1856 there was another Anglo-Chinese conflict after which the West obtained the Tientsin concessions: eleven ports to be opened to trade, a penalty payment of four million taels [a silver weight] to be made, and Westerners to be permitted to live anywhere and to preach Christianity. This last mentioned right unfortunately led to the creation of segregated Chinese Christians who enjoyed a position in society above that to which they would have been entitled in the Confucian order. It also led to a new philosophy preached by a Chinese self-styled 'Heavenly Prince' who set out the Taiping ideals – one God, Christ a prophet, redistribution of land among peasants, and the elimination of concubines and of foot-binding for women. In 1860, after ten years of battle and the loss of ten million lives, the insurrection was suppressed. The Taiping rebels were exceedingly harsh on their enemies and, as they were identified as Christians by the general populace, they exacerbated anti-Christian sentiment. In the same year, 1860, an Anglo-French force conquered Peking (Beijing), destroyed the old Summer Palace, obtained trade concessions and imposed further fines; and Russia gained 350,000 square miles of Chinese territory. The defeats of Chinese militia by the West led the Chinese to adopt some changes, without enthusiasm, such as the introduction of Western weapons, railways and telegraphs and, through Sir Robert Hart, an example, in the

Chinese Maritime Customs Service, of a bureaucracy that worked without corruption.

Gradually China lost its Zone of Pacification and the concomitant tributes it had long enjoyed: Burma went to the British, Okinawa to the Japanese, Ili to Russia, Sikkim and Korea to independence. In the first major clash of ironclad ships in the world, sixty-five large Chinese ships were outgunned by thirty-two small fast Japanese ships. The Japanese struck the first blow before declaring war. In 1895 Korea surrendered, Japan was given Taiwan, and a further huge fine was imposed on China. In the same year France gained control of Kwangchou, Germany of Tsingtao, and Britain, concerned that France, Germany, Russia and Japan were gaining 'such slices of the China melon', obtained concessions along China's richest artery, the Yangtze River.

In 1900 Hong Kong was handling forty-one per cent of China's foreign trade and 11,000 ships a year. During these wars the United States was only marginally involved in China, initially because it was a reluctant colonial power and, later, because it was engaged in taking over Hawaii, Puerto Rico and the Philippines. Cheng-Kuan-Ying summed up Chinese discontent: 'The Westerners profit themselves at the cost of others . . . when a foreign ship collides with and destroys a Chinese boat, the latter is blamed for being too slow. When a foreign stage-coach hurts a Chinese, the latter is charged with not knowing the right-of-way. When a Chinese merchant owes money to a foreign merchant, as soon as he is accused, his property is confiscated. [The Westerners] reduce the wages of their employees . . . control Customs . . . kidnap and sell our people.'

In June 1898 the young Emperor proposed new schools to teach Western knowledge but was imprisoned by the Dowager Empress as 'a running dog of the imperialists'. Anti-foreign feeling rose like a tide amongst the dispossessed, the starving and the peasants in an organisation known by the West as 'The Boxers', and by the Chinese seeking freedom as 'The Righteous and Harmonious Militia'. When the Boxers entered Peking on 13 June 1900, killing Chinese Christians, burning foreign buildings and besieging Western legations, they were attacked and beaten by a combined force of British, French, American, German, Russian, Austrian and Italian troops. In desperation the Dowager Empress introduced Western-style education and industry.

In a battle for Korea, Japan crippled seven ships of Russia's Pacific Fleet on 8 February 1904, before declaring war. In a few months Japan's 330,000 troops defeated 100,000 Russian troops. In retaliation the Russians despatched a forty-two ship fleet from St Petersburg. It had to sail around the Cape of Good Hope as Britain denied passage through the Suez Canal. The fleet arrived in need of repair and lost forty ships to the waiting Japanese fleet.

———— ∞ ————

Taku – or as near Peking as we can get,
3 Jun 1900.

My dear George, I wrote last from Amoy where we went to celebrate Queen Victoria's Birthday on 24th May. We got to

Wai-Hei-Wei on the 29th and settled down for a week's peace, but in the afternoon, owing to excited wires from the Minister, we were ordered here – to standby to land our Marines.

On 30th May we got to our present anchorage 15 miles from land. We were the first Britishers who arrived and found 6 Russians, a French, an Italian, a Yank and one Chinese ship here. A tug came out, no letters from any authority, and said the other ships were landing 100 men each. In half an hour our marines were in the tug. Our smart Sgt-Major was heard reproving a young Joey for the way he packed his valise; 'But isn't it service way?' exclaimed the youth. 'You don't want no service way now; pack it in the common-sense way.' As they shoved off they found the Frogs, Cossacks etc. returning saying they had been fired at. The pilot in our tug suggested our marines should conceal themselves and the tug went past the fort without a passenger showing though I have not yet found out how our marines got their boots under cover when they only had a 4 foot bulwark [the marines had a reputation for huge feet!]. The best of it all was that the firing from the fort was only a salute to a passing Mandarin! The blank shots that were too much for the Russians let our people in first although we arrived 48 hours after the others. Next we got another wire from the Minister saying that all European life in Peking was in danger so we landed another 80 merry men. Our 1st Lieut Wright went in charge with a Sub and 3 Mids. I believe the marines are going to Peking and the blue-jackets to Tientsin where things are also critical. They had a big fire two nights ago and saved the Chartered Bank, many getting their clothes burnt and we had to send fresh supplies. One of our Mids wrote to his servant: 'I want a pair of trousers; get anyone's; they will be compensated.'

———— ∞ ————

Ned received two reports back from First Lieutenant Wright:

Tientsin Race Club, Tientsin (port for Peking),
1 June 1900.

Dear Charlton, We got here sharp at 9 o'clock. When I arrived the Chinese band met us and played us to our quarters in grand style. We have a patrol 3 times a night on a beat just under 4 miles long . . . a terrible job. Now for my wants: I am paying a compradore 50c per man per day for food. I presume that comes out of their compensation allowance. If you can, will you send a shift of whites [change of clothes] for all hands . . . P.N. Wright.

———— ∞ ————

2 June 1900.

Dear Charlton, I have been very busy. Too busy in fact. Last night after working incessantly for 42 hours, which included reconnoitring the line for 38 miles towards Peking, I broke down entirely and went off my head. It was most annoying. My memory is an absolute blank, and yet I gave orders for the placing of two 9-man [platoons] and sending rations to the front and lots of other things. I am much better today. The Admiral sent for me today and was most complimentary.

Bayley was grand at the station yesterday. The Chinese authorities are dead set against us and refused to supply an engine. So Bayley seized one and put a guard on it and some of our stokers. There were over 5,000 Chinese collected on the platform so we fixed swords and charged from end to end. No one was hurt luckily; my did they run! Lt Perfect is working like a horse. P.N. Wright.

Ned received this report from the Assistant Paymaster:

In the train Lord knows how many miles from Peking.

Commander Charlton, Just a few words from the front. On landing at Tongku I found the Centurion's provisions in a pinnace with no one to look after them so we loaded [railway] trucks with the whole lot. I reported to Capt Bayley who immediately shunted the trucks onto a train containing Russians and French who were going up the line where a cosmopolitan crowd was mending the rails to Peking. After three hours we got to the main body. This consisted of three trains of British, American, German, Russian, French, Austrian, Italian and Japanese with an Admiral in command. Since then we have been making slow progress, about five miles a day, as the line is badly torn up. On the 11th we got into the Boxers' vicinity and had a skirmish. They ran like hares so our bag was small, about 35 killed and wounded; not pleasant, most of them were mere boys who could not run like the others. Not one had a rifle so our casualties were nil.

We hear the Imperial Army is to oppose our entry into Peking so we ought to see some fun between them and the Boxers. We are just over 2,000 strong. Asst Paymaster.

HMS *Orlando*, off Taku, 15 June 1900.

My dear Mother, We have just finished coaling although 260 officers and men out of a complement of 490 are on shore.

I have been singularly unlucky in not getting away with our men but now the Captain has gone I fear there is no chance. Our 1st Lieut Wright was in charge of the first batch and it will be a very good thing for him and expedite his promotion. I have all the joy and labour of preparing these parties for other people to reap the proceeds!

The Boxers seem a poor lot, only armed with gingalls and 3-pronged forks but they think themselves invulnerable and have defeated the Chinese army. Two of them went to expostulate to a Chinese general at the folly of the Chinese army attempting to overcome their invulnerability; the general replied by asking them if they would mind his trying it; they had not the slightest objection and were promptly stood up and shot.

One of our ABs [Able Seamen] saw a Boxer setting fire to a sleeper on one end of a bridge. The AB dropped between the lines onto the fellow and found he had a 6 foot sword; this the Boxer presented to the sailor and asked him to chop

his head off. Jack was never so flabbergasted but remembered to take him prisoner.

16 June 1900.

Things are getting more serious. The Admiral seems to be close to Peking but his bridges to his rear have been destroyed. We can send no more men except from Hong Kong or India. Two missionaries, their wives and a baby have turned up and I have made my cabin into a nursery. They expect that the other missionaries have been swamped by the flood of 3 million Boxers.

NAVAL TELEGRAPH TO *Orlando*: SAT 16 JUNE 1210 PM SEND ALL AVAILABLE MEN BY 3 PM FOR PURPOSE OF CAPTURING TAKU FORTS AT 2 AM TOMORROW. HOW MANY MEN WITH RIFLES CAN YOU LAND.

NAVAL TELEGRAPH REPLY FROM NED: 1215 PM 38 RIFLES INCLUDING MARINES, 50 SEAMEN WITH OTHER WEAPONS, 30 STOKERS IF DESIRED.

NAVAL TELEGRAPH TO *Orlando*: SEND ALL; TOMAHAWKS WITH YOUR MEN.

18 Jun 1900.

My dear Mother, As less than 100 men were left on board I asked to go myself but was refused as we might have to go to sea. The position was exciting. Here were 3 Russian, 1 English, 1 French, 1 German gunboat, 1 American, 1 Japanese and 2 English destroyers going to cover a feeble landing party of 1,500 men who were to capture a series of impregnable forts against which, according to the theorists, the big battleships lying outside could expect nothing except pulverisation. We sent 100 men; only half had rifles; when they had gone we had not a single rifle left on the ship. About 400 men went in the tug in broad daylight and passed under the forts, the captain of the Alacrity in charge.

The forts, two of which were built after the latest approved – German – models, mounted over 250 heavy guns, 100 of which were probably heavier than any gun brought against them – bar only two 4.7-inch aboard the Russian – and they were known to be well manned. But we trusted to the Chinese character and to the knowledge that these guns were of 24 different types; every nation seems to have given them something, and we knew what a hopeless mix-up of ammunition there would probably be after a time. Walls 18 feet thick, every one castlemated, and except at embrasures quite impervious to shell. Ramparts, double moats ad lib.

After dark our small boats all moved higher up the river, except one Russian who suffered heavily. This quite defeated the Chinese who had been observed laying their guns on the large ships very carefully before dark and probably many were never relaid. At 12.50 the fight had begun with shell bursting in all directions and a continuous earthquake rumble. The cannonade continued without intermission; five solid hours of gun loading for our fellows. I took careful note of the number of audible shots per minute: Average number at 1am: 32; at 2am: 22; at daybreak: 33; at 6am: 15. We thought of our poor little ships and wondered how they fared in that hailstorm; Algerine *British 6 x 4.0"*, German *8 x 3.4"*, French *2 x 5.5cm*, Russian *2 x 4.7"* and *5 x 3.0"*.

As the day broke we thought of our wretched landing party creeping up under cover towards the forts. About 5am we noticed our small craft still blazing away and UP went the new South Fort with an explosion surpassing Ada's at Alexandria. Next we saw the Algerine *followed by the* Itis *and* Lion *creeping slowly down the north shore blazing away. Then up went the Japanese flag on the north end of the North Fort and the* Orlando's *on the south end. We could see the shell from the little ships smashing into the embrasures and throwing up piles of earth until, about 6.30am occurred the*

most awful explosion it has ever been my lot to witness. The whole of the interior of the north end of the South Fort appeared to ascend in the air with thousands of projectiles darting away like rockets from the edge of the huge pillar which, in a second, shot up vertically for hundreds of feet and then bulged out and broke. We quite expected our ships to be overwhelmed by debris but they gradually loomed out and opened fire again. The Russian appeared to be ashore; we heard – afterwards – she had been badly hit with 34 killed. Soon after firing ceased and allied flags appeared on the South Fort. The Itis *came out with a badly damaged funnel, and the Japanese leader was shot. We saw nought of our two destroyers till 5pm when they came over the bar and reported the capture of 4 Chinese destroyers.*

Anxiety about our people at the front is rife; the Peking people have not communicated for ten days.

Midshipmen with captured gun on HMS Orlando - 1900.

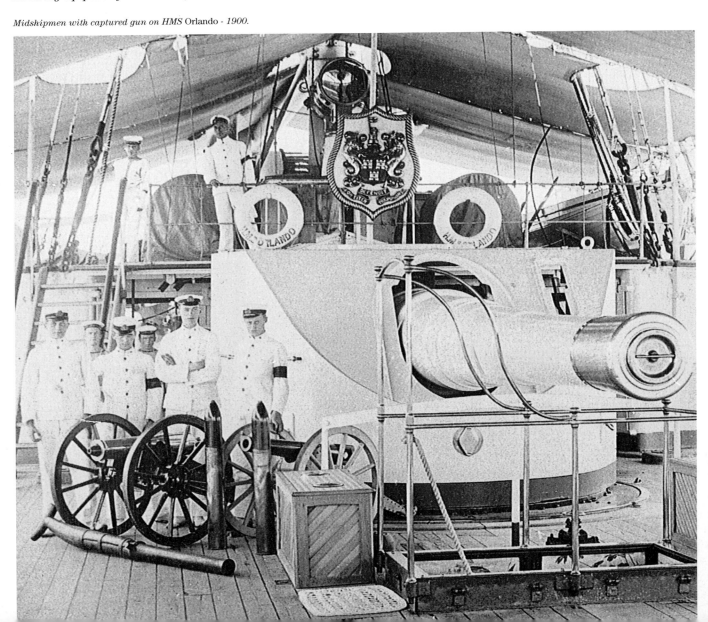

Ned received a report from Lieutenant Perfect:

Tientsin and the Front, 20 Jun 1900.

Dear Commander, We arrived here and found Wright in charge. On the morning of the 17th we had a severe battle at the station. Captain Bayley sent me with 40 'Orlandos'. We advanced by short rushes under withering fire to a village which we destroyed, killing a large number of Imperial troops en route. Wright came on the scene about 3pm before we advanced and did very good work with 9 pound Chinese guns of the latest type. Our casualties: 3 killed and 16 wounded from the Orlando.

Yesterday Captain Bayley attacked the villages on the other side of the river which were full of Imperial troops doing great damage. They met heavy resistance and he had to retire. Casualties: Wright severely wounded, left eye gone, jaw shattered and fingers of left hand badly smashed. He was marking 9 pounder shell when he was struck by a portion of a shell. Chinese still bombarding and doing considerable damage to French and English concessions. All communication absolutely cut off. Our men doing well. Mike (dog) well. Lieut Perfect.

HMS *Orlando*, Taku to Chifu (now Yent'ai), 23 June 1900.

My dear Mother, All the same vessels are inside at Taku so we get the job of running about between Wei-Hai-Wei, Chifu and Taku. We have had a rather exciting time cruising about with 350 men ashore and only about ten deck hands. There were four Chinese cruisers knocking about and in the present state of their insanity no one could quite tell what they might do. The Chifu forts train their 9.8-inch guns on us going in and out of harbour. No doubt the soldiers in them will turn and join the Boxers when they arrive. All Wednesday night we embarked troops and horses at Wei-Hai-Wei including 200 of a Chinese regiment. The latter were smart and lively in more than one sense and I was very glad to get them out of the ship at Taku.

The situation grows daily worse; no news from Peking for 15 days, Admiral's relieving party 12 days, 80 cut-off Marines 10 days. Tientsin besieged and cut off from Taku.

Our youngsters attacking the Taku Fort did splendidly, lying in the mud for hours under terrific fire from heavy guns and then rushing it at daylight, climbing on each other's shoulders to get over the parapet, the first in getting down to the gate and opening it from the inside. The Jap Commander

The Orlando's *Peking Marines.*

was helping our leader, Craddock, up. He, the Jap, got shot poor fellow. Both Japanese and Russians killed every Chinaman they saw and even tried to kill our prisoners.

———— ∞ ————

Ned received a further report from the Assistant Paymaster:

30 June 1900.

The Admiral decided to abandon the rail to Peking and march next to the river, getting supplies from Tientsin. Yang Tsun was in frightful condition, the rail was worse, grub was low and the train had been attacked by Boxers armed with Mausers so, on the 19th, we left the train to the tender mercy of the Boxers. The Germans had captured four junks in which the wounded and ammunition were placed. Our progress was fearfully slow and the next day we fought every two miles. Shot and shell were as cheap as dirt. On the 21st it was decided to make a night march past a fort. At daybreak on the 22nd we fell into as nice an ambush as you can conceive. We were going along quite comfortably when two Chinese appeared on the opposite bank. Our interpreter hailed them and said we were peaceful troops going to Peking; the reply was, 'We are Imperial troops; pass on; all is well.' So we passed. We got about 500 yards when suddenly a perfect hail of bullets and shrapnel fire burst from the opposite bank. They had let us get abreast of them in a heap and then opened fire. God only knows why only three of us were hit. The Chinese were so well under cover, with the river between us, that a frontal attack was hardly any good. The marines flanked them, crossing the river and charging with fixed bayonets. That startled the Chinese hounds and in a couple of hours their position was taken. We found a huge arsenal, hundreds of guns from 4.0" Krupp to .303" Maxims, thousands of rifles and millions of rounds of ammunition. Not one of our force knew that such a place was in there.

[The writer left the main force attempting to get to Peking and returned with a small contingent to the coast; he continues] On the 27th our rockets were answered and we got to Tientsin at 8. The town was a fearful wreck; every house in the British settlement being damaged by shell. Poor Sergt Gingell, my sole protection when I left, was one of the first men killed. Asst Paymaster.

There follows a note from Ned: 'No one seems to know how Sergt Gingell came by his death, but a Chinaman was seen carrying his head about, and was shot.' Many years later Ned received additional information:

———— ∞ ————

HMS *Commonwealth*, 14 July 1913.

Dear Admiral Charlton, I can throw some light on your note. Gingell was fatally wounded while we were securing Siku Arsenal. I helped to carry him in, and shall never forget his appeals to be 'finished' as he was shot in the intestines and suffered agonies whenever he was moved. sgd E. Murray.

The Tientsin Party, on HMS Orlando - 1900.

Chinese War Junk, Yang-Tse River - 1900.

Orlando Barracks, 3 July 1900.

Dear Com., The Chinese have just restarted shelling this settlement. I am afraid no advance on Peking can be made for 3 weeks. The news from there is decidedly hopeless. I have under my command 1 Sub, 4 Mids, 51 seamen, 5 daymen and 7 stokers and, in hospital 17. P. [presumably Lieutenant Perfect].

— ∽ —

Tientsin, 7 July 1900.

Dear Charlton, Wright is the same as ever; he just seems to hang on and is not making progress. You may let it be known that we are not living in the Garden of Eden, but I admit to having a lively time. The owner of this house was shot in bed last night by a stray bullet. You have done well considering the small number of men you had. Capt J.H. Burke.

— ∽ —

Tientsin, 7 July 1900.

Dear Com., All well! Had a hot scrap yesterday. Went out to take a 6 pounder gun at the bottom of the road. Had a 9 pounder and 200 Chinese under Major Bruce. Sorry to say unsuccessful, had to retire. Major Bruce killed. Lt Perfect.

Off Taku, 15 July 1900.

Dear Old Boy [Willie], I suppose you have seen from the papers that we have dropped in on the most extraordinary situation: Civilisation versus Barbarism. I am sure it is a carefully planned attempt to chuck out the hated foreign-devil. No news from Peking since 2nd July when they said position was hopeless.

— ∽ —

Orlando Barracks, Tientsin, 18 July 1900.

Dear Capt Charlton, I am sending down 4 boxes of loot in sealed cases. There are silver trinklets, silverware, valuable furs and Chinese clothes. Sir, I beg to propose that the officers should have what they require, then the wounded, then the remainder of the ship's company. 54 ratings are returning and they are all well with two exceptions. H. Perfect.

— ∽ —

Wusung (off Shanghai), 15 Aug 1900.

My dear Mother, We arrived in the Yangtze on the 8th and remained outside until the 10th when the tide was high enough to let us get across the bar and anchor under the Wusung forts. We could, by selecting our day, get up to

Above: An execution. in S. China, - May 1899.

Below: More effective than the British stocks.

The Khung.

Shanghai 15 miles, but then it might be a month before we could get down. The Undaunted, Marathon *and* Orlando *are moored inside the bar. The position of our ships here is almost an exact parallel to that of the* Algerine *and other small craft at Peking and the relative strengths of the forces is about the same. Everything seems quiet and friendly but, I imagine, a lot depends on the success of the relief force at Peking. A second failure there would be likely to extend the cry of 'Kill the foreign devil' right through China.*

I have bicycled all round the country near the forts and inspected their magazine. It is a great change here after Taku – we have smooth water in place of a heavy sea.

Altogether we had 8 killed and 53 wounded out of the 360 we landed at different stages. I saw Wright at Wei-Hai-Wei. He is still in a critical condition; the gash in his skull is over 3" long and nearly an inch wide; his eye is saved but he will lose one or two fingers. It is a tall price to pay even for promotion.

Wusung, 31 Aug 1900.

The relief of Peking took a heavy weight off our minds. Wright is still in a critical condition. He is a married man with a wife and child at Findon, Sussex.

People here are still very panicky. Missionaries keep coming in with horrible stories of atrocities and murders.

— ∞ —

Wusung, 10 Sept 1900.

My dear Elise, On Sunday we were delighted to get our marines back from Peking – at least 19 out of 27 of them. I had them all photographed. The odd people with them, our signal man, armourer and a sickbay steward, all did most excellent work. The sickbay man was the only qualified nurse and carried out his duties for the wounded of nine nations.

Capt Halliday, our marine officer who was up there, was badly wounded in the left shoulder and is likely to lose the use of his arm and be sent home. The worst of it is he is the most left-handed man I have ever seen, and he growls like anything because everyone tells him how lucky it wasn't his right. I only heard recently that, when shot at point blank range in the shoulder, he afterwards killed four out of his five assailants with his revolver and then walked to hospital.

— ∞ —

14 Sept 1900.

Dog 'Mike' had to be drowned in the Yangtze's yellow flood having received some internal injuries which made him howl at the slightest movement, so in the dead of night he went for a swim with a heavy fire bar attached to his neck. A prosaic ending for a fighting dog who has been through all the heavy fighting in Tientsin and taken part in two bayonet charges when he was always the first on the latter curves [buttocks] of the flying Boxers.

— ∞ —

HMS Orlando, 28 Sept 1900.

My dear Mother, Accounts keep coming in of the fearful massacres of Europeans in Shansi; people somehow seemed to have got more accustomed to the horrors this year. Where 12 months ago there would have been a howl if even a Christian convert were touched, now the English papers treat quite lightly massacres of scores of their fellow men and women. A gentleman called Hu-Tsien seems to have been the most forward. After inviting all the surrounding missionaries, wives and families into his Yamen, under promise of protection, he proceeded to behead them all, and then applied to the Empress for a substantial recognition of his services.

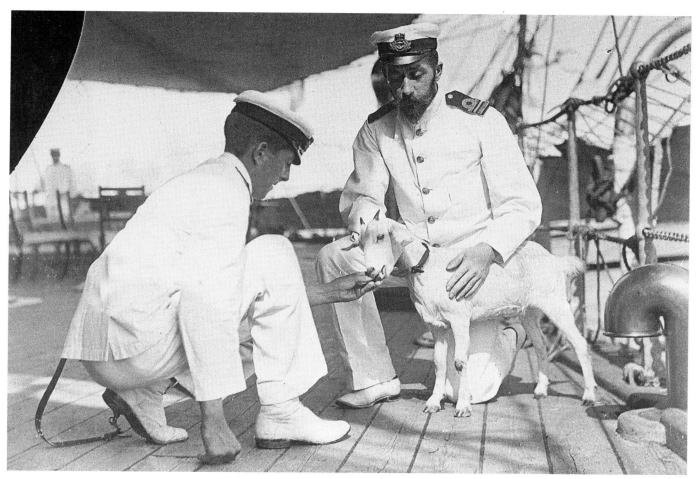

Above: 1st Lieutenant Wright (died from wounds received in Tientsin) with Sub-Lieutenant Fisher and the goat.

Below: Punishment in South China in 1900.

Above: Yangtsim, Remains of Sir E. Seymour's train.

Below: Disarmed Chinese soldiers, 1900.

Wusung Bar, 8 Oct 1900.

We hear the most wonderful stories – but this may be expected when within hail of the Shanghai Bund where dwells the 'Father of Lies' – about Shan-hai-kwan forts being surrendered to HMS Pigmy *after an ultimatum. The Mandarin in charge expressed his delight at being able to hand over to the British, although he was prepared to fight the Allies. Then the Allies appeared with 4,000 Russian troops only to find the Forts in peaceful occupation by 18 British blue-jackets.*

Our game now seems to be a pretty deep one. I suppose we shall give everything back as we did with the Taku Forts and the 4 Destroyers we captured.

We have just received orders to take Sir E. Satow to Taku where he is to become Minister (representing the British Government in Beijing).

———— ∞ ————

Taku, 18 Oct 1900.

Sir E. Satow lived with the Captain and his staff in the wardroom. Whether Foreign Office officials are supposed to have the most enormous capacities for stowing only the most expensive pâtés and vinos in contrast to the plain fare of the poor naval officer I don't know, but it is a fact that we are allowed 4 Pounds per diem for a Minister and 12/- per diem for each of his staff, whereas the value of a naval officer's rations is 9½d.

Captain Halliday V.C. HMS Orlando.

Wei-Hai-Wei, 30 Oct 1900.

Our marine officer Halliday has been recommended for the Victoria Cross. Wright left last week for home; his position is still precarious. The mere moving him to a transport set him back weeks.

———— ∞ ————

10 Nov 1900.

The Madras Regiment are already beginning to die of cold; all the cattle for the troops have rhinderpest and die at the rate of about 200 daily; typhoid is naturally bad and HMS Terrible *have lost a good many. The cattle are an awful sight; their bodies are collected and burnt.*

Last week I made a successful [hunting] expedition to the Eastern Lagoon which is out of our territory, the 10 mile radius. Lieutenant Mansell and 2 Mids accompanied me with my servant; the latter is becoming quite useful. We made a lean-to against the rocks and put up my small tent alongside. The Chinese were much interested. They are a fine race these Northerners, but quite unwashed. Owing to there being no tribute rice this year famine threatens them daily. The country seemed unusually deserted and it happened that we found out where all the people were. We were walking up the scrub when suddenly a crowd of children appeared and in a few seconds we were surrounded by hundreds of them, all with their mouths open and a big grin at the 'Foreign Devils'. I could not make it out at first but soon found out there was a Chinese theatre going on and we had hit on the children's corner. Around the stage, where the drums set up a terrific row, there must have been 5,000 people. Our four guns had evidently alarmed them as I saw the women being hurried off to the back, always a sure sign of trouble being expected, here as in other lands. We quietly pushed our way through and proceeded across the valley. It was a wonderful sight to see the crowd grouped around the little theatre, which banged away furiously trying to re-attract attention with every face turned in our direction, evidently wondering what the deuce we were doing. We got a few wild duck at the lagoon.

At Taku over 30 steamers are [stranded] on the Bar: 7 feet instead of 10.

———— ∞ ————

Taku, 19 Nov 1900.

Please return the envelope in which this reaches you as numerous small bets are to be settled on the point of the Mail leaving this afternoon, via Japan, getting to England on or before Xmas day. I do not think it possible. The Japanese Flagship is leaving for Yokohama and may possibly catch the Canadian Pacific Railway [steamer] in which case I stand to lose a bottle of port. The margin however is too small.

After coaling at WHW we came on here and have been fitted with the wireless telegraph, and are now in hourly communication with the NW Fort where they receive daily press telegrams.

Taku, 5 Dec 1900.

My dear Mother, Many thanks for writing so often; your letters are always worth reading half a dozen times over.

I have just returned from an interesting trip to Tientsin where I spent 4 days with Dr and Mrs Irwin, friends of refugee days. The [railway] line has been grabbed by the Russians and now they find it has to be given up they are hurrying all the rolling stock into Manchuria for their own use. Orders have been received by them to hand it over to the original holders, viz. British Engineers and British capital, but they delayed. From Tongku every village is a ruin; burnt, looted and everything human killed by the Russians. A lighter sunk alongside the bank marks the spot where 600 innocent coolies were shot down in cold blood by our noble Allies as they attempted to swim ashore. The men were from Chifu, all capable stevedores.

To see the soldiers of the various nations is alone worth going to Tientsin for: Cossacks on shaggy horses, French Zouaves like gigantic blue-bottles in their winter coats with red bloomers underneath. Yankees in blue shirts and slouch hats, Germans in brass helmets, Indians and Annamites wrapped so that their blue noses only are visible, gigantic Australian blue-jackets are policemen, and everywhere the nippy little Jap consisting of a rifle, a coat and a yellow hat-band. Our own white officers look very smart in 'coats, warm, British' and Canadian fur caps.

Bower gave us a pass to the arsenal and permission to take away what arms were required for HMS Orlando. I took only a new Mannlicher rifle, a Mauser carbine and a Martini-Henry rifle; the ship is so lumbered with stuff one can hardly move.

One of our Mids netted 600 Pounds in syce [silver shoes], as much as he could obtain in coolies to carry, and most of our men have opened banking accounts.

———∞———

Notes made by Ned at this time:

7 Dec   1900. Temp fell to 12°F last night (20 degrees frost).

10 Dec   1900. Hurrah! River is frozen and we have reported that we can be of no further use; any amount of craft are shut up inside.

———∞———

Chifu, 14 Dec 1900.

My dear Frank, Wireless has many advantages; we intercept the daily Reuters telegrams and once we were told we could go, I had the gear down from aloft mighty smart so that no telegraph boy could countermand it.

Ah Ping (who stole the Orlando's wardroom funds), you will be glad to hear, got 6 months at Manila for keeping a gambling hell; I have asked the Yankee police to rub it in well.

Hong Kong, 9 Jan 1901.

My dear Mother, Poor dear old Sir Adrian; he was one of my kindest friends in the world from the time I first went to sea; I cannot visualise Valletta without his kindly hospitality. What is Amy going to do? I suppose she will stick to Malta on account of her boy.

I can quite understand Frank refusing the (Royal) Yacht, although it probably means the difference between a quiet life and one of turmoil and excitement. (The offer) is a very good compliment to him. I suppose he will let it be generally known as there is no use in being bashful in this world; least of all in H.M. Navy. Tell everyone everything you have done – or imagine you have done – and what you intend to do next, and how lucky the world is to have such a person as you in existence!

———∞———

HMS *Orlando*, R.N. Sanatorium, The Peak, Hong Kong, 17 Jan 1901.

My dear Elise, The above address does not mean that Orlando has been left on the summit by a typhoon; but I have been driven up by force of circumstances, represented in this case by a Chinaman carrying a baulk of timber. I was biking along in the dark from the Elysian Fields of Happy Valley, when I observed a coolie on the starboard bow who appeared to be progressing in an orderly manner, and it was not till the end of the baulk caught me on the 'boko' that I knew what the swine was doing; as he promptly dropped the 20 foot spar in the roadway and fled, my wheel went over it, putting my light out so that my blue language was the only illumination. I was knocked a bit sillier than usual. Dr Lomas at the hospital provided me with a whiskey and soda and stitched me up. The end of the timber fortunately just missed my eye and teeth but got my nose and lip.

———∞———

Hong Kong, 28 Jan 1901.

My dear Mother, Everything here is very quiet and of course all functions except funereal ones have been cancelled until Her Majesty's obsequies have taken place. It is rather hard on the Theatre of an Australian company of children and on the Circus as these people have to get their living. As regards the Circus I ought not to have much consideration as I find out it was on one of the Circus tent spars that a Chinaman caught me in the face.

———∞———

Hong Kong, 30 Jan 1901.

My dear Frank, Mohawk left last Sat and I entrusted a parcel of 500 'Reina Victoria' to Thurwood for passage to you. These cigars are supposed to be good as our men smoke nothing but the best since they brought their loot on board. I don't intend them all for you however, so please accept 200 and give 100 apiece to our three brothers.

All is very quiet now until H.M's funeral is over. We had a great function yesterday proclaiming King Edward VII on the cricket ground near the Club. It will be curious afterwards to compare different procedures in these functions as, thanks to the glorious length of reign of Her Late Majesty (63 years), few Englishmen have any recollection of what was done on the last similar occasion, and at Hong Kong such a thing has never previously occurred. The Hong Kong Cricket Club, with their usual tact, had railed off the cricket pitch and practice nets in the middle of the parade ground so that the dais was quite eclipsed by the huge erection. Fortunately H.E. found out beforehand and, becoming furious, had it removed. The troops and seamen were formed six deep all round the ground.

Four days in the sanatorium was enough to restore my physiognomy to its usual contour. There is not much of a scar; a German student would scarcely be proud of it.

There is a fine yarn going about with regard to HMS Glory. A certain well-known officer of HMS Terrible, whom we shall call 'B', wrote to the Commander of the Glory, which had that day arrived, stating that he was a French Master and could be engaged for the Midshipmen's instruction. Having got himself up in costume, he obtained a boat from Glory and went on board. Of course the Mids started the usual style of leg pulling 'Bonjour Froggy' etc but they had rather a bad time. 'B' managed very well though his knowledge of French is small. He gave them 'dictée' [dictation], made them translate the 'dictée' into English, and removing their first papers, translate their English back into French. A form [bench] being pushed over he had it removed as 'très dangereux' and the unfortunate Mids were told 'Ah, then you do "dictée" on the stand'; and they had to stand for 1½ hours. Three times he sent up to the Officer-of-the-Watch to tell him there was too much noise, and if it were not stopped he would 'make rapport to the Captain'. The Senior Executive and others, having learnt that the French Master was giving trouble, and astounded at his presumption, came and peered at him through the casement, making such audible remarks as 'Look at the brute's tie', 'Watch him gesticulate' etc. In the end 'B' came away with all the Mids' papers with which he will be able to remind them for the rest of their lives. The Glory went to sea without fathoming the joke, but no doubt will hear of it later.

───── ∞ ─────

5 Feb 1901.

My dear Mother, There was a certain amount of contention as to a Catholic Memorial Service for Her Late Majesty, but the Italian Bishop would not allow anything to be done. Father McCymont, the new Catholic Chaplain, was rebuffed for suggesting it.

───── ∞ ─────

Wusung, 17 Apr 1901.

My bicycle, which has carried me over 8,600 miles in three years, came to a smash yesterday and will be difficult to repair. At a dyke, I attempted to ride across a single stone forming a bridge. It was a lesson to me not to get too casual.

───── ∞ ─────

1 May 1901.

We hear from Wright, our 1st Lieut, that he has got leave till September when he hopes to get his head patched up.

───── ∞ ─────

18 May 1901.

The troubles up north [in Korea] have touched us at last and we are ordered direct to Wei-Hai-Wei. I have an infant to look after in the shape of a khaki puppy, of mixed pointer breed, which some friends in Shanghai gave me.

───── ∞ ─────

Temple of Hades, Peking-in-the-Mud,
7 Jul 1901.

My dear Elise, I feel I cannot improve the shining hour of a wet day in the ancient Capital of the Celestial Kingdom except by dropping you a line.

I had the job of finding out where our men, who were killed in the siege last year, were buried, and with getting a billet in the cemetery for the stone we intend to put up. The cemetery lay right in the line of fire so our men were mostly buried in trenches where they fell. Lately the Yanks have come along and, in pursuit of their barbarous custom of sending all their dead home, they have been disturbing the poor unfortunates, and from all reports have sent one or two Welsh Fusiliers and one blue-jacket over the water as 'free born citizens'.

The approach to Peking by rail from the south is disappointing. The station used to be 6 miles outside but the Allies, requiring now no permission, have breached the walls and brought the line into the forbidden land. The city is the most astounding and interesting place I have ever struck; magnificence and extravagance are in close quarters with squalor and thrift. The Pei-Tang Cathedral, where 2,000 Christians, 20 priests and a guard of 30 French marines, without food and little ammunition, held out the siege, attracted me more than the legation. From about 8 feet above the ground the whole of the exterior is a mass of cannon ball and modern bullet marks. The organ pipes would make very good sieves. In the rear is an enormous pit, 30 yards in diameter, where a mine exploded blowing up 45 infants. The Summer Palace is now occupied by British and Italians. The Russians had the first rub at it and only managed to get away with 500 cartloads of loot, the General moaning that he was a poor man and would be unable to pay the Customs. The old Summer Palace, destroyed in 1860, is at the back of the hill. The view over Peking with its gates, pagodas and yellow-tiled Forbidden City is simply superb.

I dined with Sir E. Satow; he expressed himself indignant at Sir C. Macdonald having painted on the walls of the British Legation the legend 'Lest We Forget' and said

Peking 1901.

it was a standing insult to the Chinese nation. Why not? Let them be standingly insulted. Why, even now, I have seen it stated in home papers that the dear Chinese never did intend to wipe out the foreign devil.

I betook myself to the great Boxer stronghold of Pao-Ting-Fu. I created some sort of sensation amongst the French but they put me up at the mission and, having worked the good old yarn – 3 uncles priests, 3 aunts 'religeuses' (which happened to be true) was treated to a banquet.

—— ∞ ——

Taku, 13 July 1901.

My dear Mother, The powers are beginning to clear out and

even now the Forbidden City and Summer Palace are being closed to foreigners and returned to the Chinese.

Pao-Ting-Fu was the place where 45 missionaries were murdered and the women had such a poor time. The Catholics got away northward where they defended themselves; the Boxers burnt their new church and occupied the mission premises doing much less harm than Europeans do when they occupy a place not theirs.

—— ∞ ——

Kobe (Japan), 30 July 1901.

We got in here on the 28th after a delightful week in the Inland Sea visiting odd nooks and corners of this

The Summer Palace, Peking.

smiling country. Here I found a wire from the Commander-in-Chief ordering me home by Canadian Pacific Railway, appointed to HMS Vernon. I can only conclude that Madden has been promoted and I am to take his place. I should have liked to have finished this commission and feel rather like I am defrauding my own men after being with them for 2½ years. My servant Samuel Sanders will accompany me.

———— ∞ ————

Sumoto, Awaji, Japan,
31 July 1901.

My dear Elise, This island forms the eastern boundary of the

Inland Sea. Nothing could have equalled the beauty of the scene as we came into the harbour last night by moonlight.

Your letter about Miss Fitz's general behaviour and 'Oss-win' arrived; I am greatly rejoiced at the news as I might possibly myself have been ensnared by her charms.

———— ∞ ————

At sea on CPR *Empress of China*,
18 Aug 1901.

My dear Mother, I took passage in the ship to Yokohama and went up Fuji, a nice little climb of 12,500 feet, and then bicycled along the Tokaido to charming resorts. Japan is a place that grows on one.

The monument to the men of HMS Orlando *in Victoria Park, Portsmouth.*

Juan de Fuca Strait (Canada/USA),
27 Aug 1901.

Picked up the land this morning in a thick fog which shows only the tops of the mountains in Washington State and the wooded slopes of Vancouver Island.

Ned travelled via Banff and Niagara Falls to New York where he boarded the Cunard liner SS *Campania* to Liverpool.

The Canteen Cash Account for HMS *Orlando* for the commission 1899 to 1902 indicates that Captain J.H.T. Burke CB died on the return voyage to Britain and was buried in Aden.

Ned presented a gingall (a small cannon) from Taku to the town of Bellingham, Northumberland.

It is inscribed:

GINGALL FROM N.W. FORT TAKU CHINA JUNE 17 1900
PRESENTED TO THE TOWN OF BELLINGHAM
BY COMMANDER E. CHARLTON, R.N
H.M.S. ORLANDO.

A magnificent monument to the ten men of HMS *Orlando* who died while the ship was in North China was erected in Victoria Park, Portsmouth. The monument lists: Commander P.N. Wright, died of wounds received Tientsin; six killed at Tientsin, two en route to, and one in, Peking. It also lists the nine men, including the Captain, who died during the commission. Its central feature is a huge bell. The inscription on the bell states:

Come Pleasant Weather and Gentle Rain,
The Empire Happy, at Peace Again.

To which empire it refers might not be immediately obvious were it not written in Chinese characters; it was captured at the North West Fort, Taku on 17 June 1900.

On leaving the *Orlando* Ned received the following certificate from Captain Burke:

CERTIFICATE: Edward Francis Benedict Charlton served as Commander on HMS *Orlando* from 16 Feb 1899 to 15 Aug 1901 with sobriety, great zeal, judgement and ability.
Sgd J.H. Burke.

Subsequently he received two more certificates as a Commander from Captains on HMS *Vernon* before he became a Captain himself: 'with sobriety – and entirely to my satisfaction. An officer of marked ability and specially deserving of advancement. Sgd C.G. Robinson'; and 'with sobriety and in accordance with K.R. & A.I. (King's Regulations and Admiralty Instructions). A zealous and very able Torpedo Officer. (Signature illegible.)'

Ned, following his ambition as a young man, returned to the torpedo training ship HMS *Vernon* many times during his career. It appears that, as a single man, he regarded it as a 'home away from home'.

HMS *Vernon*, 4 June 1903.

(To) Captain Charlton RN, We have started the new long course with departure from previous years, the Lieutenants for Gunnery are doing Torpedoes, while those for Torpedoes are doing Gunnery [apparently to understand each other's requirements]. I feel very grateful, Sir, for your kindly interest in those of us who have benefited by the new scheme, and I trust as a body we shall show, by a greater devotion to duty our appreciation of the trust which has been reposed in us. James Attfield.

Inspecting Captain TBD,
11 Aug 1903.

Captain E.F.B. Charlton, Please accept my very high appreciation of the way in which you handled the 'Blue' force allotted to you. I must attribute the able defence of the Cruiser at Queenstown (Ireland) in large measure to the zealous way you carried out the additional duty with regard to the Port defences. E.G. Dicken.

On 6 Jan 1903, in a handsome document, Ned received his formal commission as a Captain in the Royal Navy:

By the Commissioners for Executing the Office of Lord High Admiral of the United Kingdom of Great Britain and Ireland. To Edward Francis Benedict Charlton Esquire hereby appointed Captain in His Majesty's Fleet.

By Virtue of the Power and Authority given to us by His Majesty's Letters Patent under the Great Seal. We do hereby constitute and appoint you a Captain in His Majesty's Fleet: Willing and requiring you from time to time to go on board and take upon you the Charge and Command of Captain in any Ship or Vessel to which you may hereafter at any time be duly appointed. Strictly Charging and Commanding all the Officers and Company of the said Ship or Vessel subordinate to you to behave themselves jointly and severally in their respective Employments with all due Respect and Obedience unto you, and you likewise to observe and Execute the General Printed Instructions and such Orders and Directions as you shall from time to time receive from us or from any other your Superior Officers for His Majesty's Service. Hereof nor you nor any of you may fail as you will answer the contrary at your Peril. And for doing this shall be your Commission.

Given under our hands and the Seal of the Office of Admiralty this sixth day of January 1903 in the Second Year of His Majesty's Reign. By Command Sgd E. MacGregor, J.A. Fisher.

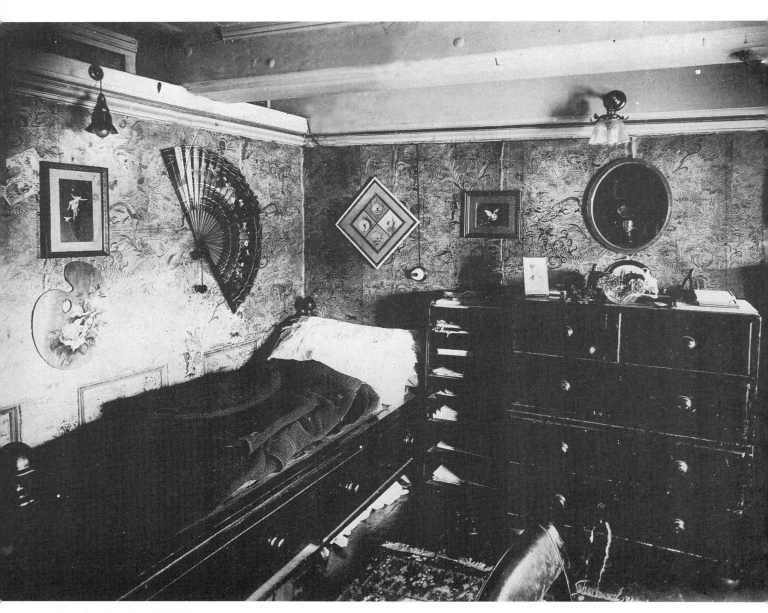

A comfortable cabin on HMS Vernon.

Marriage and Family Life

At the age of thirty-eight, for the first time in a quarter of a century, Ned was able to enjoy relatively normal family life. His records for the next decade comprise an album of photographs, a few letters to him and some newspaper cuttings in a shoebox. This period of his life is partially reconstructed from public records and statements by members of his family.

Audrey Urban advised that Ned had been acquainted with Laura Strutt for many years and found her an attractive woman, but his travels had prevented any closer friendship. Laura was born at Milford, Derbyshire on 21 April 1875, the daughter of the Hon. Arthur Strutt and Alice Strutt née de Lisle. One day Arthur, who was involved in cotton milling, endeavoured to help a child who had fallen into a mill-race with a large water-wheel, and lost his life. Some members of the Strutt family then proposed to adopt Alice's two children, Edward and Laura, so that Edward could inherit Arthur's title. Alice objected as the children would then have been brought up as Protestants. In order to circumvent family pressure, she took both her children to Catholic Spain, France and Austria for several years. Edward learnt a number of languages, joined the first Mount Everest expedition and in 1919, at the behest of the British Government, rescued the former Austrian Emperor Karl and Empress Zita from Vienna. As the royal couple left their home for the last time the Emperor's speech to his retainers was very brief, 'Meine Freunden, auf wiedersehen', and to Colonel Strutt as a sad aside, 'after 700 years'.

In 1903 Ned was invited to a weekend house party near Leicester and, on arrival, met three wealthy, titled gentlemen who, he learnt, were all seeking Laura's hand. He ascertained also that Laura was due to arrive later that day by train. Ned obtained a ride in the carriage going to collect Laura at the railway station, proposed to her on the way back, and was accepted.

A detailed report on the marriage of Captain Edward Charlton and Laura Strutt at the Church of St Mary, Cadogan Street, London, by Rev. Father Kelly on 15 December 1903 was published in *The Tablet*. It states that the bride was the only daughter of Hon. Mrs Arthur Strutt and niece of Lord Belper, that the wedding had been advanced from 30 to 15 December owing to Ned's appointment as Captain (Destroyers) of the Home Fleet from 1 January 1904. The bride was given away by her brother Captain Edward Strutt. The best man was Ned's brother Oswin. The bride wore a white mousseline satin gown, made with rows of broad tucks on the skirt, while the corsage was trimmed with a berth of pearl and crystal embroidery and some fine Limerick lace. She carried a bouquet of white flowers and ferns, and she wore a large pendant of pearls, rubies and diamonds. At the end of the service Father Kelly read a telegram from Pope Pius X bestowing his Pontifical Blessing on the newly wedded pair.

The reception for 160 guests was held at the Hyde Park Hotel. The report includes a list of presents and by whom they were given. A number of titled Catholic families appear. The list distinguishes between 100 gifts to the bride and 60 to the groom. A sample includes: to the bride from Duke of Norfolk KG, amethyst and pearl brooch; from Baroness Max von Boeselager, six silver flower vases; from Sir Percival and Lady Radcliffe, old silver casket; from Countess de Torre Diaz, ruby and diamond ring; from Miss Charlton Anne (a cousin surnamed Anne), morning tea service; from the Rev. Mother at New Hall, picture; from the servants at Milford, silver mustard, salt and pepper pots; and from Mr George Charlton, gold chain. And to the groom: from the bride, field-glasses; from Mr and Mrs W.L. Charlton (his brother Willie), Royal Navy sword; from Mr and Mrs Doran-Webb (his sister Elise), Encyclopaedia of Sport and cartridge magazine case; from Mr W. Charlton, Hesleyside, and Mrs W. Oswald Charlton, old silver teapot; from Rev H. Belassis (his uncle), portmanteau; from Lord Walter and Lady Anabel Kerr, silver tea service; from Capt. Murray Aynsley RN, salt cellars; and from the servants at 36A Victoria Road, silver bread scoop.

Ned received these congratulations from a fellow seafarer:
SMS *Zenta*, Pola, 22 Dec 1903.

Dear Charlton – delighted of your marriage advertisement I present you my best wishes and congratulations. Having got your letter but yesterday when I arrived at Pola, I beg you to excuse my late answering you. You took me really by surprise and made me a great pleasure, showing that you have not forgotten your old Cretan friend. I left the Suva Bay as instructor in the torpedo school and cruising with torpedo boats in Dalmatia. Uhlir.

The newly-wed couple spent their honeymoon at Kenry House lent by the Earl and Countess of Dunraven. *The Tablet* reports even on the vehicle used to travel to Kingston: a motor car. There are no photos of the wedding but there are two photos of attractive Kenry House showing bare-limbed trees in the December gloom. One shows 'Laura and Bill [their dog]', the other 'Ned and Bill'. From 30 April 1904 to 27 April 1905 Laura and Ned lived at Stormont, Wyke Regis, Weymouth with a beautiful view over the English Channel, and on 3 October 1904 their first child, Audrey, was born. Audrey studied at Oxford University and became a teacher at Roedean College for Girls, Johannesburg. She married Victor Urban, a chemical engineer who had served in the Austrian Army Engineers during World War I. He was initially regarded with some caution by Audrey's British relatives who asked Prince Blücher, a German in-law, to assess his bona fides. Prince Blücher not only considered him acceptable but became his best man. Audrey and Victor had six children. During World War II Audrey drove a truck for the South African Army. Laura and Ned's second daughter Marjorie was born in Hong Kong on 18 September 1906 during Ned's Far East commission. She was an artist. Ned 'gave her away' when she married Colonel Noel Parkes, Royal Artillery, in July 1930. They had five children. After her husband's death in 1951 she lived in Hastings before retiring to the village of Yelverton on Dartmoor.

Tragedy struck when Laura and Ned's third daughter was

born on 21 January 1909 for Laura died of complications only one month later. Their daughter survived and was named Laura after her mother. Ned's photo album has four photos of Northwood House, Fareham in the snow of March 1909 together with a photo of a trellis for creepers, leafless in the depth of winter, which bears the heart-rending caption: 'Laura's trellis put up by herself'. The five bleak pictures are titled. 'A white mantle of sorrow'. The next page in the album shows photos of several happy children entitled 'Imps on the Sands – Dunraven Castle, Aug 1908, taken by Laura and developed after her death'. The daughter Laura grew up strong in the Catholic faith and became a nun. She taught at several secondary and teacher training schools in the Gold Coast, now Ghana, and Nigeria before being injured in an accident and returned to England to recuperate. She then served once more in Nigeria where she was injured in a motor accident during the Biafran War. Next she started a refuge for homeless men of middle age in Birmingham; it continues to this day. Then she 'taught English in a Christian Arab-speaking School to a happy lot of Christian, Muslim, Druze and Bedhouin children' in Israel. She retired to a convent in Hastings, England.

Fareham lies midway between the great Royal Naval base of Portsmouth and the major port of Southampton. Nearby Ned met Winefride Stapleton-Bretherton. Fifteen months after Laura's untimely death, on 10 May 1910, he married 'Freda' at Rainhill, Lancashire. The ceremony was performed by the Catholic Bishop of Liverpool, Dr Whiteside. A reception was held at 'The Hall' but several festivities planned for the village were cancelled due to the death of King Edward VII. Freda was the sixth daughter of a Catholic family, which included four sons and eight daughters. They lived near Fareham for half of each year and in Lancashire for the other half. Twice a year the family, their fourteen servants and their horses travelled by hired train between their homes. In his book *Memoirs of Prince Blücher* the prince describes the Stapleton-Bretherton family. In 1832 they designed and ran mail coaches from Liverpool to London, then a twenty-four hour journey. When the era of the coach declined they switched to railways. Prince Blücher himself was the great-grandson of German Marshal 'Vorwarts' Blücher whom the Germans consider to be no less a hero of the Battle of Waterloo than the British regard the Duke of Wellington. 'Vorwarts' had run away from home at the age of fifteen and enlisted as a Hussar. He was the first foreigner to be awarded the Order of the Grand Cross of the Bath by the British. One hundred and fifty years later, when Prince Blücher married Freda's sister Evelyn, he wrote that Evelyn and he had 'a great deal in common. First of all she was a Catholic and had the cosmopolitan outlook more usual amongst aristocratic Catholic families.' Perhaps Ned felt similar empathy towards Freda.

On 2 September 1911 at Harrow-on-the-Hill in London, Freda gave birth to her first child, a daughter named Nancy. In October 1933 Nancy married Lt-Colonel Joseph Morrogh-Bernard, originally with the Royal Munster Fusiliers, and was 'given away' by Ned. Joe served also in the Egyptian Camel Corps, raised the 16th Battalion of the Durham Light Infantry

after Dunkirk, and assisted Colonel Wingate in restoring Emperor Haile Selassie to the throne. They had four children and retired to Fair Oak near Winchester.

A son was born on 30 August 1912 at Harrow-on-the-Hill. As Captain Edward Charlton, he had a distinguished career in the King's Own Yorkshire Light Infantry, was seconded to the King's African Rifles in Kenya, took part in the Abyssinia campaign to oust the Italian colonisers, and was then determined to take an even more active part in World War II. As second-in-command of the 6th Parachute Division he landed in France on D-Day. Three days later, on 9 June 1944, he was killed by a German machine-gun nest which he was attacking and which his men captured. Edward is buried at Caen. He was Mentioned in Despatches on 8 July. As Edward never married, Ned's direct male line ceased.

On 18 March 1914, her birthday, Freda gave birth to twins Christopher and Brydget at Alverstoke. Both children followed partially in Ned's footsteps. Tragically Christopher was killed as a Naval Cadet at the age of thirteen when he slipped from a cliff from which he was taking a photograph near Dartmouth Naval College, Devon. At the inquest the coroner recorded a verdict of 'accidental death', adding 'It would be a bad thing for England if boys, who hoped one day to become officers in His Majesty's Navy, were not imbued with a spirit of adventure.' Christopher's cortège, a gun-carriage drawn by eighteen bluejackets, bore the coffin to Dartmouth cemetery. The chief mourners were Sir Edward and Lady Charlton, Princess Blücher and four Stapleton-Brethertons. In recording the tragedy his youngest sister wrote: 'After the death of my brother I was given a pony by my mother; a dinghy by my father; none could replace my brother.'

Brydget joined the Foreign Office and did not marry. She never talked about her work but the writer assumes she was engaged in foreign communications as she served as a Lieutenant WRNS in cyphers during World War II. When the converted Cunard liner *Queen Mary* was ferrying some 5,000 to 10,000 United States troops per voyage from America to Britain as a prelude to the Normandy invasion, Brydget was sometimes the only female on board. Notwithstanding her warm personality she was then known as 'Frigid Brydget'. As a generous friend to Ned's many relations she provided a pivotal family link both before and after her retirement to Chichester.

Freda and Ned's last child Rosemary was born in Simonstown, in October 1917. She served as a VAD nurse during World War II and, as a very attractive young woman, featured on the cover of *Country Life* magazine. She married Anthony Acton, a District Commissioner on the Gold Coast. Tony subsequently qualified as a solicitor and practised in Bournemouth. They have three children. Rosemary supports the Campaign for Nuclear Disarmament.

The three elder children, Ned and Laura's, all attended St Leonard's Convent near Hastings where they were boarders. The five younger children, Ned and Freda's, were taught by a governess before furthering their studies at day school.

A scrap of paper in Ned's files indicates that his salary in 1910 was 892 pounds and income from mortgages on two houses, possibly inherited from Laura, was 340 pounds. In 1920 he calculated Freda's income at 130 pounds.

The Far East
Revisited –1905

In July and August 1903 Ned's base was HMS *Black Prince* from which he commanded the Torpedo Boat Flotilla on manoeuvres. In September 1903 and on subsequent occasions Ned participated in the 'War Course' and other training for senior officers on HMS *President*. From 1 January to 17 June 1904 Ned was based on HMS *Warrior* and on HMS *Erebus* as Captain (Destroyers) of the Home Fleet. The *Warrior*, the first ironclad built for the Royal Navy, was a 1st class armoured cruiser of 9,210 tons used as a depot ship for torpedo boats. *Erebus*, based at Portland, Dorset, was

originally the ironclad, HMS *Invincible*, built 1869. On 18 June 1904 Ned took command of HMS *Halcyon*, a twin-screw torpedo gunboat of 1,070 tons, before commencing his third voyage to the Far East.

Ned's bulldog Bill and racing yacht *Gadget* accompanied him on HMS *Hecla* to the Pacific in March 1905. The five-metre boat was made of wood and had a cambered cabin roof. *Hecla* was a 6,400-ton torpedo boat depot vessel used as a mother ship to half a dozen torpedo boat destroyers. The small flotilla travelled via Malta to the China Sea where Ned

Officers of HMS Halcyon, *1904; Lts Campbell, Petrie, Ned and 'Bill'.*

Top: The Home Fleet and cruisers arriving at Spithead at sunset, October 1904.
Above: Destroyers taking station ahead.

took a photo of the cruiser *Petersburg* on 7 May, twenty days before the Russian Fleet was almost annihilated by the Japanese Fleet.

On 19 May 1905 a happy programme of light opera was held in Hong Kong on the Royal Yacht HMY *Victoria and Albert*, including 'The Jolly Coppersmith', 'Nell Gwyn', 'A Country Girl' and 'The Watermelon Patch'.

Ned was once again stationed at Wei-Hai-Wei where he was engaged in countermining. This involved carrying live mines on a barge towed behind a launch. When placed in the water in an area known to contain 'enemy' mines, the countermines were detonated. The resulting explosion destroyed the 'enemy' mines. It is clear from the number of

danger flags that the use of countermines was extremely hazardous. Suitable only when the countermine-laying barges were unlikely to encounter 'enemy' fire, it was soon abandoned in favour of depth-charges.

———— ∞ ————

In September Captain Charlton received reports on two of his torpedo boat destroyers, one of which had been washed ashore at Wei-Hai-Wei:

4 Sept 1905.

My dear Captain, I regret to say that HMS Exe *is temporarily* hors de combat. *When we shall be able to take to*

Ned's yacht Gadget *being hoisted aboard HMS* Hecla.

the high sea again is doubtful. Twenty miles off the Saddles it was obvious that a typhoon was imminent. I tried to push on to make landfall but I was forced to heave to. For 18 hours I had to keep my vessel bow to the wind. At night I lost sight of HMS Dee. I fetched up here on Sunday after an experience which I trust will never fall my lot again. I have two plates where the rivets went, my provision room flooded, two large cowls were unshipped, electric lights failed, charts went, log went until I hoped the end would soon be over. Some men in HMS Dee were hurt, but not seriously. I would like some of those b***** construction people who cavil about minor defects to have been aboard. Sgd Allan Everett

------ ∞ ------

18 Sept 1905.

In 12 working days we are to have our defects completed. As far as I can see all the Dee's Berthon boats are unserviceable. I cannot test mine as my derrick was smashed. The SNO has written about my ammunition and boats so I suppose these will be sent up from Hong Kong. My wireless has packed up for good. I shall be mighty glad when my Destroyer time is up as I find small things worry me and I am getting peevish. Sgd Allan Everett.

On 24 October 1905 Captain Charlton and his crew were honoured guests at a huge reception in Kagoshima. The parade included numerous Japanese warriors in traditional armour and the crews of HMS *Hecla* and some of the small torpedo boat destroyers. The crowd was entertained with a pole dance and a dance of geisha. The 'Ladies of the Kagoshima Patriotic Association' were welcomed on board *Hecla* by the ship's officers and they in turn were photographed with officers of the 45th Imperial Japanese Regiment, the 'Heroes of Mukden'.

CERTIFICATE: The *Hecla* and five torpedo coat destroyers of the British Navy are permitted to visit Kagoshima for ten days from 21 Oct 1905. The Dept of Foreign Affairs (Japan).

Battle Squadron at Weihaiwei, China, 1904.

Four letters from Kyomi Chikami refer to the events:

———— ∽ ————

Kagoshima, 23 Oct 1905.

(To) Captain E. Charlton commanding HBM's ship Hecla, *As President of the Educational Society of the Prefecture of Kagoshima I beg to convey to you the resolution adopted by Members of the said Society at their 33rd general meeting: 'That we respectfully tender you and the fleet of our honoured Ally the warmest and sincerest welcome at the time of your honouring us with your presence. Kyomi Chikami, President.*

———— ∽ ————

25 Oct 1905.

Dear Sir, I hereby forward to you the public acknowledgement, as well as the boxes containing lacquered trays with the Imperial Crest inside, given by the Prefecture Government to those who risked their lives for the sake of their fellow human-beings. I hope you will be kind enough to distribute them among the gallant officers and men who risked their lives in jumping overboard in order to save those of others when a Japanese Junk accidentally capsized in the harbour of Kagoshima on the 23rd Oct 1905.

I cannot help admiring their action which, allow me to say, may be greatly owing to the inspiration of that immortal order given by Admiral Nelson at the Battle of

Trafalgar: 'England expects every man to do his Duty.' In the last place I have great pleasure in informing you that not a single life had to be mourned for. Kyomi Chikami, Governor.

———— ∽ ————

6 Nov 1905.

My Dear Sir, It was very kind of you to write to me before your departure. The conduct of your men during your stay here was admirable. When you favour us with another visit next Spring I hope to be able to arrange some wild boar and deer shooting for you. I suppose you have heard of someone having lost a dog at Kokubu whither your men went on an excursion. It is now safe in my charge. I feel sorrier for the dumb creature than for its master and I hope you will be kind enough to let me know the wishes of its owner. Kyomi Chikami.

———— ∽ ————

24 Dec 1905.

Dear Sir, I beg to acknowledge your esteemed favour dated 7th inst enclosing $613.64. We hardly know how to express our heartfelt thanks for the munificent gift placed at the disposal of the Ladies Patriotic Association. They told me they would at once proceed to help 'the sick and wounded sufferers from the late war in such a way as to keep alive forever the memory of your generosity, by furnishing them with artificial arms or legs, or implements of agriculture, according to the circumstances'.

I am, Dear Sir, Your obedient servant, Ky Chikami.

Officers of HMS Hecla *– March 1905. Back row: Mr Mason, Gunner (T); Lt Kiddle; Lt May, Eng Lt Hammond; Mr Holmes, Gunner; Mr Jacklinn, Chief Bosun; Mr Withell, Chief Carpenter; Mr Field, Gunner. Middle Row: Chaplain Hastings; Lt Dobbin; Lt Hastings (and Polly); Edward Charlton; Lt Alton; Paymaster Littlejohns; Fleet Surgeon Hackett. Front row: Lt Rogers; Sub Lt. Wilkinson; Mike – dog; Mr Lewis, Gunner; Asst Paymaster Barne; Surgeon Wilkinson.*

Ned distributed the Imperial trays to Sub-Lieutenant Ralph W. Wilkinson, two gunners and eight seamen. He also received a letter from a student at the time of the visit:

———— ∞ ————

The Seventh Higher School, Kagoshima,
24 Oct 1905.

Dear British Gentleman! I am very much regretted that my knowledge of English is next to impossible. I take it honour to receive your favourable visits. You are now in the Far East, left behind your native land. The Sea does not part us but (brings together) both nations. Now happily the Alliance is renewed. We both nations are to serve with our hearts for the Humanity, as Admiral Togo does who was born in Kagoshima. With full earnestness, Y. Ono, a student.

The Japanese *Chronicle* reported the official visit as follows: 'As the guests marched to the place of ceremony and formed up in front of the platform, the few British subjects in Kagoshima had no reason to be ashamed of their own little speck of mud in the far distant Atlantic. The little band of 400 did, indeed, make a right gallant show, and the welcome resounded with "Banzais". And to look at the Captain was comforting in truth. Tall and straight as an arrow, built like a grey-hound, as lithe and limber as they make them, wiry and muscular, with not one ounce of superfluous flesh upon him, he went about with such a quiet ease and self-possession that one could hardly help cheering him.' One wonders if the reporter went on to create 'Tokyo Rose' and/or 'Superman'!

From November 1906 to May 1907 Ned commanded the protected cruiser 1st class HMS *Ariadne*. He then became Captain of HMS *Magnificent*, a twin-screw battleship of 14,900 tons. As a unit of the Home Fleet HMS *Magnificent* was stationed at Sheerness on the estuary of the Thames. His papers include a photo of him with the ship's winning bayonet team, and in contrast, they include a sad letter from a retired sailor seeking his assistance:

The Russian cruiser Petersburg *taken from HMS* Hecla. Petersburg *was destroyed by the Japanese in 1905, shortly after this photograph was taken.*

The destroyer depot ship HMS Erebus *in Portland harbour.*

No. 11 Caroline Street, Belfast, 7 Jan 1908.

Dear Sir, I have took to much liberty on me as to wright to you. I am an old man of 62 years of adge and during that time I spent 46 years at Sea in Honisty and Soberity. 14 years ago my Wife sold all the belongings of my home and Desarted my Family taking with her a married man whome I know well. I got some of my Friends to take some of my family and the two younger sons I put on the Grampian *ship and paid the Government 5 years for them. The younger son asked me to go to the Eastney Barricks to the school of Music which I did. All the time he sent me word as soon as he would get a ship he would have 2 Pounds 12/- per month and he would allow me 6/- per week*

but to the presand he has never gave one Penny. I am sorry to say that my son from his boy hood has been a confounded Lyer. Hooping you will let me no if I would write to the Admiralty as it would be an act of Charity if they would make him do something for me. Thomas Huntsdale.

On 25 July 1908 Ned's brother Engineer Lieutenant Frank Charlton RN, who had served on HMS *Powerful*, *London* and other ships, was killed in a motorbike accident.

Ned took the first step on the uncertain ladder towards Flag Officer on 27 November 1908 when he was appointed Captain of HMS *Topaze*, a twin-screw protected cruiser of 3,000 tons, and a Commodore of the Second Class in charge of Destroyers at the Home Fleet 'in commission with full crews, and was further authorised and directed to hoist a Broad Pendant'. Pendants are banners flown by Flag Officers; swallow-tailed for Commodores, rectangular for Admirals. On 27 July 1909 the Admiralty appointed Ned as Captain of HMS *Boadicea*, an unarmoured cruiser of 3,300 tons, and Commodore of the First Torpedo Boat Flotilla of the Home Fleet which included HMS *Topaze*. He attended a grand dinner given by King George V and presided at a dinner of the 'Royal Navy Club 1765–1885'.

———————— ∞ ————————

Fortrose (Scotland), 1 Sept 1910.

Commodore Charlton, HMS Boadicea, *I have pleasure in enclosing a cheque for 2 Pounds being Second prize won by your yacht* Gadget *at the recent Regatta. As you are aware it came in first but it had to allow the boat that came in second 1 min 8 secs. The* Gadget *was beautifully handled throughout. Sgd W.D. Mitchell.*

Ned and his family lived at Fortrose, four miles from his base at Inverness. His daughter Audrey remembered that the *Gadget* was missing one morning. It had been inadequately moored and had drifted away during the night. Fortunately it was found undamaged off Inverness.

———————— ∞ ————————

Amongst Ned's papers is his appointment as ADC to King George V:

Admiralty, Whitehall, London,
4 Oct 1911.

Director of Naval Ordnance, I am to acquaint you that Captain Edward F.B. Charlton had been appointed a Naval Aide de Camp to his Majesty the King from 22nd ultimo. By Command.

There is no record of Ned undertaking any specific duties as ADC to the King. His period of appointment coincides with his duties as Assistant Director Torpedoes. If, as it appears, the ADC appointment was honorary, the ADT appointment was quite the opposite. The Navy was under the control of Winston Churchill, First Lord of the Admiralty. Admiral Lord Chatfield describes the era: 'There was a surge towards modern techniques which swept like a great wave over the Navy. Old wood was cut away, new growth appeared, helped by Sir John Fisher, Captain Scott and that rising force of young technically trained gunnery and torpedo officers. What had been a heresy was slowly changed to a new religion which became, consequently, the basis of advancement. When shown 80-ton gun-turrets Prime Minister Gladstone exclaimed: "Portentious weapons! I wonder the human mind can stand the strain of such a responsibility." In taking the Navy into the new era the political bosses were prepared even to use such subterfuges as calling the development of 15-inch naval guns the "12-inch Experimental".'

August – 1905. From the top: Lt Rogers; Paymaster Littlejohns; Lt Russel; Surgeon Wilkinson; Edward Charlton; Asst Paymaster Barne; Mr Hucknell and Pat – the dog.

Top: Eighteen live countermines towed to a minefield.
Middle and Above: Explosions of countermines and EC mines – prior to depth charges.

Above: The public reception at Kagoshima.

Below: Hong Kong 1905: The Aberdeen regatta with Charlton's boat Gadget *reaching across the finishing line.*

The heroes of Mukden, the 45th Imperial Japanese Regiment with the officers of Hecla *and the flotilla taken at Kagoshima, October 24, 1905.*

The bayonet team of HMS Magnificent *pose with Edward Charlton having won the Falmer Trophy at Olympia in 1908.*

Scandal and Intrigue

Marconi – 1912

Ned's appointment as Assistant Director of Torpedoes at the Admiralty came in February 1911. Under this title he was also responsible for the development of radio for naval purposes as a member of the Imperial Wireless Committee. The Committee comprised three Royal Navy Officers, two Post-Office officials and one Army officer. One of its objectives was to establish an Imperial Wireless Chain to provide a worldwide communication system for Britain in the event of war. Germany was engaged in a similar endeavour using exclusively the services of the German Telefunken Company. The British Marconi Company, founded by the inventor of radio Mr Guglielmo Marconi, was engaged to undertake the massive Imperial Chain which included the construction of huge pylons to link England with its Empire. The energetic managing director of the British Marconi Company was Mr Godfrey Isaacs, brother of Rufus Isaacs, Britain's Attorney-General. According to W.P. Jolly, Marconi's biographer, the business ventures of Rufus before he rose to a Cabinet position were 'slippery'. When the British Marconi Company was awarded the Navy contract its shares rose from two to nine pounds. Shortly before the share price rise Geoffrey Isaacs sold half his American Marconi Company shares to his brother Harry, who later sold twenty per cent of the latter to Rufus. The transactions were neither illegal nor a conflict of interest as they did not involve British Marconi Company shares, but American. Nevertheless the transaction was imprudent. The ingredients necessary for a scandal having been created, without any actual evidence an obscure journal alleged impropriety. The cry was taken up enthusiastically for several reasons: politically by the Tory opposition against the Government; economically by opposition firms, particularly Poulsen; and ideologically on the grounds that Government communication systems should not be privatised.

The Liberal Government was forced to appoint a Parliamentary Select Committee of eighteen persons to investigate the allegations. The inquiry was wide-ranging, included calling Winston Churchill as a witness, and took a year. No one was found to be corrupt in any way. Cecil Chesterton, editor of *Eye Witness*, was found guilty of publishing information without factual basis and of anti-semitic prejudice, and was fined 100 pounds. Marconi himself was awarded the GCVO by the King; Rufus Isaacs became Viceroy of India. The delay caused by the Select Committee resulted in Britain failing to establish full radio links with distant British possessions by the outbreak of war, while Germany was successful in so linking its possessions.

The index alone of Ned's evidence, which it took him four days to give under oath, runs to over 2,000 words. He was placed in the unenviable position of having to answer hundreds of questions, at a public hearing, about Navy policy, plans for radio communication, jamming etc., while endeavouring to maintain absolute security against the leaking of secret information. The *Daily News* reported Ned's evidence as follows:

A SAILOR WITNESS. The ushers called Rear-Admiral Charlton, a broad-shouldered, bronzed, clean-shaven officer. He gave his evidence in a clear ringing voice, explaining how the subject of the 'Imperial Chain' had exercised the Admiralty and how he came to the conclusion that, if the Admiralty erected the stations, naval work would suffer. Witness said at no time did he desire to give any advantage to Mr Godfrey Isaacs; his only interest was the public service. The Rear-Admiral said that the advice he gave was that if the stations were to be erected in good time, the Marconi tender should be considered.

'The Report from the Select Committee on Marconi's Wireless Telegraph Company, Limited Agreement HMSO 1913' includes all Ned's evidence; a few extracts will suffice to indicate some of his duties at the time and the difficult burden he bore as Navy spokesman:

Evidence of Mr Madge of the Post Office:

Q 5779 Lord Robert Cecil (a Tory): Were you . . . ever asked to make a technical report on the technical advantages of the Marconi as compared with the Admiralty scheme?

A 5779 Mr Madge: Not as a member of a Committee

Q 5780 Were you ever asked individually?

A 5780 Individually, yes, on several occasions

Q 5785 Whom did you go to?

A 5785 I went to see Captain Charlton who was in charge.

Q 5786 Always Captain Charlton?

A 5786 I think I am right in saying that on every occasion that I came to the Admiralty on this question I saw Captain Charlton.

Evidence of Captain Edward F.B. Charlton, ADC, RN:

Q 5811 Mr Mooney 25 November 1912: I have not yet understood whether those notes are documents of a confidential character which have passed between people at the Admiralty, or mere jottings of Mr Madge made after conversations he had at the Admiralty . . .

A 5811 Capt. Charlton: I may say that I consulted with the Secretary of the Admiralty before coming here, and he gave me general directions that I could use my discretion as to whether certain documents were produced or not, and if they were required that official application should be made to the Admiralty.

In a letter read by the chairman of the Select Committee the next day the Admiralty gave Ned permission to produce documents with the proviso: '. . . It will, however, be necessary for him to except from this permission any papers containing information in regard to war arrangements such as cannot in the interests of public safety be produced even at a private sitting of the Committee . . .'

Q 6795 The Chairman (Liberal): We shall be glad if you will give us some information with regard to the Admiralty policy towards the Imperial Chain?

A 6795 Capt. Charlton: With regard to my appointment as Assistant Director of Torpedoes, I may say that it carries with it that I am responsible in all matters connected with the design, working and development of wireless telegraphy at the Admiralty . . . Mr McKenna, who was First Lord (in February 1911) was anxious that the Admiralty should erect the stations. In consequence I sent down to the *Vernon* who are our advisors on all wireless matters. At first they said they did not see that it was possible to erect the stations on account of the amount of work it would take away from Naval purposes . . . Afterwards, under the direct orders of Mr McKenna, we made our estimates under the guidance of Mr Madge . . . All Mr Madge had to go on were the stations he had already erected in Malta, Gibraltar and in England . . .

Q 6822 Mr Mooney: The Admiralty always thought they could do it?

A 6822 Capt. Charlton: The state of pressure in the *Vernon* was very much what Capt. Hornby gives in his report here, 'The wireless department has for some years been working at very high pressure'. When certain high power stations were being built . . . design work is practically brought to a standstill. Meanwhile the development of wireless throughout the world is proceeding very rapidly . . . It is submitted that unless more time can be devoted to designing work, His Majesty's Navy instead of having the lead in wireless efficiency, as they undoubtedly have had, will soon be in a position of inferiority in this respect.

Q 6926 Mr Primrose: The side who are jamming of course cannot send any messages at all?

A 6926 Capt. Charlton: They may have two systems arranged so that one is to jam and the other to send through their own jamming. That is the ideal.

Q 7180 Mr Macmaster: You do not feel at liberty to tell us within what distance interference may be possible?

A 7180 No, because it would rather give away the nature of our apparatus; in fact it would enable anyone who wanted to interfere to put up his station at that distance.

Q 7141 Mr James Parker: You said at the time the (Wireless) Committee was determined to go on with this agreement (with Marconi).

A 7141 Capt. Charlton: I, as a member of the Committee, concurred in the decision.

Q 7164 They (the Navy) are entitled to any patents acquired by the Marconi Company during the time of the agreement?

A 7164 The Marconi Company agrees to give us information of any new invention . . . I think, on the whole, we are indebted to a considerable extent to this information which is given yearly by the Company.

Q 7165 Is there any trace of a monopoly conferred on the Marconi Company by this agreement?

A 7165 I am afraid, when there is only one person doing a thing, I do not see how you can avoid a monopoly.

Q 7187 No other Government could establish a station in Cyprus or Egypt without the permission of the British Government?

A 7187 Certainly they could not.

Q 7187 The same with regard to Mombasa?

A 7187 The same.

Q 7188 And with regard to the Cape?

A 7188 Yes.

Q 7189 And India?

A 7189 Yes, in places which belong to our own country.

Erskine Childers

The German state of Schleswig-Holstein, the original home of the Anglo-Saxons, was devastated by mighty North Sea storms in 1362 and 1634. As a result of these floods a strip of the German coast, five to thirty-five kilometres in width, was permanently inundated by the sea. Today, apart from a few sandy islands and an occasional ruined church spire, most of the land lies beneath the remorseless tides.

In 1897 Erskine Childers explored the area. He was Anglo-Irish, a Cambridge Tripos graduate and a House of Commons Committee Clerk. Alternatively sailing his shallow-draught yacht *Vixen*, later *Dulcibella*, in the channels behind the Frisian Islands, and 'kedging' it through them, he turned his adventure into a best-selling book called *The Riddle of the Sands*. Erskine wrote to the University Club, Boston, that the book 'is all based on fact, even though the story is ficticious'. The book, an exciting nautical spy story, postulated that Germany was building a fleet of barges in the dunal estuaries, that the barges would be used as landing craft in an invasion of Britain's east coast, and that Britain was doing nothing to counter this danger. The publication of the 'novel' undoubtedly spurred the creation of a new fleet (Britain's North Sea Fleet), the construction of Britain's North Sea naval base at Rosyth on the east coast of Britain, and the establishment of the Royal Naval Volunteer Reserve.

In the 1890s, Germany was flexing its muscles with the encouragement of the Kaiser and had drawn up secret plans for a possible invasion of Britain. The British Government had long seen France as the traditional enemy, and it was only in 1903, the year *The Riddle of the Sands* was published, that the Government set up a Committee of Imperial Defence under Balfour to examine the German threat, and a Royal Commission under the Duke of Norfolk to report on the need for a volunteer reserve. In 1906 the First Sea Lord wrote privately to Prince George: 'Our only probable enemy is Germany which keeps her whole fleet concentrated within a few hours of England.' Over the next few years Britain increased the armament of her battleships from twelve-inch to fifteen-inch, the weight of a single shell from 450 to 870 kg.

The two British heroes in *The Riddle of the Sands* are called 'Davies' and 'Carruthers'. It is generally accepted that 'Davies' – quick-witted, hyperactive, untidily dressed – was based on Erskine Childers himself. The model for 'Carruthers' – brave, tidy, a keen hunter – is the subject of speculation by Maldwin Drummond of the Royal Yacht Squadron, Southampton, in a book entitled *The Riddle*. He states that Captain Charlton: is unambiguously named by Herbert E. Julyan, yacht-broker, as 'Carruthers' in his book *Sixty Years of Yachts*; sailed with Erskine in his yacht *Sunbeam*, covering 1,867 miles, on a cruise of the Baltic in 1903; was, according to his confidential report, a man of splendid physique; had been in London at just the time Erskine was writing *The Riddle of the Sands*; and believed that the potential German threat to Britain's territorial integrity was insufficiently appreciated in bureaucratic circles.

On much of the actual voyage in 1897 Erskine had been accompanied by his brother Henry, a man whose characteristics did not match those of 'Carruthers'. The *Yachting Monthly*, March 1939, considers it probable that Ned was Erskine's mentor on the capabilities of torpedo boats in both offensive and defensive roles in shallow water. There is no means of proving whether or not he was a model for 'Carruthers'. In an apparent endeavour to disguise certain characters Erskine takes pains through much of the book to characterise 'Carruthers' as a land-lubber; why then does he, apparently inadvertently, disregard this characteristic in a few places and imbue him with seafaring expertise such as knowledge that 'Davies' had 'committed a grave offence against maritime law in having "cooked" his log', and 'Davies' knew that 'Carruthers' 'had done a great deal of yachting'?

Ned had returned from the Far East to take up duty on HMS *Vernon* at the end of 1901, a year after Erskine returned from fighting on the British side in the Boer War and before he commenced his 'novel'. While one can only speculate about the real identity of 'Carruthers', it seems certain that during Ned's subsequent duties at the Admiralty and as Admiral on the east coast of Britain, both at the beginning and at the end of World War I, he must have been constantly aware of Childers' hypothesis that Germany could – undetected – build an invasion fleet behind the Frisian Islands.

And there is a remarkable postscript to this story: Childers' transformation from Britain's friend into Britain's enemy. In addition to *The Riddle of the Sands*, in 1911 Childers wrote a book advocating Home Rule for Ireland. His sympathy for the cause was triggered by his experiences in South Africa where he served Britain as an artilleryman in the Boer War, and visited wounded Irish soldiers; he wrote: 'It seems impossible to believe that these are the men whom Irish patriots incite to mutiny. They are keen, simple soldiers as proud of the flag as any Britisher . . .' Britain's treatment of the Boers stirred in Childers feelings of resentment, as it reminded him strongly of the experiences of his Irish forebears: 'It seems to me that morally, if not legally, the Boers are belligerents (not rebels) who have fought honestly for their homes. Confiscation of their farms and deportation are harsh measures.'

On 5 January 1904 he married 'Molly' Osgood, an American sympathiser whose ancestors had engaged in the Boston Tea Party. In 1914 the British Government agreed to grant Dominion status to the southern eighty per cent of Ireland; conflict between the South and Ulster, the northern twenty per cent, seemed likely. The Ulster Volunteer Force in the north received 24,000 rifles without intervention by British troops. In retaliation, on 26 July 1914 the newly-weds and some friends smuggled 1,500 rifles from Hamburg into Dublin on behalf of the Irish Volunteer Force in their yacht *Asgard*; British troops intervened, confiscated nineteen rifles, and killed three civilians.

During the first years of the Great War Childers served as an airman in the Royal Navy and won the Distinguished Service Cross. In 1917 he was released from wartime naval duties to act as secretary to a convention on the implementation of Home Rule for Ireland; subsequently he was elected MP for Wicklow and became an ardent republican. Three of Ned's associates from divergent milieux were brought into contact at this time: his classmate of 1878, King George V; his sailing companion of 1903, Erskine Childers; and his fellow East African commander of 1917, General Smuts. A 'bloodthirsty' speech had been prepared for the King to read at the opening of the first Ulster Parliament. He asked Smuts, who was visiting, to prepare a conciliatory speech, which was accepted by the Cabinet. The King appealed to all Irishmen to 'stretch out the hand of forbearance'; Smuts told of how South Africa's vain struggles led almost to their annihilation. But later they were saved and regained their complete independence under the new Dominion status.' Childers replied that he had 'moved on from Home Rule'.

On 5 December 1921 the Anglo-Irish Treaty was signed, but pro-republicans like Childers would accept neither the oath of allegiance nor partition. Civil war commenced, the 'rebels' retreated southwards, and on 10 November 1922 Childers was captured by the Irish Government in possession of a small .22 pistol. He was court-martialled, sentenced, and executed by firing squad on the morning of 24 November. Rosemary Acton, Ned's youngest daughter, wrote in July 1993: 'It was a great tragedy when Erskine was executed, quite unfairly. He was no spy . . . My father was very upset. Tried to do all he could to save him (as did several members of the House of Commons). To no avail. In my father's words, "complete injustice".'

Charlton's first notice from the Admiralty of impending war. 29 July 1914.

Winning Warrior in World War One

Notwithstanding Liddell Hart's extensive histories of both world wars, he is far from dogmatic in ascribing causes for that first terrible international conflict, the Great War. Simplistic histories blame the assassination of Archduke Ferdinand, heir to the Austrian throne, at Sarajevo on 24 June 1914 by a Serbian, with the possible connivance of the Bosnian military governor, but Hart states firmly that, 'fifty years were spent in the process of making Europe explosive.' Most of the countries involved doubled their military spending in the decade prior to the war. Greed, fear, hunger or pride epitomised the outlook of many.

A list of combatants and probable military deaths was compiled from a newspaper cutting in Ned's folio, from David Shermer's *World War I*, and from other sources:

NATION	YEARS IN WAR	KNOWN DEAD	PROBABLE MOTIVATION
The Allied Powers			
BRITAIN	4.3	760,000	Retention of naval hegemony (Shermer)
BRITISH EMPIRE	4.3	250,000	Loyalty to Britain
FRANCE	4.3	1,360,000	Fear of Germany
BELGIUM	4.3	14,000	Fear of Germany
ITALY	3.5	650,000	Enmity with Austria
RUSSIA	3.6	1,700,000	Fear of Germany and of internal revolt
SERBIA	4.3	45,000	Dislike of Austria
ROMANIA	1.5	339,000	Fear of Germany
MONTENEGRO	4.3	3,000	Dislike of Austria
GREECE	1.9	5,000	Resentment of Turkey
JAPAN	4.3	300	Support its Allies
PORTUGAL	2.7	7,000	Quarrel over shipping
UNITED STATES	1.6	116,000	Restore Liberty
The Axis Powers			
GERMANY	4.3	1,900,000	Territorial and commercial hegemony
AUSTRIA-HUNGARY	4.3	1,150,000	Fear of internal revolt
TURKEY	4.3	350,000	Fear of Russia and West
BULGARIA	3.3	88,000	Assist Austria

During the course of the war neither the Allies nor the Axis achieved clear naval ascendancy, although German U-boats sank many Allied ships and the Royal Navy largely achieved its objective of blockading Germany. In the battles for the former German colonies the Allies were generally successful. On the main front, the trenches in France, both sides lost thousands of men each day and achieved nothing except stalemate until 1918 when the addition of 250,000 United States troops per month gave the Allies victory on 11 November 1918. In 1915 Churchill attempted the war's major diversion, a logical attempt to bypass the deadlock in France by attacking 'the soft under-belly of Europe' through the Dardanelles and Gallipoli. This would have eliminated two Axis powers – Turkey and Bulgaria – if it had been successful; unfortunately it failed and Churchill resigned from the Cabinet.

On 13 May 1913 Ned had been promoted to Rear-Admiral. The ranks of Admiral were formally established during Cromwell's Commonwealth. Three categories were created: Admiral (full), Vice-Admiral (deputy) and Rear(guard) - Admiral, as well as three great fleets, the Red, the White and the Blue. Admirals of each rank fly a distinctive rectangular flag.

———— ∞ ————

HM Yacht *Victoria and Albert*, 12 May 1913.

Rear-Admiral E.F.B. Charlton Sir, May we offer our humble and heartiest congratulations on your promotion to Flag rank.
Sgd by six Seamen, late 'Orlando's 1899–1902.'

———— ∞ ————

Letter from a retired servant to Ned's mother:

Rose and Crown Hotel, Blackhill, 10 June 1913.

My Very Dear Madam, I heard a few days ago that Captain Charlton had been made an Admiral. I am very pleased that you have been spared through your recent illness to see that day.
I am dear Madam, Yr obedient Serv't, Anne Kimpson.

———— ∞ ————

60 Strada Irlandese, Malta, 23 Sept 1913.

Dear Admiral Charlton, You may imagine my great surprise and immense pleasure [at your promotion] . . . I too have been promoted to 'Domestic Prelate of His Holiness', a high distinction in the Catholic Church. I am sending you a small crucifix blessed by the Holy Father. J. Cassar.

On being congratulated on his appointment by the Bellingham District Council, Ned wrote and thanked them, adding, 'I have been very fortunate in arriving at Flag Rank when just turned 48, and must attribute my good luck in a great measure to having been able occasionally to refresh myself by a visit to my forefathers in the pure air of North Tyne.'

Home and Atlantic Fleets at Scapa Flow - 17 April 1909.

CONFIDENTIAL The Woolsack, Mimizan, 22 Dec 1913.

Dear Admiral Charlton, It has given me much pleasure to submit your name to the King for one of the new Civil C.B.s recently instituted for Naval Officers. With my best wishes. (sgd) Winston S. Churchill.

On 5 March 1914, Ned's mother, Margaret Charlton, died at 38A Victoria Road, Kensington, aged seventy-six and fortified by the rites of the Church.

———— ∞ ————

Admiralty, Whitehall, 1 Jul 1914.

Dear Admiral Charlton, (handwritten) I am glad to offer you the appointment of Rear-Admiral in the Home Fleet at Portsmouth. Your services as ADT at the Admiralty have given satisfaction. I hope you will be equally successful in a seagoing command.
Yours sincerely, sgd Winston S. Churchill.

———— ∞ ————

In his wartime letters home Ned did not draw attention to the physical danger to himself. It is evident however that he was aware of the risks as he sent the following confidential letter to Oswin, his lawyer, executor and brother, at the start of the war. It was found, not in Ned's folios, but in Oswin's estate:

21 Sept 1914.

The North Sea is a dear old friend and I would as soon lay there as anywhere else. This mine seeking is dangerous work against a hidden enemy whom it is impossible to locate exactly and therefore it is advisable to leave a note behind.

If I remain in the North Sea, a brass plate, costing not more than 30 Pounds, may be put up at Bellingham in the chapel. Should my remains be recovered, let them be buried quietly at Fareham with my dear Laura. No new stone. An inscription may be cut into the present stone. In case of my death over this work, remember I am as much at the front as if killed on the field of battle now raging round Rheims. My widow should be entitled to full award of pension.

I feel disturbed at having saddled my dear Freda with a somewhat expensive house for another seven years but if she finds her income, without mine, would not allow her to live there, perhaps some way may be found of getting out of it.

If a proposal for adoption of one of my elder children be

made it could be accepted. Mrs Radcliffe is to have nothing to do with them [a Lady Maud Radcliffe is recorded as a friend of the bride's at Laura and Ned's wedding].

I feel I can do no more for them than to give my life for my country. Au revoir,

Edward F.B. Charlton.

———— ∞ ————

In Ned's 1914–18 folio the chronological sequence used in previous folios is abandoned in favour of an alphabetical system, i.e. Ascension Island; Admiralty House; . . . Zanzibar; Zeppelin. The folio was apparently put together after the war by Ned as the index is in his handwriting; he kept his letters home separately. The folio commences with a twenty-seven-verse parody of Rudyard Kipling's 'Now this is the Law of the Jungle' entitled 'The Laws of the Navy'. They were collected by Ned in February 1904. Five follow:

> Now these are the Laws of the Navy,
> unwritten and varied they be, And he that
> is wise will observe them,
> going down in his ship to the sea.

> If you win through an African jungle,
> unmentioned at home in the Press, Heed it not.
> None seeth the piston; it driveth the ship
> none the less.

> On the strength of one link in the
> cable dependeth the might of the chain, Who
> knows when thou may'st be tested? so live that
> thou beareth the strain.

> So thou, when thou neareth promotion,
> and the cap which is gilded be nigh,
> Give heed to thy words and thy actions lest
> others be weary thereby.

> Now these are the laws of the Navy, and many
> and mighty are they, But the bow and the stern of
> the Law, and the hull and the keel are – OBEY.

Rear-Admiral Charlton's call to duty came two weeks before the war started and prevented him from taking up his appointment as Commander-in-Chief of the Home Fleet at Portsmouth.

Admiral Commanding Minesweepers – 1914

Ned's collection of newspaper cuttings gives an overall picture of minesweeping warfare. When war was declared, Germany sent out surface raiders to sow the North Sea with explosive mines that generally sunk any ship that struck them. The mines were moored to the seabed by a wire cable which kept them hidden below the surface. The North Sea was ideal for mine warfare as it is generally shallow and the water is almost opaque. The Admiralty looked to the British steam fishing trawlers for counter measures. The principal bases would be the Humber ports of Grimsby and Hull on the coast of Yorkshire. Within a week thirty-four trawlers were put into action and in the succeeding weeks 160 vessels were added, almost all manned by North Sea fishermen. As British casualties from German mines were significant it was decided, after debating whether all shipping on the east coast of Britain should be discontinued, to fix a channel around the coast, which would be buoyed all the way, for safe passage of British and Allied ships. This 'Fairway' or 'War Channel' would be swept daily for mines.

The total number of vessels engaged in minesweeping during the war was 2,858 of which 444 were lost including 250 trawlers, 125 drifters and sixty-nine others, mostly yachts or small paddle steamers. On average five men died in each sweeper lost. In one sector, fifty-six Allied ships were sunk by mines, but 1,029 mines were destroyed. Initially the minesweepers went out in pairs abreast dragging a wire sweep between them. Later they generally went out in sections of six to eight and each sweeper cleared a strip about 150 metres wide. Using a paravane, a device like a kite which kept the sweep well to one side of the towing vessel, the sweeper dragged serrated wire which cut the wire cable anchoring the mine to the sea bed. When the mine floated to the surface it was destroyed by rifle fire in the early stages of the war and, in the later stages, by small cannon. One or two Naval Reserve officers often accompanied each section.

In the first months of the war, as the first Admiral ever designated to command minesweepers, Ned was exceptionally busy setting up the mine defence system. One of his first actions was to fly over a minefield in a seaplane to see whether mines could be seen from the air; alas they could not, although this later became possible in the clearer waters of the Mediterranean. As early as October 1914 a battleship, HMS *Audacious*, was sunk by a mine. Ned devised a system by which 'Q-messages' were sent to all ships once a minefield was discovered. On 16 December 1914 German battle-cruisers bombarded three east coast towns killing 120 civilians. Only later did the Royal Navy realise that the bombardment served to cover the laying of 100 mines by the German mine-layer *Kolberg*. Ned went to inspect operations and wrote short letters home on scraps of paper. The first letter was from Scarborough shortly after that popular east coast holiday resort had been shelled by the German Navy:

Pier Hotel, Scarborough, 30 Dec 1914.

My dear Freda, I send you some postcards which show the damage clearly . . . they had 57 panes of glass broken in this house alone.
We had a rather amusing day in the Brighton Queen; *this vessel is one of the first of the Paddle Sweepers and runs 17 knots. We swept towards Scarboro' and the sweepers came right up to the Castle. When they eased up their sweeps, up came the mines and, after a few rifle shots, these exploded with considerable noise so that the people thought it was the return of the Germans and started running. However as we went on quietly they appeared to become reassured.*

Brighton Queen, Farne Islands, 13 Jan 1915.

My cabin is very comfortable. The hot baths make up for a good deal; there are no less than seven bathrooms and it would not be surprising if the Brighton Queen *ran out of water before she ran out of coal. The Duke (Valencay) certainly had a very good idea of comfort and knew what was useful in a seagoing vessel; for instance there are three chronometers whereas only the largest vessels usually carry more than one.*

As the mines were anchored to the seabed they were of course closer to the surface at low tide than at high. Initially sweepers were lost as a consequence of sweeping at low tide. Ned issued instructions that no sweeping was to be undertaken within two hours of low tide.

In January 1915 Ned travelled north to confer with his counterparts in the defence of the east coast and to appraise them of mine defence strategy. For part of the journey he travelled in his small flagship HMS *Sagitta*

HMS *Sagitta* at sea off Moray Firth, 19 Jan 1915.

My dear Freda, It was a deadly slow train to Petershead last night, two hours to do 33 miles. Sir G. Armstrong [an old shipmate as a Midshipman; later editor of The Globe] *met me at the station and conducted me through the pitch dark town to Admiral Simpson.*

HMS Sugitta.

Hoisting in a mine.

Handling a mine.

Dinghy making mines safe.

Swimming to the mine to cut the seals. Lt-Comm Garnett in the water.

Approaching the mine.

A contemplative sweeper.

127

Damaged trawler at Scarborough - Dec 1914.

————— ∞ —————

Scapa Flow.

It is quite a treat to see a few [battle] ships again. Had a long interview with C-in-C [Home Fleets] (Admiral Jellicoe) and expect to start back tomorrow after some experiments. I hear the Victor sank off the North Coast of Ireland. She had on board 'Karl Graves', the special German spy who had been captured from a Norwegian vessel on his way to America; no-one saved. Serve him right but hard luck on the vessel.

————— ∞ —————

Cromarty, 21 Jan 1915.

I saw Rear-Admiral Pears and paid my respects to [Admiral] Calthorpe who was there with his Squadron and wanted me to dine, but the weather was too uncertain so we had the gates opened at 11.15am and passed over the minefield, the hills around all covered with deep snow.

————— ∞ —————

Off Rosyth, 22 Jan 1915.

Saw my Admirals (Lowry, Bradford and Beatty) (respectively E. Coast Scotland, 3rd Battle Squadron and Battle-cruiser Fleet) and am off to the Humber . . . have managed to get two coast lights turned on.

————— ∞ —————

Train, Hull to King's X, 23 Jan 1915.

We had quite a pleasant night and the two coast lights enabled us to navigate without trouble and pass through the Scarborough minefield just as day was breaking. [Admiral] Fisher, I see, is laid up with a cold but I suppose I shall be able to interview him.

I have had your despatch case with me the whole time; it has been most useful and has been admired by the C-in-C himself.

————— ∞ —————

In the early days of the war the German torpedoes had many successes but British torpedoes achieved little. While some British torpedoes are known to have been set to run too deep, a major problem was that the Germans had fewer merchant ships and consequently presented fewer targets. This lack of targets, as well as design faults, reduced the effectiveness of early British mines. Admiral Lord Fisher, whom his biographer Marder describes as regarded by the Royal Navy 'either as a genius who raised the efficiency of the Fleet to a peak never reached before, or as an evil old man who played havoc with naval discipline and efficiency', was recalled from retirement early in the war and was scathing of Ned and other torpedomen in several of his letters: 'Our torpedoes seem to be filled with sawdust!

Outside the W/T House.

Pistol Practice.

Admiral and cat.

Navigation Class.

In Firth of Forth, Jan 1915.

Cat overboard.

There's a heavy reckoning coming to everyone connected with *Vernon* during the last four years. I hope to get a good many officers disgraced for it.'

Also from Fisher

Admiralty, 8 Feb 1918.

My beloved Jellicoe, I fear I sent you a 'thunder and lightning' letter yesterday, being in an aggressive mood, having just had a row with Charlton over the mine-sweeping, which I do not think well organised as it should be one big scheme; and not so much done as I had hoped by his recent visit to everyone up and down the coast . . . some of Charlton's work now is QUITE SILLY in searching areas that by no possibility will EVER be traversed [laid with German mines]. I am going to join up [put] Admiral Ommanney in the job.

and

19 May 1915.

To H.H. Asquith (Prime Minister), If the following four conditions are agreed to, I can guarantee the successful termination of the War:

1 *That Mr Winston Churchill is not in the Cabinet . . .*
2 *That [Fisher's deputy] Sir A.K. Wilson leave the Admiralty*
3 *That there shall be an entire new Board of the Admiralty*
4 *That I should have complete professional charge of the war at sea etc . . . Fisher.*

In an appendix Fisher proposed numerous staff changes including terminating the services of Ommanney, whom he had favoured for Ned's position only three months earlier, transferring Ned elsewhere and replacing him with Vice-Admiral Oliver. Only two days later Fisher no longer supported Oliver but favoured a fourth candidate, Admiral Madden. However, he had come to accept that Germany might sow mines in numerous locations and that anti-mine action was vital:

Secret and Private, 21 May 1915.

Dear Jellicoe, The mine-sweeping is really THE one chief thing in the War in view of the certainty now (very near us) of every yard of the North Sea being infested with mines. Charlton is quite unfit for so immense a job and Madden is the ONLY MAN.

───── ∞ ─────

The Torpedomen, published in 1993, states: 'Fisher's outburst was both intemperate and unfair. If anyone was responsible for the Admiralty's inability to develop effective weapons it was he [Fisher] who had so consistently opposed the creation of a Naval Staff.' Torpedoes had already proved themselves to be even more devastating than mines and it is surprising that Fisher continued to describe mines as 'THE one chief thing in the War'. As the originator of the oft·

Almost fatally damaged by a mine, HMS Lilac *finally struggled to Aberdeen for repair July 1915.*

CL mine explodes behind Sagitta, *rather too close to be pleasant – April 1915.*

Above: HMS Lilac *after being mined arrives at Peterhead. Draught of water forward 32ft, aft 12ft.*

Below: Admiral of mine sweepers, Officers and crew of HMS Sagitta – *March 1915*

misquoted *mal mot* 'Never explain, Never deny, Never apologise', Fisher was never likely to rest quietly on his pre-war laurels. The PM rejected his ultimatum of 19 May and accepted his resignation from the post of First Sea Lord.

———— ∞ ————

Admiralty, 3 Feb 1915.

My dear Freda, Fortunately, although the sea is too big to sweep throughout, it is also too big to mine everywhere and one must have a bit of luck sometimes.

———— ∞ ————

HMS *Sagitta*, Eastbourne, 25 Feb 1915.

The Brighton Queen *will have to go to Pompey [Portsmouth] as her stern is leaking due to a slight misunderstanding with the destroyer* Cygnet *who mistook her for Leda and rammed her. [Leda; a mythical swan mounted by Zeus; the Brighton Queen was later sunk by a mine off Dunkirk.]*

———— ∞ ————

HMS *Sagitta*, at sea, 25 Apr 1915.

After a duck hunt tomorrow morning I am going to look at one of the new sweepers just launched.

———— ∞ ————

13 May 1915.

Trial was a very successful one; so Newcastle has the honour of getting the first of the new type to complete her trials.

Ned kept in touch with Lieutenant Haig of HMS *Sagitta* during later stages of the war. His certificate of service to Lieutenant Haig is on the identical form to the numerous certificates he himself had received over the years but is more comprehensive and ignores the need to report on sobriety!

CERTIFICATE: Donald M. Haig served as Sub-Lieut and Lieut RNR on HMS *Zarefah* and *Sagitta* from 24 Aug 1914 to 6 Dec 1915 and conducted himself very much to my satisfaction. Mr Haig was promoted to Lieut on 30 Dec 1914 and has been in command of *Sagitta* since 29 June 1915. A very good watch keeper and reliable Navigator. The vessels were employed on mine sweeping operations from Sept 1914 and were exceedingly useful both when carrying my Flag and on independent cruises in all parts of the North Sea and Channel. Sgd Rear-Adm E. Charlton.

In one of his letters to Ned, Lieutenant Haig tells the 'remarkable tale of a stoker, who after *Arethusa* was struck, climbed up inside the funnel and down the funnel guys to the deck. He was stark naked and rather scorched but otherwise all right although he had no recollection how or where he lost his clothes. The ship took the mine under her boiler room and the boilers must have gone through her bottom, otherwise the man could not have got up the funnel.'

One of the reports Ned received was from the Master of the SS *Zero*; it brings home the mine hazard in the White Sea off northern Russia:

Finished loading homeward cargo 10 July 1915. Admiral Ivanovsky told us we had two Russian officials on board with valuable documents and had made arrangements for the Sapad *and* Yuch *to sweep ahead of us. We got underway on 13th but had to anchor due to thick fog. On 14th fog lifted but their sweeping gear fouled. At 10pm a ship of the Murman Line came up, full of people, towing four lifeboats with people and also a steam trawler towing two boats, also with people. As two of our steamers were overdue I signalled them but got no reply. At 11.30 pm the British Sweeper* Bombardier *directed us to 'stop instantly'. He had four Hull sweepers under his command. Several loud explosions occurred shaking our ship from stem to stern. We anchored and the men in the sweepers, who had not stopped for three days, got some sleep. We learnt that the men in the lifeboats were from the* Urania. *Next day more mines were swept, one blowing the paint off the* Ganton. *At 0.20am on 18th we proceeded; in 6 days they had destroyed over 50 mines. I thought it best to give you this report in detail as I feel the seriousness of the mine danger in the White Sea has not yet reached England and little help can be expected from the Russians in Archangel. We had on board 5 saloon passengers including two finance officials carrying thirty million in 16 packages; also 10 men from the mined* Arndale *and* Drumloist. *sgd H.E. French.*

———— ∞ ————

Ned described another incident which he witnessed himself:

On 1 Sept 1915 I was engaged in looking after the sweepers in a yacht manned throughout by RNR and RNVR officers, most of whom were undergraduates from Cambridge University. It was a misty day and mines, we had reason to believe, had been laid somewhere in the 'Fairway'. While searching we observed a mine blow up alongside a steamer about a mile away to the northward. Fortunately for us perhaps, we were heading south and had to turn around to close her. Between us and the steamer was a Patrol Trawler heading north. Without the slightest hesitation this little vessel made a bee-line for the disabled ship which we could see was in a bad way with one boat hanging vertically from a davit. When the trawler had got within about 150 yards of her there was a terrific explosion, the trawler's stern cocked up in the air and her still-revolving propeller had disappeared under water before the pieces had finished falling. We stopped at once and picked up seven survivors. We observed the bulky form of a man floating on the surface with his head under water. The bow wash seemed to dislodge some air out of his clothing and his body disappeared; a man in our bows immediately dived after him, and both were hauled on board together. The unconscious man was treated by our doctor but I regret to say his efforts were of no avail. The man turned out to be the mate, and a fisherman, and left a widow and eleven children.

As a result of this type of incident, and perhaps his own concern for his large family, Ned made representations to the Treasury to have the pension paid to widows and dependants who 'Died in Naval Service' increased to the higher rate paid to dependants of those 'Killed in Action'. The effort was successful and the words 'Killed in the performance of Naval or Military duty' were substituted in February 1916 by the Treasury in place of the words 'Killed in Action', thus enabling the dependants of minesweeper men killed on duty to be more fairly recompensed.

During the first half of 1915 the Royal Navy was at a loss to explain the sprouting of many small isolated minefields and suspected that the mines 'had been sown by neutral fishing boats in the pay of an unscrupulous enemy'. On 2 July 1915 the German submarine *UC-2* was accidentally rammed and sunk by the coaster *Cottingham*. The submarine was salvaged by the British who discovered that it carried twelve mines which could be sown while the U-boat remained submerged. Once the riddle was resolved the UC-class mine-laying submarines were attacked with vigour. Of the seventy-nine constructed, fifty-two were destroyed; in the German Navy they became known as the 'sisters of sorrow'.

Ned recorded for the Ushaw school magazine some humorous aspects of these tragic times:

One youngster wrote to his father, a vicar, saying, 'You always told me, father, when in danger to look for help from above. I did so yesterday when being attacked by shellfire from a submarine, and there above was an aeroplane trying to bomb us.'

The sweeper *Columbia* radioed: 'Enemy aeroplane overhead dropping bombs.' The ship's cook and wireless operator, amongst others, fired at the plane with rifles and managed to knock a bit out of it. The plane crashed in the sea near the Dutch coast, the crew being rescued by a British fishing boat whose skipper berated them solidly for the five days of the return trip. Radio contact with the *Columbia* was however lost so Ned raced to the rescue and semaphored on arrival, 'What are you doing?' Reply: 'Picking up fish killed by bomb explosions.' 'Why don't you answer my wireless signals?' Reply: 'Wireless operator is collecting the fish.'

On another sweep the *Columbia* was sunk by two German torpedo boats which were unaware that it had just sent off a SOS message. The Germans circled cautiously round the lone survivor, a crew member who made a rude sign at them. A British torpedo boat and a trawler raced up and managed to sink both enemy vessels – bringing a smile to the face of the survivor.

A light vessel hailed a returning sweeper early in the war when sweepers worked in pairs: 'Where's your mate?' 'The b*****'s blown up.' 'What are you going to do?' 'Going back to get another b*****.'

On one occasion, when an enemy submarine appeared close to a minesweeping section, she was promptly rammed by the nearest trawler, which almost grounded on top of her. As the fishing boat slid over the submarine its engineer rushed on deck with a coal hammer and delivered a violent blow at the periscope. As a result the submarine surfaced and surrendered to a torpedo boat. The submarine's crew were saved though they took the precaution of sinking their vessel. The trawler's crew were handsomely rewarded by the Admiralty.

After the war Admiral Charlton was deputed by King George V to present decorations to some of the unsung minesweeping heroes. At the presentation Ned read the official report on an incident which Lieutenant MacCabe had presented to the Admiralty in 1918, and which he described as a fisherman's fight: 'The convoy was returning from Iceland when the submarine appeared about 7,000 yards away and opened fire with shell and shrapnel hitting the *Aisne* several times. The enemy vessel was of a large type, probably 300 feet long, and fitted with guns of 6.0 inch calibre and one, if not two, smaller ones. The officer summoned his flotilla to form line ahead and follow him, and they swung into formation with the precision of warships. One of the crew of *Aisne* was killed and four wounded. The shooting from the submarine at first was good; her speed was such that she might have steered in rings round the trawlers; and her armament was sufficient to blow the lesser craft out of the water. The fishermen kept their fire going until they were threatened with lack of ammunition. When the leading trawler, the *Conan Doyle*, found herself with only 15 rounds left she signalled "Prepare to ram", but it did not come to that. The submarine was closing to shorter range, and the second trawler in the line managed to hit her with a shell.' The U-boat disappeared, minus its forward gun, and possibly sank.

In addition to receiving five Distinguished Service Crosses and nine Distinguished Service Medals, members of the flotilla were granted an award after the war totalling 500 pounds – 18 pounds 10/5d to each skipper and 3 pounds 14/1d to each crew member.

The classic account of minesweeping in World War I is *Swept Channels* by Taffrail. He brings to life some of the difficulties encountered by Ned as the first Admiral of Minesweepers and details the growth of minesweeping from six old torpedo-gunboats to vast flotillas stationed in sixty-one ports. At the start of the war one sweeper was lost for every five mines destroyed; as experience grew the loss rate dropped to one vessel for eighty-five mines.

The Germans laid 43,636 mines during the war; the Allies 170,000. Six hours after the outbreak of war the first German mines were laid by the *Konigin Luise*. She was spotted by a British fishing trawler which reported her 'throwing things overboard'. The Royal Navy sank her but the next day the cruiser HMS *Amphion* struck one of the newly laid mines with the loss of 151 lives. Not only was Ned's task complicated by the secrecy with which the U-boats laid mines at night but also because the Germans resorted to delayed action mines whose mechanisms became active as long as thirty days after their release. A total of 357 trawlers were taken over as sweepers in the first month of the war; a further 315 in October 1914. A new naval rank of 'Skipper' was created; in fact the build-up of skippers was so rapid that insufficient uniforms were available; each was therefore given an officer's cap, a badge and a set of brass buttons which he was invited to sew onto his best suit! Taffrail states: The difficulties and perplexities confronting Rear-Admiral Charlton were enormous but he was well known throughout the service as a practical organiser full of initiative and resource . . . A yacht, the *Zarefah*, was allocated to him as flagship and in this vessel he visited the various ports on the East Coast to see matters for himself. Protective minefields were laid down to hamper the U-boats. The first dozen war-built minesweepers were ordered on 1 Jan 1915. During the war one minesweeper was laid down every six-and-a-half days. The German submarines got to know the swept channels so well that on one occasion the sweepers merely 'pretended' to sweep a certain area with the result that German submarine *UC-44* blew up in the minefield previously laid by its compatriots! By the end of 1915, 7,888 officers and men were employed in the British Minesweeping Service and a total of 5,169 mines were accounted for. Minesweeping continued long after the war ended; in Nov 1918 it was estimated that 20,000 mines remained undetected.

The East Africa Campaign – 1916

Africa is now considered to be the cradle of the human species but in the fourteenth century it was regarded as the 'Dark Continent' until 'discovered' by intrepid Portuguese explorers, who established the colonies of Guinea, Angola and Mozambique circa 1500. In fact, India had traded with Zanzibar much earlier, the Arabs had been capturing slaves along the East African coast for centuries, and the African tribes themselves had been gradually migrating south; however they had not quite reached the Cape of Good Hope when, in 1650, the Dutch decided to occupy it as a resupply post for their ships sailing to the Far East. In time it became a colony and there were eight 'Kaffir' wars at the interface of European and African migration.

As a consequence of the Napoleonic wars in Europe, the Cape became a British colony and, in 1820, the British landed settlers. A few thousand Boers were disenchanted, undertook the perilous Great Trek into the interior, and established the republics of the Transvaal and the Orange Free State. Meanwhile Britain dreamt of, and to a large extent acquired, British territory from Cape to Cairo. France took much of North Africa, Belgium the Congo, while the Germans colonised South-West Africa, the Cameroons and German East Africa (Tanganyika/Tanzania). In the latter half of the nineteenth century gold and diamonds were discovered in the Boer republics and Britain decided to annex them with some help from disaffected residents. This was attempted, at

first without success in the Battle of Majuba Hill in 1881 and in the Jamieson Raid in 1895. In the 1899–1901 Boer War, known as the Second Freedom War by the Boers, the British were successful. In 1910 South Africa was given self-government. The former Boer General, Botha, became Prime Minister and, forgetting past differences, brought South Africa into World War I on the Allied side. His first priority was to conquer German South-West Africa which was achieved in 1915; his second to conquer German East Africa where German forces, under General von Lettow-Vorbeck, had attacked Kenya. Lieutenant-General Smuts took charge of the campaign and was assisted by the Royal Navy which blockaded all ports and destroyed the German cruiser *Konigsberg* in the Rufiji River in July 1915. At this stage Ned was appointed Commander-in-Chief of the Cape Station:

— ∽ —

29 Oct 1915.

Dear Admiral Charlton, I have much pleasure in offering you the command of Cape of Good Hope Station.
Your services at the Admiralty as Admiral Commanding Mine Sweepers have given satisfaction and I hope you will be equally successful at the Cape. (Lord) A. Balfour.

— ∽ —

After a short spell on HMS *Hyacinth*, Ned said farewell to Freda at Devonport on 30 December 1915 and travelled to South Africa on his flagship, the cruiser HMS *Vengeance*. His personal staff included Flag Lieutenant-Commander W.F. Cullinan, who was to serve continuously with Ned for the next seven years, Flag Lt-Com C. Goolden, Fleet Surgeon R.H.J. Browne, and three clerks. Ned wrote home frequently, sometimes using a code such as 'Passed the Wine Island this morning' [Madeira?], 'making for your youngest brother's island' [St Vincents, Cape Verde?]. The officers and men of his former flagship HMS *Sagitta* sent Freda a gift for Ned 'as a small token of the respect and, to express it accurately I should add, affection in which your husband was held'.

— ∽ —

HMS *Vengeance*, at sea, 4 Jan 1916.

My dear Audrey [his eldest daughter], Today we had a splendid rat hunt in my cabin; the long tail of a large rat was seen hanging out below my Dardanelles picture. We got the ship's large white cat and gave him a chair to climb on, but he found it difficult to balance himself as the ship was rolling. At last he got hold of the tip of the rat's tail and bit it; the rat bolted behind a cupboard followed by the cat. There was a lot of squealing and we thought Master Rat was done for until he suddenly bolted and I knocked him over with a stick. The cat is a splendid ratter and has killed quite a lot. I am afraid you won't have any rats in your cabins [when you follow] as the rats always travel third class in passenger ships. The white cat came from HMS Illustrious *with the men, and was born on her; when he was a kitten he fell down a hatchway and is stone deaf as a consequence. He has got a*

HMS Vengeance, *the flagship in times of peace.*

certificate just like a blue-jacket and has been rated 'Cat, First Class' after joining as 'Kitten, Third Class'. He also has a 'Hurt Certificate' for the accident which states that he was 'on duty looking for rats' and was sober at the time.

———— ∞ ————

6 Jan 1916.

My dear Freda, A very good cinema show last night; all the latest films. Our Commander was the first person to start them in ships and was given in consequence over a quarter of a million feet of film. The machine cost 37 Pounds and they put 200 Pounds from the canteen for as many films as they want.

Had four officers to dinner again last night and the table looked quite well with your table centres and just enough silver. I shall leave the greater part of it at Admiralty House.

———— ∞ ————

At sea, 10 Jan 1916.

After a short stay at your brother's isle, I was astounded at there being such a barren place in the world. Nothing but a vast heap of cinders with a picturesquely coloured town at the head of the bay full of interned German steamers. The colour

of the houses was its only beauty, Portuguese law forbidding houses being painted white! Instead of the prettiest of all Emblems, the blue and white of Monarchical Portugal, they now fly a hideous red and green republican abomination.

———— ∞ ————

12 Jan 1916.

They say there is mail leaving today which we shall just miss [later note by Ned; it was the Appam with the Governor of Sierra Leone and 800,000 pounds on board; it was captured by the German raider Moewe].

———— ∞ ————

17 Jan 1916.

(King) 'Neptune' and [sea goddess] 'Amphitrite' arrived on board in the traditional manner over the forecastle and marched aft with the band and were received by me on the Quarterdeck. 'Amphitrite' (the Chief Quartermaster, aged 53 and weighing 19 stone) was a jewel. I welcomed them and told them it was thirty years since I last had that pleasure; 'Amphitrite was then a lithe and lissome lass but no doubt the change in her appearance had been brought about by the many Naiads and Tritons she had since brought into the *underworld and that it now looked like twins.' The big cup was filled with champagne, 4 bottles, and passed around the whole troupe and, while the band played 'Rule Britannia' and 'Neptune', they passed out over the stern to return to Davy Jones to receive a consignment of Huns.*

———— ∞ ————

23 Jan 1916.

Tomorrow we should reach our port in German South-West Africa (as it was) where coal awaits us.

Just had prayers in my fore cabin. There are a large number of Catholics on board, over 100, I should think.

———— ∞ ————

Ned arrived at Admiralty House, Simonstown, Cape of Good Hope on 28 January and spent ten days becoming acquainted with his new station. He wrote to Freda giving details of the large house on the seashore where she would be bringing the seven children. It had several servants including cook, gardener and contract laundry team; also a tennis court and six stables.

———— ∞ ————

Cape Town, 3 Feb 1916.

My dear Freda, I have almost purchased a five-seater Hupmobile, an American car which is very popular out here. General Botha has one; consequently spare parts are easily obtainable. We ran in one which had done 1,400 miles for show purposes; it was a powerful car and travelled beautifully and was very comfortable. Self-starter, electric light and all the latest improvements. Curtains are fitted to open and swing with the doors so that occupants can get out without removing them. (The car cost 400 pounds).

Am sending you a box of peaches which should arrive about 5th Mar.

———— ∞ ————

In March 1916, Freda Charlton travelled to Cape Town on the *Balmoral Castle* with her seven children and the children's nurse 'Scuttie' Hoban from the Catholic village of Arundel. She had previously looked after Laura and Ned's children. She told Audrey that she found it difficult working for Freda because of her strident voice, but put up with it 'for the good of her soul'. In contrast to Laura, Freda preferred outdoor activities to reading.

In his flagship HMS *Vengeance* Ned travelled northward through the Indian Ocean. He met the overall commander, General Smuts, in Durban and in Mombasa. He then drove to Serengeti near Mount Kilimanjaro for a third discussion to co-ordinate strategy. He inspected the Royal Naval Marine 4.0-inch battery in action at Salaita Hill, where the Allies had been rebuffed by the Germans in February 1916, and observed the hill being recaptured on 8 March 1916 by South African and Marine Forces. In the same month HMS *Hyacinth* shelled one of the *Konigsberg*'s huge guns which had been removed from the German cruiser and placed as a

shore defence weapon near Tanga; twenty-five German Askaris were killed during the shelling.

In 1890 Britain had received a Protectorate over the spice island of Zanzibar in exchange for relinquishing sovereignty over the strategic island of Heligoland off the German coast. A photo of the Sultan of Zanzibar paying an official visit to Ned on HMS *Vengeance* on 27 March 1916 is used at the front of this book. On the same day, in a tragic accident, two of the Sultan's guard were killed whilst attempting to fire a twenty-one gun salute in honour of King George V. In April the Khoja Ismaili community in Zanzibar expressed their gratification to Ned, in an address delivered in an embossed silver cylinder, for the magnificent work done by the Royal Navy in protecting trade throughout the world. Ned thanked the community: 'I am satisfied that when the blessings of peace are again given to us, the Countries under the Dominion of HIS MAJESTY the KING EMPEROR will speedily become more prosperous than ever before. This cannot be done without sacrifices . . . The end is not yet in sight but rest assured that this war can have only one ending and that will be the complete and final victory for the arms of Allied Nations.'

———— ∞ ————

General Smuts kept in contact with Ned:

Marching, 6 May 1916.

My dear Admiral, [handwritten] Many thanks for sending me Commander Rawley so promptly. I was sorry Cull [a naval pilot] had to go but he really looks unwell. (separate reports indicate that he had crash-landed no fewer than eight times!)

Macdonald has reported adversely on the personnel of the Naval Armoured Car Section, but his remarks would apply to practically the whole of this field force which is suffering from malaria and dysentery. However we can't all go to England to recuperate and will have to see our mission through whatever proportion of sickness we may have.

At some stage Tanga will again have to be dealt with and I hope a little later to discuss this operation with you.

J.C. Smuts.

———— ∞ ————

Moshi, 9 June 1916.

Dear Admiral Charlton, Many thanks for your letter. I appreciate the points you make against your prolonged absence from the fleet and shall be quite satisfied if Capt Bridgeman could come to discuss plays. There is no great urgency as the enemy seems to be clearing from the Usambara and may evacuate Tanga at an early date. In that case my force will swing south to the central railway. When we have occupied Morogoro, the reduction of Dar-es-Salaam will become more important in order to give us a new sea base and line of supply.

Our joy at the Naval victory in the North Sea has been dampened by the tragic death of (Allied Field Marshal) Lord Kitchener and the loss of HMS Hampshire (a battleship sunk by a mine).

Yours sincerely J.C. Smuts.

Top: 'Slight' accident to the armoured train caused by the enemy, near Maktau – 1916.
Above: Marine 4-inch battery in action.

On 21 September 1916 the *Cape Argus* reported:

'The *Tabora* of 5,000 tons had been described by the Germans as an armed auxiliary as far back as August 1914. Nevertheless the Germans at Dar-es-Salaam seemed to have decided on trying to deceive the British. They repainted the ship and ran up the Red Cross flag. The naval authorities doubted her character due to the great amount of hammering which could be heard going on – which would not be the case if patients were on board. In order to be quite sure they asked permission to inspect the ship, offering to go blind-folded in a German boat but this was declined. The naval 6.0 inch guns were directed at the *Tabora* and she was seen to roll over on her side without loss of life.'

CERTIFICATE: Rear-Admiral Charlton was mentioned in a Despatch from Lieut-General the Hon J.C. Smuts K.C. on 27 Oct 1916 for gallant and distinguished services in the Field.

Sgd Winston Churchill.

Ned was also Mentioned in Despatches by Lieutenant-General Sir J.L. van Deventer KCMG on 30 September 1918.

NAVAL SIGNAL: 29 Oct 1916 from *Challenger* to SNO (to be coded and decoded) SEND FIRST OPPORTUNITY 100 FORMS A1, 500 FORMS A2, 12 INDELIBLE PENCILS, 1 DEPOT SUPPLY LEDGER etc . . . VERY URGENT REQUIRED, PRACTICALLY NO STATIONERY HERE.

A handwritten note has been added by Ned underlining the words 'practically no stationery here' with the words 'a very good job too. This is our wireless energy exploited by the military – an example of want of forethought – waste of time. E.C.'

On 18 November 1916 Admiral Charlton issued a précis of naval operations on the coast of German East Africa during August 1916:

On 1 Aug, at daylight, the port of Saadani was seized by a landing party from two of HM Ships covered by fire from two monitors. The landing party was assisted by 50 Zanzibar African Rifles [ZAR]. Saadani is the principal coastal port between Bagamoyo and Pagani and consists of a fort and 2,000 inhabitants. The opposition was slight and the fort was occupied, the enemy patrols contenting themselves with sniping from the bush. One ZAR was killed and 2 seamen wounded. The fort was found to contain numerous slave irons and chains. On 3 Aug the Germans counter-attacked but this was not pushed home. They were shelled by the British and retired. The naval landing party was gradually relieved by the 2nd West Indian Regiment.

On 2 and 4 Aug the trenches at Bagamoyo were shelled and on 6 and 11 Aug gun positions at Dar-es-Salaam were bombarded, the whole coast being kept under surveillance by seaplanes and a kite balloon. On 13 Aug a seaplane's engine broke up, the plane descended to Kingani and the crew were rescued by a ship's boat. Kingwere Ferry, seven miles from Bagamoyo, was strongly held by the Germans who rendered its use impracticable to the British troops. The river is fifty yards wide and the Kingani River thus presented a considerable obstacle, as did crocodiles. Boats could only cross the dangerous bar at high tide and would then take many hours to cover the 19 miles during which they would be exposed to fire from the south bank.

On 15 Aug the Navy attacked Bagamoyo which was held by the Germans 4 miles up the river. The Marines, seamen from HMS Vengeance and HMS Challenger and 54 ZARs landed in the ship's boats, the heavy ships bombarding the trenches behind the town. The town was also attacked by bombs from seaplanes. The Germans fired on the boats from a 4.1 inch gun from the Konigsberg, pom-poms and Maxims. The landing party kept low on the beach where the 4.1", 30 feet back from the ridge, could not be depressed. The 4.1" was attacked by three 3-pound guns carried by a tug captured previously at Tanga and two steam boats – one being the Admiral's barge. The gun was captured and with the aid of 100 men, put on board ship and taken to Zanzibar. The heavy mounting had been moved from Rufiji to Tanga by 500 porters.

The bulk of the Germans under Captains von Bock and von Boedecke were based close to the French Catholic mission. The Captains had rejected Bishop Vogt's expostulation that they should not base themselves so close to his mission. On the day of the attack, a church feast day, the Church was crowded, but the bishop, an Alsatian, by his excellent example, prevented a panic and none of the women or children was injured though the Church was badly damaged.

The mission is 400 yards from the beach. The pom-pom at this point was knocked out by a direct hit from the British monitor HMS Severn. Captain von Boedecke was killed, and the remaining Germans tried to pass round the town and face the landing party. Some whites and askaris deserted on the way, the balance were charged by the Marines and Naval Brigade. On the German side Captain von Bock was killed; on the British side Captain Thomas, a sergeant and 2 ZAR were killed. With both commanders killed, the Germans lost all initiative and the British took possession of the town. Kingwere Ferry was shelled by indirect fire using a seaplane as a spotter and the enemy fled, allowing the British troops to cross. One mule was taken by a crocodile. The German defenders numbered 60 whites and 350 askaris; the British attackers 216 officers and seamen, 66 Marines and 54 ZAR. The attack on Bagamoyo proved crucial. The Government House and Boma were burnt out. The hospital which flew 2 Red Cross flags and the German flag contained no sick except for one case of gonorrhoea; the doctor had left. A large amount of military equipment and ammunition was found in the hospital which had evidently been used as living quarters by the white soldiery.

———— ∞ ————

A description by one on the receiving end of the bombardment is given by the Bishop of Bagamoyo (translated from the French):

Bagamoyo, 18 Aug 1916.

My dear Père, At last after two long years of enforced silence we can give you our news. Two Brothers, one Priest and the Rev Mother have died of illness . . . All except four of our Brothers were impressed into service . . . We have not suffered any serious deprivations. As regards the war, I don't know what the censor will pass. The first bombardment of Bagamoyo by the Pegasus took place on 23 Aug 1914, the last most terrible on 15 Aug 1916. None of those who took refuge have been killed or wounded; this can only be explained by a special protection of the good God. The officers of the English Navy have been very good to us. Admiral Charlton invited me on board HMS Vengeance and this morning paid a short visit. His visit will make a good impression in favour of the mission, but Capt Dickson told me that the military may have to intern all missionaries. There's the jar! I have asked the Admiral to say a word in our favour.

The bombardment of 15 Aug commenced at 5.15am. by our clock. I proceeded at once to the confessional. The shells fell close to the mission. The church trembled, and I trembled too! I think everybody confessed well. I asked myself whether we should go outside the church where the palms were falling nearby, but seeing all the persons in the church I put my confidence in Our Blessed Lady. My feet and hands were cold but I was calm. One felt that death was near. Father Gallery said Mass. During communion the church shook violently. We heard the noise of a great fall. It was a little side tower which had been struck.

I awaited a precipitous rush from the church but there

The Hima River Bridge.

was no panic. The shells continued to fall close by. I said we should go to our big house by the side door away from the sea. We went out then. There were still about 50 in the choir when there was a terrible explosion and the baptistry chapel collapsed . . .

With affectionate Salutations, + Francis Xavier Vogt.

———————∽∽———————

Ned continued his official report on the East African naval campaign during the latter half of August 1916: 'On 19 Aug, Mikindami Camp was bombarded and on 20 Aug the British Army relieved the naval forces occupying Bagamoyo and the ships returned to Zanzibar. On 21 Aug the British feigned a landing at Dar-es-Salaam, opening vigorous fire. The Germans responded with two heavy guns on shore which fired 80 rounds ineffectually and their position was then heavily shelled by the large ships and they were silenced. The harbour mouth and gun positions at Dar-es-Salaam were bombarded and the fire was returned vigorously. One ship carried out a night bombardment on the railway station, an attack which had great effect on the German's subsequent decision to surrender. On 22 Aug explosions began to take place in Dar-es-Salaam. From 22 Aug to 3 Sept the British

continued the bombardment. Ned prepared an ultimatum: 'TO THE MILITARY GOVERNOR OF DAR-ES-SALAAM, YOU HAVE DONE REMARKABLY WELL. SURRENDER NOW OR THE TOWN WILL BE BOMBARDED', but this was amended to a joint demand from the military commander and himself.

What happened next is described by a young Reserve Lieutenant named Charlewood who was in command of a whaler, HMS *Echo*, and had had no sleep for twenty-four hours: 'I lay down on the bridge and fell asleep only to be aroused an hour later with a message for me to report immediately on the flagship. I could not imagine why the Admiral should want to see me at that hour and searched my conscience for some breach of duty committed. Within his cabin Admiral Charlton put my mind at ease when he informed me it was his intention to demand the surrender of Dar-es-Salaam, and that in consideration of my long service on the coast and my knowledge of the port, he had decided I should be the officer to receive it. HMS *Echo* was to enter Dar-es-Salaam harbour under a white flag, which was to be kept flying unless fired upon. I was highly flattered by the honour but was too overwrought to make fitting acknowledgement. The Admiral understood, shook hands and told me to get as much sleep as possible. Shortly after 5

Above: Admiral Charlton ascending in Kite balloon from Manica.

Left: Photo of bombardment of Bagamoyo taken from a spotter plane on 15 August 1916.

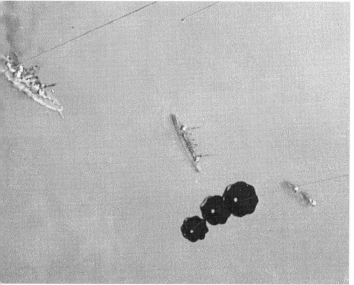

Above: Photo of fleet from a Kite balloon, – left, Vengeance, *middle,* Challenger, *right,* Himalaya.

Above: A seaplane from Zanzibar.

Above: HMS Vengeance, *'The Old Hundred', Captors of Saadani, Bagamoyo and Dar-es-Salaam at Zanzibar, August 1916.*

Below: Admiral Charlton with captured German guns at Bagamoyo on 15 August 1916.

am we weighed anchor with a large white sheet at the fore masthead. The Admiral had transferred to HMS *Challenger* (with a smaller draft than the flagship) and stood nearby to support us if necessary.' When they reached the blockship the *Echo*'s boat was sent ashore with a white flag and after thirty minutes the deputy burgomaster offered unconditional surrender.

On 4 September 1916 Ned advised Reuters that Dar-es-Salaam had been surrendered to a joint army/naval force. Several naval and flying officers were decorated with CMG, DSC, or DSO, Charlewood receiving the DSO. Admiral Charlton ascended in a balloon above his fleet and flew in a seaplane over Zanzibar. The SS *Feld-Marshal* was captured and repaired. Ned requested the Bishop of Dar-es-Salaam to blot out the Kaiser's coat of arms in the Catholic cathedral.

— ∞ —

The Sultan of Zanzibar wrote to Ned:

The Palace, 23 Aug 1916.

My dear Friend Admiral Charlton, In acknowledgement of your kind letter of yesterday (advising) the capture of Bagamoyo in which Zanzibar African Rifles participated, and did excellent service, and your kind desire that I should accept the young hippopotamus which was captured, I accept the very well thought of present.

I thank you from the very bottom of my heart in freeing us from the barbarism of our common enemy.

— ∞ —

Lieutenant Charlewood reports in respect of the hippopotamus, 'a cement-lined pool was constructed for it in Victoria Gardens, where it lived happily and provided entertainment for many years'. He also gives a story about Ned: 'The Admiral was a keen fisherman, and I had often seen a line towing from the stern of his flagship. As his ship was never able to skirt the reefs as closely as our whalers, I was not surprised he had no success. He asked whether we caught many fish on our patrols, to which I replied in the affirmative. Then he said, "When you catch a fish do you stop the ship?" I suspected a trap, but judged the truth was best, so I replied, "Yes, Sir!" "Quite right, too!" he bellowed. "If I ever caught a fish I'd stop the whole d***** fleet!" I imagined a string of flags being repeated down the line: "STOP INSTANTLY, ADMIRAL HAS CAUGHT A FISH"!'

On 7 May 1918 the Sultan awarded Vice-Admiral Sir Edward Charlton the Brilliant Star of Zanzibar of the First Class.

The Portuguese allies were supposed to attack German East Africa from Mozambique but did not in fact invade, their commander eventually being recalled to Lisbon to answer for his inaction. On 17 October 1916 Ned was guest of honour on the Portuguese NRP *Adamastor*. If the menu is to be believed he was served with; Madeira, champagne, porto and liquors, French hors-d'oeuvre, Serbian soup, Belgian fish, Montenegrin tongue, Russian chicken and champignons, British turkey, Japanese curried crab, Italian asparagus, Portuguese sweet rice, and Romanian cocoa.

Ned wrote about a hundred letters to Freda while on duty in East Africa; they report on less momentous matters than his official despatches:

— ∞ —

HMS *Vengeance* at sea, 11 Feb 1916.

My dear Freda, We are just getting into our first port of call (Durban). Following their usual policy with me, my Lords are starting the old game of taking my ships away and giving me no others in their place. I really believe it is because I am too complacent and do not growl sufficiently. Two ships have been sent to other parts on successive days.

General Smuts left yesterday; I received him at the Station. He certainly has a very businesslike air about him.

Have just missed a great meeting of Catholic Bishops here; full description in the newspaper of the Mayor's reception and the dresses of all the ladies. The Lady Mayoress received her guests in 'tinsel net and red roses at the waist'; I hope there was something else.

— ∞ —

(Mombasa), 20 Feb 1916.

Just moored in this snug harbour, the principal port in British East Africa. Passed the Challenger *outside pulling the* Comrie Castle *off the reef; she was successful. Our Marines and 12-pound battery are already at the front.*

— ∞ —

24 Feb 1916.

K. Dalglish [a relative of his mother's family, the Bellasis] is here in the (Royal Australian Navy ship) Pioneer; *he has grown into a fine big man; there is a vacancy up country with our guns but I hardly like to send him as his family has already suffered so badly (two brothers and a brother-in-law killed).*

I agree with the German Censor that your writing is much improved; I suppose printing it prevents your rapid thoughts getting ahead of your pen [Freda's letters to her sister Evelyn in Berlin were censored by the Germans].

— ∞ —

Uganda Railway, en route Voi to Mombasa, 10 Mar 1916.

General Smuts received me most kindly and I had an interesting discussion. I saw our Marines, naval guns from the unfortunate Pegasus, *armoured cars and aeroplanes which are the Navy's share. I witnessed the attack on Salaita Hill and went up it with General Tighe and Colonel Graham and picked up a 12-pound shrapnel shell base, from one of the guns brought out on* Vengeance, *in the centre of the redoubt on top of the hill (Colonel Graham was killed the next day).*

143

Off Cape Delgado, 30 Mar 1916.

The Sultan of Zanzibar came off to the ship with 14 Notables, all most picturesque Arabs. He came in his state barge presented by Queen Victoria, a beautiful boat with 16 oars. He was seated in his silver chair under a canopy.

———— ∞ ————

Mafia Island, 10 Apr 1916.

One of the (German auxiliary cruiser) Emden's life-buoys arrived here in the middle of February having drifted right across the Indian Ocean, 3,280 miles, in a little over a year.

———— ∞ ————

15 Apr 1916.

A collier called Northumbria, *and which ought to have known better with a name like that, broke down ten miles off the enemy coast with 5,000 tons of coal. Fortunately* Challenger *was near and was able to get her to safety.*

———— ∞ ————

3 May 1916.

Got into Grand Comoro this morning; it is a fine big island with an active volcano nearly 8,000 feet high. I went on shore and called on the Resident, a young Frenchman. I could only stay a couple of hours or should have liked to climb the mountain but the Resident said it would be difficult on account of the natives. I asked why he wanted natives and he said, 'to carry one up, of course'. He then told me the Governor of the Islands 'climbed' up in this manner some years ago and on arrival near the top 17 natives fell dead from the cold. He did not mention the probable cause of this disaster was the cartage of a fat old Governor and the effects on the hearts of the natives of much exertion under great change of pressure.

———— ∞ ————

14 Jun 1916.

You are quite wrong about my being more interested in the elder children than in yours; I think I am inordinately fond of Nancy and Eddie and very proud of the twins.

———— ∞ ————

22 Jun 1916.

Glad to hear you are getting efficient in driving the car; also pleased to hear about the boat sailing; it is not necessary to give whiskey to the seamen after a sail; tea or beer should suffice. Half a bottle of beer is ample, but many would prefer tea with the maids thrown in! [As Freda could not swim, the sailing was particularly adventurous.]

17 Jul 1916.

They have tried to persuade me to pull down Bismarck's statue but I have refused. If it were the Kaiser's, it might be different. I propose to inscribe on the pedestal of Bismarck; 'His advice to his country was "Never quarrel with England or Russia",' and leave it at that.

———— ∞ ————

HMS *Vengeance,* Tanga, 14 Jul 1916.

The Ascot game arrived and we (four senior officers) had a game after dinner. It came in well as an amusement to say nothing of the small gamble resulting. But in future I shall have counters instead of money as it is rather hard to stop the men's Crown and Anchor boards and allow worse gambling in my cabin.

———— ∞ ————

At sea approaching Dar-es-Salaam, 22 Aug 1916.

The Bishop (of Bagamoyo) ought to be given a medal for bravery, if one could be given to an enemy subject. As he has 420 schools and over 20,000 native children under instruction in his diocese, I do not intend to allow the Military to remove him.

We were relieved by the 2nd West India Regiment and within half an hour three of them had raped a woman in front of her husband. It was disappointing after Commander Watson's great success in keeping order.

Yesterday morning Zanzibar had a great show; it was more like the triumphant return of a Roman Emperor. I sent over the captured guns with orders that they were to be exhibited.

The procession through the streets included:

- *The Sultan of Zanzibar's brass band,*
- *Black [Vestal] Virgins strewing flowers,*
- *200 coolies towing the* Konigsberg *gun,*
- *100 Seamen from HMS* Thistle *and HMAS* Pioneer,
- *5 captured camels, white Muscat donkey, baby hippopotamus,*
- *130 ZAR under Colour Sergeant Smith of HMS* Pegasus, *and HMAS* Pioneer's *brass band.*

And just off shore: HMS Vengeance, *followed by* Manica *with her kite balloon up 2,000 feet, followed by a seaplane.*

———— ∞ ————

Ned had transferred to HMS *Challenger* and mentions his own activities on the day of the procession: 'After bombarding Dar-es-Salaam we got back in time for a game of golf.' One of the Germans who was bombarded in Dar-es-Salaam subsequently criticised the Royal Navy for shelling the city during the day and then returning to Zanzibar for whiskey and soda. Ned noted: 'This was incorrect; it was gin and tonic!'

Dar-es-Salaam, 5 Sept 1916.

My dear Freda, My cabin is beginning to be quite a museum with two carved Indian chairs, bust of the Kaiser with the order of the black pig round his neck, the Arms of Tanga, a German ensign and a leather sofa from the Dar-es-Salaam Court House.

— ∞ —

20 Sept 1916.

I was hurt to see you considered the surrender of Dar-es-Salaam a foregone conclusion; it was nothing of the sort. [Though the German East African coast was in Allied hands by September 1916, the German forces in the interior continued to elude capture until the armistice two years later.]

— ∞ —

HMS *Hyacinth* at Zanzibar, 14 Oct 1916.

I see from the English papers that my godson, Philip Bellasis, has gone to the Happy Hunting Ground at Delville Wood, following so many of his family. I have written to poor Aunt Marie.

— ∞ —

Ned was asked to write for the Ushaw College magazine and, in addition to describing the naval campaign, gave this story:

On the beach at Bagamoyo were observed three small native boys, aged say 10, 9 and 7, watching with glittering eyes the re-embarkation of the ZAR. The eldest, who had made friends with the Sergeant, said he was an orphan and starving and would they take him with them? After much consideration the married but childless Sergeant applied to adopt the lad and the Commanding Officer agreed. The 9-year-old summoned up his courage and a good-natured Zanzibari of similar circumstances was found ready to adopt him. They both got on board when there was a fearful howl of dismay from the youngest who dashed into the water and held onto the boat's side. He said he was a Zanzibari whose mother lived on the island; his father, who had brought him across two years ago, had been killed by the Germans. He was old enough to remember the name of his mother's residence and a soldier was found who collaborated the story. All three were taken over on the Battleship. The next day the Commanding Officer, who was playing a round of golf at Zanzibar, was waylaid by a buxom black lady who fell at and embraced his feet and thanked him for restoring her boy.

In mid-November 1916 Ned returned to Simonstown and joined in family life with Freda and their seven children. Ned and Freda visited the grave of her brother, Captain Robert Stapleton-Bretherton, who had been killed at the battle of Spion Kop in the Boer War.

In a report in the *Morning Post* dated 18 January 1917, General Smuts paid tribute to ten Generals engaged in the successful East African campaign and added: 'My heartiest thanks are due to Rear-Admiral E.F.B. Charlton C.B. and all ranks of the Royal Navy for the very able and thorough manner in which they have furthered my plans, not only by occupying points along the coast, sometimes without military assistance, but by enabling a change of base to be carried out first to Tanga and then to Dar-es-Salaam.'

In 1917 the SS *Tyndareus* was severely damaged off Cape Town when a 60ft x 20ft hole was blown in her side. After 'the mishap' – a torpedo strike – the bow drew forty-six feet and the stern twelve (instead of being roughly equal). Ned reported on the event to the Admiralty as follows:

'The behaviour of the Battalion of the Middlesex Regiment, on board the steamship *Tyndareus*, after the accident to that ship, there being a large quantity of water on board, and the ship apparently sinking by the head in a heavy swell, was most praiseworthy, and equal to the Birkenhead tradition of the British army on the same spot. It was only due to this that no lives were lost in the boats. The ship was saved by the coolness and perserverence of the Captain, Officers, engineers and engine-room staff.'

The reply included a message from the King:

'Please express to the officer commanding the Battalion of the Middlesex Regiment my admiration of the conduct displayed by all ranks on the occasion of the accident to *Tyndareus*. In their discipline and courage they worthily upheld the splendid tradition of the Birkenhead, ever cherished in the annals of the British Army.
George R.I.'

After the war it was learnt that nineteen ships torpedoed off Cape Town were victims of the giant German submarine *U-155*.

— ∞ —

Ned was patron of the Boy Scouts in the Cape and Freda assisted with many of their activities, including goalkeeper at soccer! The founder of the movement wrote to him:

The Boy Scouts Association, London,
12 Mar 1917.

*Dear Admiral, I feel I must express to you my very sincere thanks for what you have done for the Boy Scouts Movement in Cape Town and for your encouraging comments on the work of the scouts in connection with the Royal Navy.
Sgd Baden-Powell.*

— ∞ —

Ned continued with duties such as chairing meetings of the United Services Institute, the Dockyard Rifle Club, and the Wesleyan Soldiers and Sailors Home where the Committee increased the number of beds from seventy to ninety-five. In 1917 the 'Sailors Home' took in 1,415 Royal Navy men, 168 British, Swedish, Spanish, Russian and Japanese seamen who had been torpedoed, and 1,764 merchant seamen. He opened the Moslem Bazaar in aid of the Governor General's Fund, saying, 'It had been gratifying to see what excellent work was being done by our Moslem compatriots in every British port.' Ned also sponsored a variety entertainment entitled 'Swat that Baby' put on by officers and seamen at Cape Town, admission 3/-.

On 13 October 1917 Freda gave birth to their last child, a daughter named Rosemary.

In February 1918 a letter to the editor complained of the infrequency of mail to Tristan da Cunha. Ned wrote to Mr Glass on the island and received a detailed reply which essentially confirmed the infrequency. He established that the small island, which had no harbour, had adequate cattle, sheep, geese and pigs to feed the inhabitants and obtained a complete census of the population, handwritten, on one foolscap page. It listed twenty married families with sixty-five children, five widows with seven children and 'Miss E. Cotton, old maid, have two girls living with her'. The significant number of widows was the result of a tragedy in which thirteen able-bodied men were drowned while returning from a passing vessel. In 1922 the same writer informed Ned that only three vessels had visited the island since 7 October 1920, and added:

'I received the Knife Which you send me and thank you Very Much and it came useful to me for travelling round the mountains for the young Sea birds. We have a Minister and his wife on the island and they keep school and also have started the Scout boys. The population of the island have increase to 129 and all is well.

Yours Sincerely, R.F. Glass.'

Ned's visitors book for 1917 records not only the names of the captains who visited Admiralty House but also consuls from Argentina, Belgium, France, Netherlands, Norway, Portugal, Russia, Siam, Sweden and the United States.

Japanese naval ships assisted in the defence of the Cape:

HIJMS *Niitaka*, 27 Sept 1917.

It owes quite to your Excellencies careful attention we were received with warm welcome during our co-operation with HM Ships.
Sgd Captain T. Inuzuka.

HIJMS *Tsushima*, 1 Jan 1918.

Will you do me the honour of receiving this very humble doll of 'Momotaro', one of the brave heroes in the old tales of Japan.
Sgd Captain N. Komatsu.

HIJMS *Yakumo*, Singapore, 18 June 1918.

I thank you for your kindness which you had extended to Officers and men which will be appreciated by the Imperial Japanese Navy.
Sgd Vice-Admiral I. Takeshita.

On 24 January 1918 Ned and Freda attended the wedding of the Governor-General's daughter, the Hon. Doreen Buxton, to Major Charles Fitzroy, and in the same month attended the wedding of the daughter of one of their Malayan contract-laundry women.

In February 1918 the old German Club in Cape Town was reopened by the Governor-General as the Union Jack Club. The large gathering included Prime Minister General Botha.

Ned gave a speech:

I am very glad of the opportunity to thank the South African Garrison Institute and the Union Government for the very handsome benefit they have conferred on the Navy in providing the Club for our Seamen and Marines.

I have heard some remarks made that this place is far too good for the common sailor, and it would be more suitable for one of the crack clubs of Cape Town. But the common sailor today is a very different being from the man we read of in Marryat, though his spirit and character remain precisely the same. He is now a highly educated being with a good knowledge of mathematics, and in many cases skilled at mechanical work. No longer the crude but ignorant person who drank rum out of coconuts (laughter).

With our seamen of the Navy I include our brother seamen in the R.N.R., R.N.V.R. and Merchant Navy who are doing so remarkably well (applause).

Sentry at Britain's Front Door - 1918

In February 1918 Ned was promoted to Vice-Admiral and was awarded the KCMG. General Botha wrote to him:

Prime Minister's Office, Cape Town, 3 Apr 1918.

Dear Sir Edward, Your work here has been most successful and the departure of yourself and Lady Charlton will be a great loss to us. God's blessing on you both,
Yours sincerely,
Louis Botha.

On 10 May 1918 General Botha again wrote to him to thank him for a huge captured naval mine which had been sent by Ned to be exhibited in Pretoria.

During his 1914–15 term as Admiral Commanding Minesweepers Ned had gained exceptional knowledge of the defences of the east coast of Britain. In 1918 the Government was still wary of a possible invasion by the Germans along this coast. Ned was recalled urgently, and travelled by cruiser to Sierra Leone where a new HMS *Britannia* collected him to return him home as rapidly as possible. Ned took up his duties as Admiral of the East Coast with HMS *Amethyst* as his flagship. His family returned on RMS *Galway Castle*; it was sunk on its following voyage to the Cape. HMS *Britannia* was lost off Gibraltar only three months later.

On 1 July 1918 King George V noted in his diary. 'Saw Adml. Charlton who has just come home from the Cape.'

— ∽ —

HM Naval Base, Granton near Edinburgh,
27 Jul 1918.

Dear Admiral Charlton, As regards the Escort Trawlers from here coaling at Immingham, I hope to obviate that by making them take a deck cargo (of coal).

You may talk about you being 'makee-learn' and new to the work but since you've been here the Trawlers have come back almost before we expected them.
Thanks so much. J.A. Searton.

> NAVAL SIGNAL: FROM SNO TYNE TO VAEC DANISH BARQUE *Freda* 55–15N 0–8W SHOT FIRED BY SUBMARINE, CREW ABANDONED SHIP. NEXT SHOT STRUCK BOAT KILLING 6 WOUNDING 4. BOAT CLOSED BY 2 SUBMARINES LAST SEEN 1700 ON 13TH STEERING NE. *Freda* LAST SEEN DISMASTED WITH BOWS OPENED OUT. CARGO PIT PROPS.

Ned added: 'Keep this, probably still afloat. EC 21.8.18.'

Despite the Armistice being only a month away, these were hazardous times. Ned inspected the vast array of net mines with glass floats being manufactured by a hardy band of women at Immingham. The net mines had already ensnared the German mine-layer *UC-21*. Ned also supplied intelligence to United States seaplane bombers which operated from Killingholme and which had attacked, and probably destroyed, a number of U-boats.

When the devastating 'War to end all Wars' drew to a close Ned was again able to enjoy some family life. Freda and the eight children ranging from one to fourteen years lived in the little seaside resort of Felixstowe. Each working day Ned was conveyed in style by launch across the estuary of the Stour to his headquarters in Harwich. Each morning his dog accompanied him, only to disappear for unknown adventures upon arrival. Each evening without fail the dog was waiting at the jetty when Ned departed for home. Many WRNS were stationed on the east coast and Ned had to deal with at least one personality clash:

Women's Royal Naval Service, London,
27 Jul 1919.

Dear Admiral Charlton, We should miss Miss Isemonger if we demobilised her; only sometimes she makes us feel quite frantic; invariably does the opposite of what she is told to do. It is a little difficult when one ventures to suggest to Miss Isemonger that her hat is not quite uniform and she turns on one and says, 'Really, I have no time to devote to millinery!' The reason for any delay in appointing her was that knowing of great difficulties with her as a VAD I hesitated before accepting her as an WRNS officer and waited until I had seen her work. This impressed me as good and I therefore faced the probable difficulties involved by her personality. Katherine (illegible).

— ∽ —

Ned wrote a personal letter to Miss Isemonger:

Dear Miss Isemonger, I have received your letter in which you say many bitter and ungenerous things. I can only tell you that having worked with WRNS since the inception of the Service I have never encountered the favouritism and petty jealousies of which you write.

It will probably interest you to know that a year ago we wrote to the Admiralty to know if women already serving in Naval Bases, who were absorbed into the WRNS, might count their civilian service prior to enrolment. Their Lordships' reply was in the negative. I have taken the trouble to explain because I want you to realise that these matters are dealt with in principle and not in relation to individuals.
Yours sincerely,
E. Charlton.

— ∽ —

A memorial service to the 57,000 British seamen lost in World War I was held at St Paul's on 12 June 1919. In addressing the huge gathering which included the King, Admirals Beatty, de Chair, Charlton and others, the Archbishop of Canterbury quoted Shakespeare's immortal lines: '. . . this sceptred isle,/ . . . This fortress built by Nature for herself/ . . . This precious stone set in the silver sea, . . .' and concluded: 'Through the testing fires we have striven to reach the height of an ennobling trust. We are not afraid to link it with our prayers for the bettering of the world, for the coming of the Kingdom of the Prince of Peace.'

On 28 June 1919 the Humber Conservancy Board in Hull wrote to the Admiralty, 'expressing the cordial thanks of the Board for the invaluable and successful efforts made by Vice-Admiral Charlton and his predecessors Nicholson and Ballard in enabling commercial navigation to be maintained on the Humber under war conditions'.

As the first Admiral of Mine Sweepers, Ned had the honour of having his flag carried before him at the head of the minesweeping contingent in the great parade held in London on Peace Day, 19 July 1919.

Above: The remains of German Super Zeppelin L70, shot down in the Wash in August 1918, being brought to Immingham by the trawler Scumber *for use as scrap metal.*

Below: A U-boat sunk in the North Sea, salvaged from twenty-six fathoms and brought into Newcastle. The bodies of fourteen German seamen were recovered. No torpedoes had been fired.

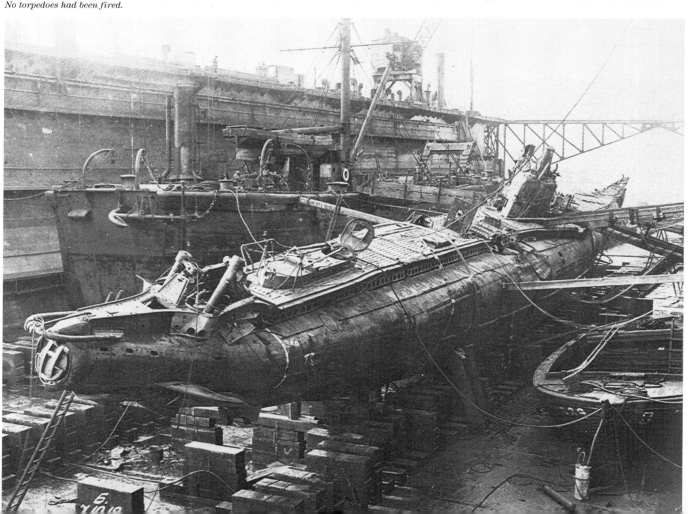

Ned's duties on the east coast of Britain ceased in 1919 when the naval establishments on the Humber and Tyne reverted to the Nore Command. He was fifty-three and must have known that the retirement age for Admirals was fast approaching, but he had one more major duty to perform for the nation in occupied Europe – where he already had unusual connections.

Above: Both pictures are of convoys off the N.E. coast – 1918.

Below: HM Destroyer Whitley *carrying out steam trials – 8 October 1918.*

Top: Minesweepers in Grimsby Harbour, August 1918.
Above: Immingham Docks – 1918.
Right: Flotilla heading north to join the Grand Fleet, taken off Flamborough Head – 4 October 1918.

The Peace Treaty
of Versailles – 1919

Thirty-two nations met in Paris in 1919 in a bid to establish permanent world peace by means of five major treaties with the vanquished, who were not allowed to participate in the process. The major determination in respect of Germany, the 'Treaty of Versailles', was made by French President Clemenceau – known as 'The Tiger' – by British Prime Minister Lloyd George and by United States President Woodrow Wilson. Several of the victorious Allies sought revenge, which Wilson endeavoured to temper. Initially he strove hard for universal disarmament but was forced to compromise and accept no more than partial disarmament, and that of the Axis only, in order to obtain acceptance of his second great proposal: the establishment of a 'League of Nations' which would henceforward arbitrate disagreements before they led to war (the League foundered when the Senate of the United States voted against the concept). The procedures of the conference were complex and included a small central council, some seventy advisory committees and a plenary conference.

The treaties adopted the principle of 'self-determination for ethnic groups' which led to the greatest single re-demarcation of national boundaries and the greatest interchange of colony ownerships the world has ever known. France received a mandate over Syria, the Cameroons and south-west Germany (Alsace-Lorraine); Britain a mandate over German East Africa (Tanganyika) and Palestine; South Africa over South-West Africa; Australia over former German Papua New Guinea etc. Some former countries were re-created, others created *ab initio*: Poland, Finland, Latvia, Lithuania, Estonia, Czechoslovakia, Hungary and Yugoslavia. The former empires of Austria and Turkey were reduced to a minute fraction of their original domain. Finally, against the advice of Churchill and of Smuts, the victors imposed a huge fine, impossible to pay, of $33 billion on the losers. Germany's combat forces were restricted to 100,000 soldiers and 15,000 seamen; they were forbidden to own and operate submarines and military aircraft; conscription was prohibited. Prince Blücher likened the French demand for reparations to a 'bull rushing wildly at a red flag hung on a wall, well in stride to its own destruction'.

The Allies entered World War I with the primary objective of destroying German hegemony. The ultimate outcome of the war and of subsequent treaties was very different from the objective and was largely unpredicted: the Austrian and Ottoman Empires were destroyed; the United States of America became the world's greatest power; the power of France and Britain was attenuated; the Russian Empire turned Communist; Japan became ascendant over China; Germany lost its colonies (its resentment became extreme and flared into another war only twenty-one years later); and national and ethnic vanity was reinforced in many places, including Germany, Croatia, Bosnia and Serbia.

In February 1919 Ned was appointed President of the Allied Naval Armistice Committee (PANAC), one of the advisory committees to the Paris Conference which formulated the Treaty of Versailles. In respect of Naval Power the Treaty determined that in future the German Navy would be limited to six battleships of 10,000 tons, six light cruisers, twelve destroyers, twelve torpedo-boats and no submarines. The motives and the 'behind-the-scenes' deals between the numerous political leaders on the central council and at the plenary conference may never be known in full, but it seems reasonable to assume that Ned, as President of the Allied Naval Armistice Committee, was in as good a position as any public servant to know the intent of the Treaty in respect of the German Navy, and we know from his letters that, as a much travelled and temperate man, he also knew the prevalence and the dangers of xenophobic hatred. The following examples are taken from Ned's folio and indicate his awareness of this delicate issue.

———— ∞ ————

A captured German letter reproduced in 'News from Enemy Sources No. 3 (Confidential)' issued by Intelligence Section, General Staff:

Tanga, German East Africa, 8 Mar 1916.

Dear Karl, It is very gratifying to hear of our great success and that we have thoroughly beaten these English pigs. I am sorry I cannot tell you about the blockade runner. But I hear from home that we are at last beating the French. The Russians and the macaroni-eating monkeys will then have had enough. The whole war will be over in the autumn. God will make it so for His chosen people.   Fritz.

- In the German-controlled French newspaper *La Correspondance Politique de L'Europe Central* dated 17 May 1917: '(French) General Joffre is assuredly not flattered by the familiarity with which he is treated in the United States, where he is generally spoken of as "Papa Joffre". He must regret not enjoying the popularity of the late Admiral Dewey when the latter returned from Manila, where his ironclads had sunk the wooden vessels of Spanish Admiral Montaya.' (Ned's photos of 1900 depict the sunken Spanish ships as ironclads.)

- An anonymous letter sent on the occasion of the temporary grounding of the *Galway Castle* off East London, South Africa.

14 Oct 1917.

The Union Castle Co, We thank you for providing a sight which gladdens our hearts. Bah! We have had to stick your blatant arrogance, but now 'Our Day' will soon be here and you will soon be very small puppies instead of the kaffir-fostering curs you are now. When Africa is ours and you d*** Britishers are cleaning our boots . . .

- Sir David Beatty's speech on board HMS *Lion* 24 November 1918 when he sent out the First Cruiser Squadron of the British Grand Fleet to bring in the surrendered German High Sea Fleet to Scapa Flow Harbour:

'Officers and Men of the First Cruiser Squadron going away to perform your final duty. England owes the Grand Fleet a great debt . . . the War was won by the Sea Power of England . . . We never dreamt that the last time we would see [the German High Sea Fleet would be] when they were shepherded in by the Grand Fleet. It is a pitiful sight to see these great ships expecting them to have the same courage as we expect from men whose work lies on the waters . . . their end is a proper end for a foe who has proved himself lacking in chivalry. From the beginning his tactics and behaviour have been contemptible. The First Battle Cruiser Squadron has been selected because it was the first to take care of them and I am sure you will think it an honour to conduct them to their last resting place (laughter). I want to ask any of you who have dealings with the High Sea Fleet to remember what they have done in the past. No clapping them on the back and giving them a cigarette. I have said in the memorandum you have to meet them with courtesy – cold courtesy. They are beneath contempt and should be treated with contempt . . . Remember he is a despicable beast . . .'

• To the Editor of the *Evening News*: 'Sir, I suppose all the ships of the Grand Fleet which ventured out to sea about once a year will be awarded bars [to their medals] but the men who went to sea continuously, day after day, winter and summer, are not to receive one. Sgd A Disgusted Minesweeper.

• Press report on Ned's speech to minesweeper men in Hull where he must have been amused to hear himself introduced as the son of a Newcastle 'docker':

'Before the War it was no exaggeration to say that fifty per cent of the men of the (British) merchant marine were aliens and many were men of an objectionable nature. Lascars and Chinese were no doubt invaluable in tropical climates but besides these there were Dagoes, Huns, Levantines and mongrels without number who could certainly be dispensed with if we could have British ships for the British (applause). To supplant the above-mentioned foreigners, the conditions of life on board British ships must be made to attract the best men (applause). In his early days, said Admiral Charlton, with the inquisitiveness of a small boy, he used to find his way forward to the men's quarters and see the way in which they lived. Although over forty years ago, he had no hesitation in saying that nothing in connection with the sea had altered to date so little as the accommodation of seamen. The same narrow, congested quarters, the same fleabags to sleep in, the same want of decency and moderate comfort. Not so the passenger accommodation which had improved beyond all knowledge. He was not one who did not appreciate comfort, but there was a great deal of difference between moderate comfort and senseless luxury (applause). What did they want with swimming baths, racquet courts, marble mantle pieces and mirrors at sea? Gaudily lit saloons and Brussels carpets? (applause).

In January 1920 Vice-Admiral Sir Edward Charlton left London in the battleship HMS *Malaya*, 27,500 tons, to take up his duties as President of the Naval Inter-Allied Commission of Control in Berlin (PNIAC). He was accompanied by French Admiral Dumesnil, Italian Admiral Orsini and Japanese Captain Sakonje; the four officers comprised the Naval Commission. In securing naval reparations from Germany the agreed percentages were: Britain 70%, France and Italy 11% each, Japan 8%. Ned left 303 pages in three files with extracts of letters home for the period January 1920 to June 1921. It seems likely that his intention was to make a comprehensive folio but this was not done. Other pages must have existed but, apart from the last page, numbered 620, they are missing. 'A Pan-German Tract of Hate' taken from the tabloid *Vorwarts* dated 16 February 1920 precedes the first letter and it appears that Ned may have intended to use it as a foreword to the proposed folio. The translation is summarised:

THE END OF GERMAN SHAME

None of the occupying forces shall leave our soil alive; in no part of the world shall we accord them peace until every German has been avenged ten fold, one hundred fold. Neither Lloyd George nor Clemenceau nor Wilson; no one shall die a natural death.

If Germany has been defeated, the German people have not. There are still sufficient German men of honour to avenge our shame.

You, the enemy, will suffer a peace as terrible as ours if you do not renounce your Treaty.

———— ∽ ————

HMS *Malaya*, North Sea once more,
16 Jan 1920.

[To Lady Charlton; presumably retrieved later and retyped by his secretary] We had a splendid view of you as we went out and I suppose you had the same of us; somewhere, when we were off the Victory, *I heard Eddie's shout of 'Daddy' and then all the others in rotation. It would have been an impressive sight, the big Battleship with three Admirals' flags flying, but what a day! It reminded me somewhat of our departure in HMS* Orlando *in February 1899 when we saluted the C-in-C from the same spot and hoisted our jib and it was just a similar sort of day, thick mist, cold and drizzle.*

Just outside the Nab a steamer reported a mine but I expect it was only wreckage.

The two destroyers accompanying us are the British Turquoise *and the French* Oise; *consequently the former has been christened the* Turk Oise.

— ∽ —

Off Wilhelmshaven (Germany),
17 Jan 1920.

Whether purposely or not we do not know, but two Light-vessels were adrift in the swept fairway off the German coast.

The German Naval Peace Commission (GNPC) came on board today and we had our first meeting. They were wearing their old pattern Imperial uniform and flying the pre-war German Naval flag which we saluted, and got the salute returned.

— ∽ —

18 Jan 1920.

I read prayers in the chapel, the French and Italian Admirals attending – mainly I think because I told them it would be one fifth the time of the others.

— ∽ —

19 Jan 1920.

We have been busy interviewing the GNPC and have been all over their dockyard. Except for the ships engaged in mine sweeping it is in an advanced state of decay like a half-awakened 'City of the Dead'. They had a bad explosion here, some 40,000 shells going up and killing a lot of people.

— ∽ —

HMS *Malaya*, Wilhelmshaven, 20 Jan 1920.

We visited the new German Cruisers which they are to hand over in compensation for [scuttling their fleet at] Scapa Flow. The GNPC did not like it at all and said they would not be responsible as the crews were out of hand.

We got rather a jar today; the Malaya *cannot get through the (Kiel) Canal as the authorities have neglected the dredging, so we have transferred to the cruiser* Coventry, *4,500 tons.*

— ∽ —

HMS *Coventry*, Kiel Canal, 23 Jan 1920.

The fortifications at Heligoland were marvellous; the Germans have proposed seven years to break them up and this does not seem an unreasonable time if it really is to be destroyed.

Owing to fog we were delayed at Brunsbuttel; the tide had fallen so we stuck (luckily after the GNPC had landed) and remained there from 6pm to 1am. There was no damage but she is an unpleasantly large ship to have ashore. Fortunately it was dark and the Germans saw nothing.

HMS *Coventry*, at Kiel, 24 Jan 1920.

Today we had a glance around the dockyards and I was interested to see where the Blücher *was launched.*

You should have seen the 100-ton crane coming alongside to lift out the car weighing two tons. It and the spare parts are now on the train.

— ∽ —

In train to Berlin, 25 Jan 1920.

Commodore von Gagen is the President of the GNPC; he is really a young Captain specially promoted and seems willing enough.

The mark is down to 220 to one Pound, less than one penny compared with one shilling pre-war.

'Mary' [Ned's parrot] was left in Malaya *and was very talkative. She gave the Engineer Commander a shock one day as he heard fearful noises coming from the steering engine and it was quite a long time before he realised it was a parrot.*

— ∽ —

Hotel Bristol, Berlin, 26 Jan 1920.

I got your letter from Milford describing the return of the weeping trio (three eldest girls to boarding school).

— ∽ —

At the same time that Ned established his Naval Commission, an Allied Military Commission under French General Nollet established its headquarters in Berlin as did British General Bingham who was head of the Inter-Allied Commission of Control and responsible for political matters. In respect of the Naval Commission a newspaper cutting at the time reports a brother Admiral remarking to the press in respect of Ned: 'He is an obstinate devil and not likely to be bounced by the Germans.' Another newspaper report of the time paints the following overall picture:

Reuters correspondent says that the Germans seemed to be impressed with the importance of getting on with the work, and there is every reason to believe that they will do their utmost to carry out their treaty obligations.

During an inspection of the Konigsberg *the German crew sang 'Deutschland uber alles' and 'Wacht an Rhein'. It is believed that this was not a demonstration of hostility, but merely a desire on the part of the sailors to show that the spirit of the German Navy was not depressed. Discipline appears in every case to be excellent.*

The four battleships at Wilhelmshaven, which are to be sent to England, are in such neglected condition that the ashes raked out in November 1918 are still lying on the floors, while on the foredeck of one battleship a pigsty has been installed.

Up to the present, 300 merchant ships over 1,600 tons have been handed over. It was further stipulated that the

Allies should receive all ships of 1,000 tons or over under construction. Instead of completing these, however, the Germans declared that they had not the necessary material, but the Commissioners discovered that they were putting new ships on the slips – of 995 tons each. The necessary steps have been taken.

———— ∽ ————

27 Jan 1920.

My dear Freda, the first great military conference of Nollet's with the Germans fell through completely; [German] General von Cramond, of the old type, claiming the right to run the show.

As they could not even decide who should sit down first, all our Commission walked out.

The mark has tumbled to 440 to the Pound today.

———— ∽ ————

30 Jan 1920.

One really felt last night that the war had not been fought for nothing when we found a ragged German soldier begging in the Unter den Linden and graciously helped him with the magnificent donation of one mark. That, and driving around Berlin in my British (Talbot) car made out of a bit of Super Zeppelin, afforded a lot of inward satisfaction.

A Highland soldier in Berlin was heard to remark the other day after a walk along the Unter den Linden: 'Man, 'aa fairly bursts with pride when 'aa think that every man 'aa sees here hates me for all he is worth.'

Countess Orsini told me that a league of German aristocrats has been formed to abstain from connection with the Allies, so I do not expect that (Princess) Evelyn (Blücher) will be able to introduce many of her friends to me even if I wanted to know them.

———— ∽ ————

By the time Ned made a speech in 1923 he had more sympathy for unemployed German soldiers: 'Of Army Officers there are about 33,000 out of work. One I knew, who was formerly a Major in a Cavalry Regiment at Potsdam, now has a pension of 900 marks per month, equal to about fourpence.'

The British staff of the Naval Inter-Allied Commission included four Royal Navy Captains and two WRNS secretaries who helped Ned with the considerable amount of entertaining he was required to do for the other delegations. They were clearly resourceful women in a city where Englishwomen were rare. References to them in Ned's letters to Freda follow:

- 31 Jan 1920. The (two secretary) WRNS started work ten minutes after their arrival (Miss Stephen and Miss Raye).
- 7 Feb 1920. Miss Raye went back to Cologne (Köln) to look for their luggage.

- 8 Feb 1920. Miss Raye was very fortunate to get their baggage; she got to Ercoelen, where it had been traced to, on the Belgian frontier, and they all swore it was not there. However she insisted on searching the station and in one store found the place piled up to the ceiling with hen-coops and live chickens, and sacks of corn stacked on top, which they said had recently arrived. She made them pull down the sacks until they could see behind, and there was all their luggage neatly stacked. Coming through Germany they tried to take the other young woman's luggage away from Miss Raye as it was not hers but she is a good German scholar and defeated them.
- 4 Mar 1920. Miss Stephen had a nasty throat on Tuesday and a high temperature. I hope she will not have to go as she is a wonderful worker and coder. The Secretary (Flag Captain Cullinan who had worked with Ned in Simonstown and was as a consequence well known to Freda) works them pretty hard and they never leave the office before 7pm but they are accustomed to that; when we got to Immingham [in 1918] the two of them had been working for over twelve months, watch on and watch off, day and night, at their desks which the one on duty never left even for meals. Of course they had the great interest of receiving all the latest news about submarines, Zeppelins, fights and sinkings.
- 11 Feb 1920. I should like to have put off the dinner last night on account of poor Weekes' death (a staff officer) but it was too late. We had six ladies and twelve men and the Hotel rather spread itself to do us well. There was an ante room, dining room and a third room where the service came through and the band was stowed. The table looked very pretty; in fact the flower shops of Berlin are the best things here. There was a big mass of flowers in the centre and each lady had a spray. The table was elliptical, or what you would call an oblong circle, twelve feet on its shorter axis. The ladies were Lady Kilmarnock, Countess Orsini and her daughter, Mme Dumesnil and Misses Raye and Stephen. We had no Royal toasts and the ladies went out first in the English fashion. The wines were served with the courses which is very economical but leads to an awful mixture inside for which reason the Englishman generally prefers to start with one and stick to it. I am going to wait a fortnight for my next dinner which will be for men only, having now gone through all the women we possess.
- 19 Sept. 1920. Fortunately something generally turns up to enliven matters when things are dull; half this Hotel was burnt out last night. Downs, who lives with the servants at the back of our office, came over about 3.30am and asked me if I knew the Bristol was on fire. I replied, 'Where is the *Bristol*; is she alongside or in the stream?' (as early as 1653 the Navy had named a frigate the *Bristol*) and it took me some

time to realise he meant this hotel. There is always so much row in the Linden between 3 and 4am that a few fire engines, and Huns shouting 'Fire' failed to disturb us. On going into the passage one saw a fine blaze on the other side of the quadrangle and the wind blowing the flames and sparks directly towards us, so we packed up and prepared to quit. The only one of us that did anything useful however was Miss Stephen, who in the absence of the Flag Commander was doing Flag Lieutenant duty and, entirely on her own initiative, ordered all British cars round to the Bristol immediately. And they were all waiting outside by the time we had packed and would have been invaluable had we had to leave; so there is some use in women sometimes! The automatic fire alarms are said to have acted splendidly. Altogether the place had a lucky escape but there is a million marks' damage.

- 21 Jan 1921. Our people had been furious with Miss Raye (now Mrs Anderson) as she never acknowledged her wedding present. Today came the explanation to Miss Stephen. They live three miles from a Post Office and the handyman had been stealing all letters and parcels. Now she and her husband are off to India and she has to acknowledge all her wedding gifts again.
- 19 Mar 1921. I send you some very good photos taken by Miss Stephen with a new camera she has got.
- 25 Mar 1921. Miss Sharpley [who replaced Miss Raye] had an unpleasant experience at the Ice Palace; she dropped her pocket book and turned to pick it up. A man two or three yards away waved his hand and disappeared into the crowd.
- 13 May 1921. Miss Sharpley was in a bad collision in Trafalgar Square on Monday and was thrown off the top front seat (of an open double-deck bus) onto the pavement but not badly damaged; she was removed to Charing Cross Hospital and will be well in a week; the woman who fell on top of her was killed.

———— ∞ ————

Berlin, 3 Feb 1920.

Darling Freda, I hope the influenza wave will not come your way; we certainly have it here; Wibner is very ill [note by Ned, he subsequently died].

I dined with General Bingham at the Adlon Hotel; Generals Robertson and Kilmarnock were there; Bingham considered it a historic dinner, the principal soldier, sailor and diplomat in Germany all being present.

The Bristol is, I think, the best of the Berlin hotels.

I generally have for:-

Breakfast:	*one boiled egg, an orange and tea*	*19 marks*
Lunch:	*soup, fish, chicken and a sweet*	*25 marks*
	small bottle of wine	*16 marks*
Dinner:	*Almost similar*	
	(chicken, turkey or goose)	*25 marks*

10% is added on for waiting, which is slow but sure.

4 Feb 1920.

The Scapa Flow prisoners are coming in today and had a great reception at Wilhelmshaven; we saw the preparations and thought they were for us until we saw the 'Welcome to the Fatherland'!

———— ∞ ————

11 Feb 1920.

I received a wonderful document from Geneva from the 'Fêtes de la Liberté'. They asked me to attach my signature with a 'pensée' on the superhuman grandeur of the Allies' heroes in the war so I wrote:

> *'My best and only wish is:*
> *May the friends of our youth in Battle,*
> *Be the companions of our old age in Peace.'*

Not quite original but an old quotation slightly added to. The envelope had been opened by the Germans although addressed to me as PNIAC so I am having the liaison Officer's blood. His face has been reduced from a double sea-boot to a Lancashire clog.

———— ∞ ————

16 Feb 1920.

The Consul-General Arty told us a most amusing story of an Irish soldier's adventures. He belonged to the Irish Guards and, as a corporal, got taken prisoner just when the Germans were trying to induce the Irish soldiers to fight against us. About thirty, including this man, agreed to join up on condition that they should not be required to fight, that they might wear their own uniform and choose their own employment. They chose a green uniform interspersed with shamrocks, which the Germans, who carried out their demands implicitly, had specially woven for them; and for their employ they chose work in a Munich Brewery where they spent the remainder of the war.

When the Revolution broke out a party of six of these heroes found themselves in Berlin and got hold of a field machine-gun which they managed to get to the top of the Brandenburg Gate, the principal archway at the end of the Unter den Linden. They got their gun into action on the mob, playing it alternately on whichever side seemed to be getting the better of the scrap, quite impartially as to whether they were Revolutionaries or Government people, so long as they kept the fight going and were damaging the enemy.

I often wish you were out here, but until things are more settled, wives are better away.

We are at a deadlock with the Latins [Ned's name for the French and Italian Admirals when they acted in concert against him] who are always trying to get behind the Treaty and get more out of it than was intended. For instance they want the Germans to allow us access to all their wireless stations, so that they can find out all about them, whereas the Treaty only gives us access to 'Commercial Messages'.

Your loving husband, Ned.

Ned wrote occasionally to his elder son Edward:

18 Feb 1920.

My dear Eddie, As this is the first real letter I have written to you, in return for your first letter to me, I write on the paper with an Admiral's Flag which I only use on state occasions.

This is a funny place; on account of our ships having blockaded the Germans and prevented wool and other things coming into Germany, the people have had to make use of paper. I saw a man wearing paper clothes and we have paper table cloths and paper curtains. The bicycles have no rubber on their wheels and motor cars often have (coil) springs right round (the rims of) their wheels.

Please give my love to everyone and pray for poor Weekes who deserved to go straight to Heaven. Your loving Daddy.

———— ∞ ————

15 Feb 1921.

We had two very nice days skating on beautiful black ice; that is before any snow had fallen on it.

I see in the German papers that their old battleship Baden *has been sunk in experiments between the Isle of Wight and the mainland. Did you see this or hear the explosions?*

I carried out some of the same sort on my old ship, the Hood *of happy memory, and we did them in Stokes Bay just behind the bathing huts, but she did not sink.*

———— ∞ ————

24 Mar 1921.

I shall have to call you something else than Eddie soon; it is too childish. You cannot be Ned while I remain in this world, and Neddy is what they call the donkeys in Northumberland. Ted I do not like, so it will have to be Edward. How do you like that?

Fighting was going on in the streets of Hamburg yesterday so I do not know whether I shall be able to get home in ten days' time.

———— ∞ ————

Wilhelmstrasse 67a, Berlin,
19 Feb 1920.

My dear Freda, Things are moving very slowly and there seems to be a contentious point in every clause of the Treaty. Of course the Huns choose what suits them best but our Allies are more troublesome than they are.

———— ∞ ————

24 Feb 1920.

The son of Count Zeppelin turned up today and wanted to be left as a supernumerary on the Naval Books as he is managing the naval court-martial board until trials come under civil law. We allowed it, although the French objected.

25 Feb 1920.

Lovely day which should suit Coventry *arriving at Heligoland with her destruction party.*

———— ∞ ————

27 Feb 1920.

I do not think there is much chance of my early promotion as I am still seventh on the list of Vice-Admirals and nearly all above me are young and active. So perhaps you had better order another lot of visiting cards. One can cross out the 'Vice' almost as easy as going to confession.

———— ∞ ————

4 Mar 1920.

It is rather disgusting the Headmasters ousting all the Catholic boys from the Osborne interview, but I should not hesitate to talk to the Second Sea Lord about it. [Osborne College on the Isle of Wight had replaced HMS Britannia *for Royal Naval Officer Training.]*

———— ∞ ————

The Kapp Putsche – 1920

7 Mar 1920.

My dear Freda, One of my Sub-commissions was assaulted by a mob in the streets of Bremen yesterday; I am consulting with General Nollet as this is the fourth case inside a week.

We have an officer going to England tonight so I am sending a parcel for you; the beads you can wear in mourning and the drop [pendant] when you come out. I also send a present (an Iron Cross) for 'Mary' [his parrot] on account of her gallant conduct and speech on her passage to Kiel, quite equivalent to what many similar decorations were given for.

———— ∞ ————

11 Mar 1920.

Our people came back from Bremen where they had a narrow escape from being thrown into the River Weser by a mob of about a hundred scoundrels. They were kicked and beaten, accompanied by shouts of 'Beat them to death' and showers of horse dung. The police did very well and saved them. [The unsuccessful Kapp Putsche to take over the German Government occurred on the night of 12 March 1920.]

———— ∞ ————

14 Mar 1920.

We are now threatened with a General Strike. I imagine it is caused by Labour against Militarists.

16 Mar 1920.

As we heard there was no dinner at the Hotel yesterday we decided to go out but found the front door locked. I got out by the back afterwards but the streets were in darkness and there was nothing of interest going on except a little desultory shooting.

A German Taube aeroplane dropped a pamphlet outside Ned's office at noon on 16 March 1916. The translation reads: *'German Men and Women! The black-marketeers and usurers will be packed off with an iron fist. Under our honest Government Germany will resume its former pride.'*

— ∞ —

18 Mar 1920.

My dear Freda, Your birthday and the twins. The trains are expected to be running again tonight. 5pm. The 'New' troops marched out and the old ones in. We strolled back to the office and had hardly got inside before there was a good deal of firing in the Unter den Linden; guns, machine-guns and hand grenades, one of the latter dropping where we had been standing. I shall not forget your birthday in Berlin.

— ∞ —

19 Mar 1920.

My dear Freda, I told you we had just got back when firing broke out; that was comparatively slight. When the next detachment of [German disaffected] Naval Brigade followed, the Flag Commander and Dutch Minister saw the whole thing which was a quite unjustifiable attack by the Military on the unarmed mob. In passing through the Brandenburg Gate, the officers bringing up the rear deliberately turned and emptied their revolvers into the crowd who had not even a brick to throw. Just afterwards six soldiers rushed out and seized an old man of about 60, knocked him down and beat him with rifle butts leaving his body lying there. Another party of six came out and did the same thing to a harmless youth of 17. The firing became general, a good many being killed and their bodies laid out in front of the hotel.

During the lunch hour, I saw a car with four officers going down the Linden and calling out to clear the streets. At the Brandenburg Gate there was an explosion which disposed of three street cleaners. This really looks like civil war.

A British Tommy, by accident, threw a bucket of water out of his quarters over a German sergeant who was passing; the latter came in, storming with indignation, but was told he had no business there; if he had a complaint he must make it through his Government. 'But,' he said, 'we have no Government.' 'Very well', the Tommy replied, 'go away and find one.'

— ∞ —

23 Mar 1920.

Admiralty asked today if the situation in Heligoland was satisfactory. Nothing about us. I propose replying: 'Heligoland situation quite satisfactory. Drink plentiful.

Tennis courts nearly complete. Golf course ready. Balls expected daily by seaplane.'

There was a heavy scrap at Kopenick on Sunday so it was just as well we did not pursue our journey over the bridge; the officers who examined our papers and many others having been killed defending it.

— ∞ —

In a speech in 1923 Ned gave details of the insurrection:

The Third Division or Erhard's Brigade was an independent lot of freebooters or filibusters who had been fighting and creating trouble. On 8 Mar we woke up to find Berlin in their possession; the German Government retired to Leipzig and the Security Police to the country. The whole Brigade was camped around Wilhelmstrasse. They treated us quite correctly and were anxious to get us to acknowledge them as the Government in being. The move was by no means popular with the people and the German Government in retaliation declared a general strike which was carried out fully so that the usurpers found out that although they had possession of the city, they had no machinery to run it and consequently decided to clear out.

Just after the Kapp Putsche we had given instructions for the Germans to send over certain warships [to the Allies] but they said they could not obtain enough coal to deliver them on account of the required monthly supplies to France [as reparations]. We applied to the Coal Commission who said that, as it was not a great quantity, the Germans could supply it if they used a little more effort. We told them this and shortly afterwards found ourselves one morning without any hot water in the Hotels for our morning baths; we complained at once and were told that cutting off the supply of coal to the Hotels was part of the special effort they were making. A bright specimen of German humour!

— ∞ —

27 Mar 1920.

My dear Freda, I am sending the Easter eggs for the elder children by parcel post. Audrey's egg has spellikins, Marjorie's marbles and Laura's small paper dolls for dressing.

General Bingham went on leave last night; he looks very seedy. He has worried a good deal during the disturbances.

Orsini goes to Munich on Sunday to put his son in a German school; I do not think I would do that if I were Italian.

— ∞ —

28 Mar 1920.

I spent the forenoon at the Kaiser Frederick's Museum where there are a lot of excellent pictures and loot from all parts, as in our British Museum.

The Japanese Attaché turned up and I am going to call on him in uniform tomorrow as they are so extraordinarily loyal to us and deserve a bit of a show to call attention to their presence.

31 Mar 1920.

Did I tell you that at St Mary's, where I go to church on Sunday, I got into a seat and saw 'von Bock' on three brass labels and afterwards a widow and a small girl came in. I made enquiries and found out she was the widow of the von Bock we killed at Bagamoyo. Rather curious we should be kneeling in the same bench and worshipping the same God. I do not think she would have appreciated it, had she known. How would you like to have the German who had been instrumental in killing your husband kneeling alongside you at St Anne's?

— ∽ —

9 Apr 1920.

Two of the surrendered battleships have arrived at Rosyth.

— ∽ —

10 Apr 1920.

Three months since the Peace Treaty came into force. Their Army should be reduced to 200,000 today. The Navy has been cut down to the [required] number, 15,000, now that all the officers at Kiel have been thrown out and a self-appointed Sub-Lieutenant is in charge of Kiel yard.

— ∽ —

13 Apr 1920.

The German Commodore has just been to see me. He wanted to tell me about the actual situation at the Naval Ports where the Warrant Officers are at present in command, but are quarrelling with the Petty Officers, and the men are doing likewise.

— ∽ —

22 Apr 1920.

A convoy of ships to be surrendered started for France; ten of them altogether and they seem to be behaving like ten little nigger boys. They consisted of one battleship, one cruiser and eight destroyers. The battleship Thuringen *first fell out with boiler trouble, then one destroyer caught fire and one went aground . . . The attempt by our Latin Allies to seize the* Augsberg, *the one and only cruiser told off for Japan, failed ignominiously; some time ago I discovered Article 437 of the Treaty which says that, in the event of an equality of votes, the Chairman shall be entitled to a second vote. I have never used this power and kept it up my sleeve. As I considered the attempt by France, backed by Italy, to get the* Augsberg *was purely rapacity, I got a simple vote taken on what should be the ship's destination, which resulted as expected in 'Two for' Japan and 'Two against'. This was received with smiles by the Latins. Then I read out Article 437 and gave my second vote for Japan.*

24 Apr 1920.

I looked in at the Cubist Art Department, National Gallery; most appalling; many pictures were not equal to those done by Eddie or Nancy, and much less intelligible.

— ∽ —

3 May 1920.

Two sad occurrences reached me yesterday. First [Flying Officer] Moon, who flew at Rufigi, was killed in a seaplane. Second a very bad accident to Admiral Orsini. His party and the French Admiral had gone out in three cars. The Italian driver was scorching as usual, and Dumesnil, who drives very fast, said he could not keep up. The leading car suddenly ran off the road into a tree, took a bound into the air and landed in a field. Orsini is the worst injured, skull cracked for five or six inches right across the forehead; Flag Lieutenant, thigh broken; and Orsini's daughter, arm broken. Madame Orsini, the German wife, was pitched into the mud and is in a hopeless state of nerves. If Orsini recovers he will be unfit for the Commission for at least six months. I hope it will not capsize my plans. The car was 'demolir'.

— ∽ —

Ned returned to England for leave in HMS *Danae* on 9 May and went back to Bremen in HMS *Dragon* on 26 May 1920.

— ∽ —

HMS *Dragon*, anchored somewhere off Heligoland, 27 May 1920.

Here we are in the North Sea in a dense fog. This evening after picking up the Channel buoys through the swept mine fields most successfully all day, we were just expecting to make another buoy with a staff and triangle on top when the missing buoy was reported right ahead. It loomed up large and we ported to clear it while we discussed whether it was a triangle or diamond on top, when the object under discussion flew away, being a seagull, and left a mine with one horn [detonator] standing up and covered with barnacles. We spent some time sinking it.

— ∽ —

On way up the River Weser, 30 May 1920.

They have made wonderful progress at Heligoland. Nearly all the turrets are now completely disabled.

— ∽ —

4 Jun 1920.

I do not think the new Governess's inability to teach will do any harm; she is certain to open up the children's minds in some new direction. It does not matter much at their age.

6 Jun 1920.

I lunched with the American minister and enquired from his staff about cars; full approval of Hupmobiles but they volunteered that the Dodge had done the best service of any war car.

[Prince] Gebhard [Blücher] dined last night and I had the two ladies, the Secretary and Soutter. He was most informative and can be very charming.

―――――― ∞ ――――――

11 Jun 1920.

I am to be allowed to see Admiral Orsini at the end of the month; his eyes are going to be all right. His substitute, Commander Gonzenbach, we can keep in order. He was very nearly thrown in the Weser at Bremen last March but managed to take shelter in a place of accommodation for Damen and got 18 Pounds damages out of the Huns for a new coat; his being torn.

―――――― ∞ ――――――

13 Jun 1920.

I had a nice afternoon sail on the Wann See yesterday. There was a good breeze and we made our way as far as the Potsdam bridge. Thousands of boats out; it is absurd to say that these people have no money to pay indemnities. Let them sell their yachts, their gloriously appointed motor boats and their luxurious cars to pay for their sins; we are more heavily taxed than they are (seven times) I believe.

Gebhard was very little changed except eight years older instead of six. We avoided all reference to the war; I only said his countrymen did not know what they had done during the war and that they had been kept filled up with lies; he agreed as to there being liars everywhere. My officers said he was exactly like an English country gentleman.

―――――― ∞ ――――――

14 Jun 1920.

I heard from Dragon *today that they had got another mine on the way back; that makes six on the two trips. Another has sunk an English tug off the Dutch coast after she had towed a German ship all the way from Chile.*

―――――― ∞ ――――――

23 Jun 1920.

I saw in the Morning Post *that one of the German Battleships that we had got surrendered had fouled the piers, and was now lying across them, beneath the high level bridge at Newcastle-on-Tyne. It would be rather a nice revenge for the old ship if she manages to bring down the bridge, which is one of Stephenson's masterpieces.*

In July Ned travelled to Brussels for discussions on the progress of destruction with the British Prime Minister Lloyd George, Belgian Premier Delacroix, French President Millerand, German politicians Fehrenbach, von Simons and Wirth, Captain von Muller – former commander of the *Emden* – and many others. The Germans, who were suspected of prevarication by the French but not by Ned, wanted to extend the deadline to 1 October 1921; French General Foch made it 1 September 1920. Ned reports, 'The Germans signed the ridiculous conditions but their Minister of Defence resigned.'

Ned attended a dinner given by King Albert of Belgium and then returned to Berlin by train telling Freda that the countryside looked well with every inch cultivated. His chauffeur drove the car back enduring about ten punctures on the 1,200-mile round trip. General Bingham returned by car and was involved in an accident with two Belgians on a motorcycle when leaving Spa. Ned states: 'The cycle was on the wrong side of the road but the General's chauffeur, as was to be expected, also went to the wrong side in the emergency. No-one was much hurt except the Belgians, the cycle and the car.'

―――――― ∞ ――――――

23 Jul 1920.

Darling Freda, We took a holiday yesterday afternoon and spent it on the Wann See. The day before, without any warning to us, the Military took a holiday on account of Belgian National Day so I gave our people one on account of the Sultan of Zanzibar's birthday which comes any day of the year one likes to fix it.

―――――― ∞ ――――――

27 July 1920.

I dined at the Bristol with Gebhard last night. He still asserts that we wanted the war and that we were more prepared for it than Germany. Of course I did not agree with such nonsense. He says we had 500 ships specially commissioned before the war broke out. Probably someone had added up the ships' names in the Navy List.

You seem rather disappointed with the Dodge but, if Stocker advises buying, you can do so.

―――――― ∞ ――――――

30 Jul 1920.

Admiral Dumesnil went on leave to Paris last night with the avowed intention of upsetting the whole work of the Commission (but his conduct by this time is too well known there and he carries no weight). He is sacking his chief adviser whom he calls a traitor whenever he agrees with anything we propose.

The book by Freda's sister Princess Evelyn Blücher, *An English Wife in Berlin*, was published at this time. Ned gives occasional comment:

- 15 Jul 1920. I have just had an interview with the American Commissioner who was full of praise for Evelyn's book and said she had been very fair to all of them.
- 8 Aug 1920. Evelyn was delighted with the result of her book and quite rightly.
- 9 Aug 1920. The Kaiser has written for two copies. Evelyn says I first gave her the idea of publishing her diary over some remark I made, but I cannot remember doing so.
- 20 Oct 1920. Evelyn turned up yesterday and dined with me in my room as Gebhard was attending an important dinner in the dining room; Gebhard came up for coffee about 11pm.
- Evelyn's article in the *Nineteenth Century* was edited by Marillier and comes out next issue. The first paragraph is very good and written by her but there are few traces of her in the rest which is the usual specious argument against disarmament.
- 11 Nov 1920. Great excitement today; a parcel arrived at the German Post Office for me from Harrods. I swore it was for use in the Control Commission, and after much travelling, Dalton secured it and it was opened amidst breathless excitement and contained six bottles of asthma cure for Evelyn from Edith [one of Freda and Evelyn's many sisters].
- 2 Mar 1921. I lunched with Mme Rizoff, formerly wife of the Bulgarian Minister here (now dead), and the daughter of the King of Montenegro by an Albanian shepherdess. Quite nice looking; she is the shepherdess alluded to in Evelyn's book which has great sales in America. A Silesian coal magnate was also there; von Twinkler.
- 17 Mar 1921. Evelyn said she heard from England that you were the only person remaining in the land with eight servants. They do not seem to be much help except for Budd and the cook. I wish I could be with you and the twins on your birthday.

The enthusiastic reception of Evelyn's book was in some ways remarkable; she had not always sailed such smooth seas.

At a court ball in 1908 the Kaiser of Germany asked Countess Blücher to launch the German armoured cruiser *Blücher*. In his *Memoirs of Prince Blücher* the Prince writes, 'She of course accepted the honour, looking upon it in a way as a compliment to England . . . It was said by experts that the *Blücher* was one of the best armoured cruisers ever built. I did not at the time she was launched realise that, as such, she was looked upon by the British Admiralty as a distinct challenge – the upstart German Navy squaring its fists.' The *Blücher* weighed 15,550 tons and carried twelve 8.2" and eight 5.9" guns. The brass plaque commemorating the occasion stated:

Blücher – This ship of the Kaiser's factory in Kiel was built between May 1906 and Oct 1909 and was baptised on 11 Apr 1909 by Countess Blücher of Wahlstatt.

The Chemnitz *Tageblatt* described the occasion: 'To the amazement, not to say vivid horror, of those present, the lady in question christened the cruiser in English, even pronouncing the name in anything but a German fashion. Only the presence of the Kaiser prevented a loud outburst of indignation against the "unpatriotic" lady.'

In her book Evelyn tells how her sister Freda and Ned came to say farewell to them in London on 28 July 1914 after the Blüchers had been requested by the German Embassy to leave Britain forthwith. At the same time that Evelyn left for Berlin with her husband, who worked for the German Red Cross, her brothers-in-law Herbert and Ned were rejoining the Royal Navy and her brothers Freddie, Edmund, Vincent and Wilfred were joining their British regiments, the last named to die at Ypres.

At the Battle of the Dogger Bank on 24 January 1915, the precursor to the awesome but indecisive Battle of Jutland, the German cruiser *Blücher* was struck by a direct hit at 17,000 yards from the 13.5" guns of HMS *Lion*. When her crew were struggling in the water, British destroyers attempted to engage in rescue work but could not come close as the sinking *Blücher* was mistaken by a German Zeppelin for a British ship and bombed. Of 1,130 men on board 870 lives were lost. The captain was saved and, when brought ashore in England, was escorted by Herbert Throckmorton. The Captain told Herbert that the *Blücher* had been launched by an English lady. 'I know', replied Herbert, 'She's my sister-in-law.' Herbert was married to Evelyn and Freda's sister Ethel. A replacement cruiser *Blücher* was sunk off Oslo in World War II; one wonders whether navy ships should be named after army generals!

While in Berlin, Evelyn was able to receive letters weekly from her sisters Edith and Monica, and occasionally from Freda. She tells how she discussed the vexed question whether German commanders had sunk Allied ships bearing the Red Cross. 'Some, women especially, are horrified at the stories told. My sister Freda, on her long dangerous journey to the Cape, took seven small children with her, and made them wear life-belts all the time. When I showed some German ladies the photographs of the twins of two years of age standing on deck, each girt with a huge life-belt, tears came to their eyes and they said, "Do people really think that the Germans are so cruel as to want to sink ships with women and children on them?"'

On 28 November 1917 Freda Charlton wrote to Evelyn from Cape Town mentioning a curious coincidence: 'The officers under her husband's command were ordered to bring in all foreign rifles found in South Africa and, amongst others, was brought in one with my husband's [Blücher's] monogram engraved on it.' He had used it to hunt wildebeest in the Orange Free State before the Boer War.

At the beginning of the war the Kaiser had called Evelyn and her two fellow exiles – Princesses Pless and Munster –

'The Three Graces'. Later, due to their undisguisable sympathies, he renamed them 'The Three Disgraces'.

After winning a race for veterans at the British sports in Berlin, Ned had three weeks' leave in England in August 1920. On his return he took his daughter Marjorie to Heligoland and gave a party for about one hundred children of the island. He inspected the work of disarmament which is described at length in the *Daily Telegraph* of 31 August 1920:

'Before the war the Germans transformed Heligoland into something very like a stationary ship of war. The island, which is a mile long and a fifth of a square mile in area, was honeycombed with subterranean chambers. In these there was accommodation for everyone and everything needed to fight the fortress . . . the command stations were armoured cupolas sunk in concrete-lined pits. From the centre of each rose a periscope. In these the first Allied Officers to reach the island found silhouettes of all vessels of the Allies. There were half a dozen such controls. There were two powerful searchlights mounted on disappearing platforms. The main armament of the island consisted of eight 12-inch naval guns, four 6-inch, eight 11-inch howitzers and numbers of anti-aircraft guns . . . in the dissection of the guns and armour plates, a new oxy-hydrogen process is being employed. It is a German invention first put into practice only a few months ago. The flame bites its way through the centre of the breech of a 12-inch gun in about a minute. By this process the guns are cut into lengths of three or four feet each. With steel at its present price the debris will realise a large sum.'

In a speech in 1923 Ned gave additional information on Heligoland:

'The Island, which had been British for some eighty years, was transferred to the Germans in 1890 for much important territory on the East Coast of Africa; the islanders then living had the option of remaining British Subjects, and we also retained the right to have a Lloyds signal station there, and for British fishermen to dry their nets when required. Four days before Britain entered the war the British Heligolanders were thrown in prison.' In respect of the destruction, explosives were used to blow up concrete and some metals, while oxy-hydrogen or oxy-acetylene was used for cutting steel and pure oxygen for burning cast-iron. 'On one occasion about thirty searchlights had to be destroyed; they were large mirrors about 4ft 6in in diameter and we had given permission for them to be used for commercial purposes if they could be cut down to a smaller size. This had been found impossible; consequently the edict went forward that they were to be destroyed. The German workmen refused to destroy them and stood laughing at our presumed impotence. The British Engineer Commander, a man of noble build and an old rugby football player, got hold of a sledge hammer and smashed the lot. The workmen were so impressed they gave somewhat of a cheer for his pluck'

29 Sept 1920.

Darling Freda, Another big 40,000-ton dock has started from Kiel and if this fine weather lasts the old dock may even get to its destination, Portland [England], but it takes some time to get round Denmark at the rate of three knots.

———— ∞ ————

10 Oct 1920.

The dock arrived in Portland after 12 days; worth 1¾ million Pounds as she floats. I am very pleased with the work of our people and at their having kept on good terms with the Germans while handing over. The French get nothing as they always quarrel. All the experts are writing to me now over their paravane inventions to know who suggested it first; I have not got the records. Captain Preston is one of the most deserving and he has put in no claim at all, possibly because he thinks it was in the ordinary run of duty.

———— ∞ ————

15 Oct 1920.

The Social Democrats of Germany passed a vote of censure on me today which gives me a great deal of pleasure. They object to our carrying out the Peace Treaty so far as it concerns the destruction of submarine diesel engines, pretending we want to destroy all diesels. As the submarine ones cannot be converted economically [to civilian use] and can at any time be reconverted for use in submarines we have to insist on their destruction. They always omit in their arguments the Article which says: 'all Submarines have to be destroyed entirely – integralement' – and pretend these may be kept for commercial purposes.

———— ∞ ————

19 Oct 1920.

Orsini turned up at the main Commission meeting yesterday for the first time since his accident; his brain seems all right but his eyesight has been seriously affected.

———— ∞ ————

24 Oct 1920.

The Algemeine Zeitung, a semi-official Government paper, made an attack on the Naval Commission yesterday and said that I personally, Admiral Charlton, was interested in the motor industry (wish I were) and consequently wished to destroy that of Germany. I was amused when Dr von Simons, 'The man' of Germany, sent one of his Ministers to apologise for what they had said was a printer's error and explained that the Government had nothing to do with it. [The British Ambassador] D'Abernon appears to think that we ought to reply to the newspaper attacks but I said we were not here to argue with the Germans but to control them. Unless smashed,

Marshal Foch, Generals Weygund and Bingham with Admiral Charlton to the right, Belgium 1920.

Charlton inspects destruction of German 30cm guns at Heligoland.

the engines can be recovered for use in submarines; only 2% of the submarine diesels are now in use commercially. I believe they have sold many of the others to Neutrals and possibly even to our Allies. The 'strafe' continues.

———— ∽ ————

15 Nov 1920.

I received a letter from Lord Derby today; it apologises for my having had to call him, with the remainder of the Council of Ambassadors, a lot of scoundrels and, although he expresses regret for the Council, he makes no attempt to mend their ways.

———— ∽ ————

18 Nov 1920.

Gebhard had a small dinner party of eight in what is now known as the Admiral's dining room; it was excellent. The reputation of the chef here is now well established as the best in Germany.

———— ∽ ————

20 Nov 1920.

General Bingham had a nice little party of fourteen last night at the Adlon including Gebhard and Evelyn. She leaves tonight for Silesia. It has been very nice having them here and I shall miss them.

Admiral Fatou [who had replaced Admiral Dumesnil], on his own and without asking my advice, has gone away on a dockyard tour in the Oise, the French gunboat to which the Germans object because the crew turn their backs 'en masse' whenever they pass a German man-of-war and make disgusting noises. The Germans say 'What are these monkeys doing here now? Where have they sprung from? We never saw them during the war!' Naturally the Germans objected to the Oise. (Subsequently Fatou thought better of it and undertook the inspection without the gunboat). Besides there is a French transport going to Wilhelmshaven to embark equipment to which the Peace Treaty does not entitle them but which the Germans have got sick of refusing. As they will be there some time and cannot help their objectionable habits, more trouble is likely to result. I have told the Council of Ambassadors it is dishonourable to seize a thing they have no pretence of being entitled to, and when asked to guarantee payment, decide they will wait until they get it – and then refuse payment. The Latins appear to have persuaded the Ambassadors to do their dirty work and then will expect me to carry it out and put all the onus on the Commission.

———— ∽ ————

22 Nov 1920.

I return the pamphlet which is most objectionable and I should have got up and left if it had been read while I was in church. We cannot allow politics in the Catholic pulpits in England or countenance them by sitting through their reception.

Went by special permit to the Kaiser's Schloss at the end of the Unter den Linden. The one he always used in Berlin, where all sorts of wickedness was hatched, and from which the sailors were driven out during the Revolution [in March] by field and machine-gun fire. 1,250 rooms; it is now being turned into a museum. Many of our English Royalty were there in pictures, especially Queen Victoria [the Kaiser's grandmother]. General Bingham's mother was there in a picture of Emperor Frederick's wedding; she was a lady-in-waiting. The Kaiser's private dining room was small and unpretentious. Very little damage was done inside by the bombardment. The Kaiser's own glass screen, which he had to keep the draughts away, and incidentally keep himself in shadow while he lighted up his visitors face, had been pierced by three machine-gun bullets so someone must have known where he was likely to be, but I think he had skedaddled to Holland the day before.

The Council (of Ambassadors) have got themselves in a hole over the light Cruiser equipment for France and Italy which they have enforced, though it is nowhere in the Treaty, but as all the onus would have been put on me, I protested strongly against such dishonesty and there will be a fine row about it shortly. They propose to tell the Germans, AFTER THEY HAVE GOT IT, that they are not going to pay for it. Lord Derby thought that the protest meant that I had stopped the embarkation and complained to the First (Sea) Lord who said I must withdraw or allow it to proceed. But I had never stopped it and having made my protest, said I had never meant to call them personally a lot of dishonest scoundrels; which they are collectively. Lord Derby wrote quite a nice letter apologising for being a collective scoundrel and there the matter stands for the present. We are in a strong position as their decisions will never stand the light of day. It is a dirty game, POLITICS.

In World War I British officers received prize money for their participation. Ned's share was gazetted in December 1920 and came to 1,500 pounds from which he bought the Dodge car for Freda and put 500 pounds on deposit.

Admiral Callaghan died and Ned became No.3 on the Vice-Admirals' seniority list. He returned to England on the destroyer HMS *Carysfort* on 17 December 1920 and subsequently went back to the Continent on the *Pieter De Conink*, 'said to be the fastest passenger steamer in the world'.

In 1921 Ned continued his duties as PNIAC in Berlin while Freda continued to run their home at Eastern House, Alverstoke, Hampshire. They wrote to each other almost daily. Ned continued to give several dinners each month, attend numerous official functions and organise a monthly dinner-dance at the Hotel Bristol where the senior Naval delegation staff lived. These dances were attended by eighty to a hundred members of both the Naval and Military Commissions and their friends who made up their own tables and paid fifty marks per head to the hotel.

163

Ned's staff car in Berlin. A British Talbot made in part from scrap metal salvaged from a German Super Zeppelin.

Ned frequently played sport; golf until the Berlin Golf Club barred all Control Commission delegates in retaliation for British Golf Clubs barring German players; then ice skating and ice hockey in winter, and yachting in summer. In addition to his Naval officers, Ned was often accompanied at the dinners, dinner-dances and sailing picnics by his WRNS secretaries, by Evelyn, by Countess Orsini, and occasionally by visiting relatives from England, including Freda's sister Monica. Freda complained that all the photos he sent to her include women. Ned replied that he missed her and in numerous letters asked her to come to Berlin as it was now safer, but she did not visit Berlin. Her journey to South Africa appears to have been her only overseas trip after her marriage. Perhaps she saw her duty as running their home which included eight children and eight servants. Although many Germans suffered deprivation after the war, the staff of the Allied Commissions enjoyed good food and an active social life. Ned apparently avoided all impropriety. He wrote to Freda on 18 February 1921: 'The latest incident at the Adlon would provide ample subject matter for a French play; it is almost unbelievable but absolutely true; rather lengthy but I will write it out and you will probably come out post-haste to save me from similar danger':

Scene; Adlon Hotel main hall very full for afternoon tea;

noisy band. At one table a good looking German lady, well dressed, living in hotel, but with husband gone away for two days, is having tea alone. A gentleman of comely German appearance enters and orders tea at a table nearby; depressed at the absence of his wife for a few days. After a few glances at each other, he suggests they have tea together mutually cheering each other up. Afterwards a walk in the Tier Garten, dinner, a visit to a cafe-dansante accompanied by much German champagne, they thoroughly enjoyed themselves. He offered to see her home; 'But I am staying at the Adlon,' she said, 'So am I,' he replied, and they returned there full of life. His room was on the first floor and he gave her the number. She said, 'Mine is on the fourth,' but she got out of the lift with him on the first. At about 3am she had occasion to get up and, putting on her fur necklet over her chemisette, she went in the passage in search of the 'Damen'. The passages were long and she took some time finding it. On the way back she discovered that she had forgotten the number of his room and the key for her room was with her clothes in his room.

Steps approached and a well-dressed man who had also dined not too wisely, found a charming lady on the verge of tears. She appealed for help and told how her key was in a gentleman's room, number unknown. He replied, 'I am the man you are looking for,' and conducted her to his room. He turned out to be the Dutch Consul and had to leave at 6am to catch a train to meet his wife in Holland. He left his companion sleeping, paid his bill and caught his train.

About 9am a maid entered and found the lady sleeping. Awakening, partially oblivious to the night's events, she found herself in a strange room with no clothes except a fur tippet, and decided the man had stolen her clothes and all her jewellery and decided to report it. Herr Adlon, the stout and groggy old Manager, was sent for and decided it was a matter for the Police. They investigated, telegraphed the frontier post, dragged the Consul off the train and three Policemen brought him back to Berlin. Meanwhile the first man awoke, found no lady but clothes and jewellery and reported their presence to the Manager.

The police collected compensation from all three guilty persons and also from the Manager who should not allow such goings-on at his hotel.

Ned ends the story to Freda, 'This could of course not happen at such a respectable hotel as the Bristol. But will you please tell me what I must do if I find a lone lady wandering about in her chemisette at 3am?'

Ned was called to a meeting of the Council of Ambassadors in Paris and attended a dinner for sixty given by the President of France at the Elysée Palace wearing his 'Légion d'Honneur'. He renewed his acquaintance with the Comte de Dion, the motor vehicle pioneer, whom he had met sailing in Brittany twenty-five years previously, and lunched with Admiral Grasset who had served with him on the Naval Armistice Committee and who had just become First Sea Lord of France. Ned was indignant to find that the Sacre Coeur Convent, which his mother had attended, had been turned into the Musée Rodin 'full of disgusting sculpture though no doubt very clever'. At Freda's request he went shopping for stockings for her in the 'Bon Marché' – presumably not dressed as an Admiral! Ned was overruled by the Council of Ambassadors in respect of the diesel engines for submarines and the Germans were allowed to retain them.

Freda, possibly appraised by her sister Evelyn, advised Ned to be cautious fraternising with 'G', a German man, not Gebhard but possibly Gebhard's brother Gustav. Ned replies that he has only been out twice with 'G', once to the theatre and once to the Scala, and avoids any discussions on politics or war matters although such have been attempted. In Silesia a referendum strongly supported reunion with Germany; Gebhard expressed his pleasure that British troops were there to maintain peace.

— ∞ —

11 Feb 1921.

My dear Freda, Had to call on the Japanese Ambassador. I wore my sword and 'Star of the Rising Sun' . . .

— ∞ —

13 Feb 1921.

Gebhard turned up this afternoon from Pless and dined with us. He was fined 100 marks, or ten days' imprisonment, for having imported six arrows (for archery purposes on the lawn) without permission, which looks as though the German Government is keeping a close watch on armaments!

— ∞ —

27 Feb 1921.

We had a smash in the car which might have been very serious but our chauffeur did very well; a taxi coming down a side street at full speed ran into us amidships and lifted us onto the pavement, quite six feet. Entirely the taxi's fault as we had seen three cars pass just before and Arty [Lord d'Abernon] remarked on them before it occurred, so we were going slowly and blowing our horn when the other fellow swooped down without any notice whatever. We just avoided a tree and turned into the road again, quite undamaged beyond a little paint. Fortunately it is a well built car and heavy. Bits of the taxi flew about but the occupants were civil and said it was their driver's fault. I looked anxiously at the tree and wondered if my head would have been thick enough to break it as Orsini's did when his encountered the nine inch apple tree.

— ∞ —

11 Mar 1921.

One of our typists working in Fontaine's office at 5 Pounds a month turns out to be a Princess Krapotkin, Russian, and is doing well and a very nice woman [Capt. Fontaine was Ned's Chief of Staff].

— ∞ —

17 Mar 1921.

The attempt to blow up the Tower of Victory was probably Communistic to enrage the people against our Commissions. The papers said it was done by foreigners but the dynamite and fittings were all German Government material which foreigners would be unlikely to have.

We hardly realise how little some of these Continentals know of the World, especially the French who are great home lovers. Of the five French Generals who went over to the London Conference, including Foch and Nollet, Bingham tells me not one of them had been in England before and three of them had never set foot on a ship before.

— ∞ —

25 Mar 1921.

I have just shifted the ribbon of my typewriter and want to try it. It is rather amusing to find a notice on the spool which I got in Immingham in 1918: 'Keep your old metal spool. Your country gains two ounces of metal and you are providing more shells to fire at the Huns.' Now we are taking shells away from them by the million and destroying them.

15 May 1921.

I did not write (yesterday) as I have just spent thirty-six hours in the boat; I went down to the East End where it was built. A military officer had bought a motor boat and offered me a tow round the 25 miles of canals to the Wann See but his boat would not start. So Dalton [Ned's servant] and I started off hoping they would overtake us but they never did. I thoroughly enjoyed the splendid exercise of pulling and towing the yacht and the dinghy over the distance, to say nothing of the thirst obtained. We plugged along, alternately pulling and towing, along the banks until 7pm when I sent Dalton to telephone for the car which was waiting at the Wann See. It never arrived so I sent Dalton to Berlin by train and slept very well in the boat in spite of the German holiday-makers.

At 7am Dalton returned and we resumed our procession. After some hours of toil we reached a lock where the keeper wanted payment for a broken down motor boat. I found he wanted two marks and paid him (2d). After that we again plugged along towing or sailing between bridges (40 of them). We were told we could not tow or sail as both were 'verboten' but continued doing so on the opposite side to the objector.

At 8pm, after only a light breakfast, we arrived at Wann See. I knew my buoy was being arranged, but not exactly which, so I seized the nearest and was roundly cursed in abominable German by Major Clutterbuck, much to my amusement and his subsequent discomposure. Dalton, who is usually very quiet, had a thirst which exceeded mine and we soon managed to get through a quantity of beer which even the Germans appreciated.

— ∞ —

23 May 1921.

If you happen to be near the Marine shops in Portsmouth you might get me a R.Y.S. Burgee, the smallest obtainable, as I want to fly it on the Wann See. (Ned had been elected a Naval member of the Royal Yacht Squadron in 1918.)

General Nollet leaves for a rush visit to Heligoland in an endeavour to prove it really was a soldier's possession. He will find it difficult as it was always manned by the German Navy.

— ∞ —

26 May 1921

The Reparation Commission has at last woken up and is endeavouring to collar all the money we have made out of 'Arisings Naval'. On account of the word 'Surrender' which occurs in regard to the disposition of Naval War Material, but does not occur in the Military Article, we have destroyed the relevant German Naval material and sold the results. So far we have got 18 million marks, 70% of which goes to our Admiralty, 11% each to France and Italy, and 8% to Japan. The Reparation Commission want to collar this

but we have all paid our shares to our respective Admiralties and so they will have difficulty extracting it. Our Admiralty has written a furious letter to them and told the Council of Ambassadors that they are trying to flout no less than four of their own Supreme decisions.

— ∞ —

30 May 1921.

Many thanks for the flags. The boat is 20 feet long, seven foot beam and four foot draught; a centre-board cutter (named Niac*).*

— ∞ —

4 Jun 1921.

The King's Birthday went off well. I called on the Ambassador in uniform with my staff at 10am and then went out sailing with the Secretary and the two ladies and flew all our flags. It created quite a commotion amongst the Germans but your small jack and the boat's ensign were just right for a festa day. We lunched in the reeds under the shadow of the sail and then made for home so as to be sure of getting back for the Ambassador's dinner. The dinner was for 32 and I wore my K.C.M.G.

— ∞ —

8 Jun 1921.

Gebhard showed me Evelyn's letter (searching for the grave of Evelyn and Freda's brother) at Ypres. As successful as possible, but very sad.

Ned was promoted from Vice-Admiral to Admiral on 5 July 1921. About the same time he received the Knighthood of St Gregory from Pope Benedict XV.

From November 1921 to February 1922 the Wann See froze over and the Commission members enjoyed ice yachting. The Germans, battling against inflation and insurrection, complained that the whole time of their Foreign Minister was being occupied in answering notes of complaints regarding the non-execution of details of the Treaty of Versailles. Lord d'Abernon records that in the two months preceding 20 March 1922 there were forty-two complaints, nine from the French Embassy, twenty-five from General Nollet, three from Admiral Charlton and five from Air-Commodore Masterman.

On 1 February 1922 Lord d'Abernon held a costume ball at the British Embassy attended by the German Chancellor, Dr Wirth, the new Minister for Foreign Affairs, Dr Rathenau, and the entire Diplomatic Corps in Berlin. Ned attended in a Louis XIV costume while Gebhard went as the Great Elector Frederick of Brandenburg. The ball was reported on by the *Berliner Tageblatt* which commended the accuracy of detail of the costumes. The *Deutsche Zeitung* used it on 4 February 'not to discuss the delicacy of enemy foreigners to have such a luxurious feast in half-desperate freezing Berlin' but as an opportunity to attack Berlin Jewry for fomenting a railway

Ned pottering around his yacht, the Niac *on the Wann See.*

strike. It continues: 'Reports are coming in that Boleshevist wire-pullers are again at work and that Russian-Jew money is being successful.' On 28 June 1922 Dr Rathenau was assassinated.

Lord d'Abernon reported: 'The year 1922 has brought the operations of the Commission of Control to a point not far from the complete execution of their programme – certainly far beyond the point where any danger need be feared . . . ' On 11 January 1923 France occupied the Ruhr portion of Germany against the advice of its Allies. The Germans effected passive resistance and devalued their currency to 18 billion to the pound. The last note Ned has on Berlin, apparently written about 1933, includes the following: 'As for the Treaty of Versailles, one of its chief framers, no less a person than Clemenceau himself, is credited with the cynical but truthful remark that "it contains all the elements for a just and durable war"!'

— ∞ —

After completing his duties as PNIAC Ned received the following letter:

Admiralty, 17 Jan 1923.

Sir, I am commanded by My Lords Commissioners to convey to you Their appreciation of the tact and firmness which you have displayed in the exercise of your difficult duties. sgd Charles Walker.

Lord d'Abernon wrote to the Foreign Secretary:

Berlin, 18 Jan 1923.

My Lord Marquess, I have the honour to report that Admiral Sir Edward Charlton, K.C.B., K.C.M.G., left here on 15 Jan, having completed his term of service.

The British section of the Naval Commission has now been reduced to two officers.

Admiral Charlton has given me the following statement about the amount of naval war materiel destroyed and the amount awaiting destruction:

	No or weight	Destroyed to 31 Dec	Remaining to be destroyed
Guns	Tons	9,625	19
Gun Mountings etc.	Tons	17,399	31
Ammunition & explosives	Tons	45,122	191
Mines & accessories	Tons	48,566	nil
Torpedoes	No	5,364	nil
Miscellaneous war materiel	Tons	133,100	1,126

As your Lordships will see the work has been done very thoroughly. I am anxious to bring to Your Lordship's notice the great services rendered by Admiral Charlton in the difficult and delicate work of the Naval Commission of Control. I should be glad if Your Lordship considered it

167

appropriate to inform the Admiralty how efficient this officer has shown himself to be.

The transparent honesty of his character, the sincerity of his speech, and his hearty seamanlike manner, have ensured him the confidence and respect of all those with whom he has been brought into relations.

He is a fine specimen of the British sailor.

sgd d'Abernon.

———— ⸂⸃ ————

A copy of the above was sent to Ned under cover of the following letter:

Admiralty, 4 Apr 1923

Admiral Sir Edward F.B. Charlton, Eastern House, Alverstoke, Hampshire. In transmitting Lord d'Abernon's

letter, the Secretary of State for Foreign Affairs states that this tribute to your services has been read with a great deal of satisfaction.

sgd Charles Walker.

Forty-five years after obtaining his first report, Ned had received his last. On 7 February 1923 King George V noted in his diary, 'Saw Charlton on his ceasing to be President of Naval Commission in Berlin.' During his career Ned was awarded the following medals: KCB (Knight Commander of the Bath); KCMG (Knight Commander of St Michael and St George); Knight Commander of St Gregory the Great; Star of Zanzibar (First Class); Grand Cordon of the Order of the Rising Sun (Japan); Medal of the Royal Humane Society; Commander of the Legion of Honour (France); Cross of Malta; ECB Civil Class; Egyptian Medal 1882; Khedive Star; Chinese Medal 1900; 1914–15 Star; General Service Medal; Victory Medal; Papal Medal.

Vice Admiral Charlton examines a document, Capt Fanshaw stands behind him, Berlin 1922.

Retirement

Admiralty SW1, 10 Mar 1924.

Sir, Having laid before My Lords Commissioners your letter of 3rd inst, requesting that you may be permitted to retire in order to facilitate promotion of junior officers, I am commanded by their Lordships to inform you that they have been pleased to approve your request, and that accordingly you have been placed on the Retired List of Admirals with effect from 3rd March 1924.
sgd Charles Walker.

———— ∞ ————

Freda and Ned went to live at 'Priddens', Hill Head, Hampshire where they installed a telescope in an upstairs room so as to be able to observe the ships passing through the Solent on their way to and from the mighty port of Southampton. His interest in the development of his children is apparent from the newspaper cuttings he kept of their athletic and riding achievements. Ned made frequent use of his yacht *Niac* and won many races on the Solent because its shallow-draught, centre-board design for use on inland lakes made it inherently faster than sea-going boats. For the same reason it was less stable. In a letter dated 30 July 1993 Sister Laura says: 'The *Niac* capsized during a race. I saw Freda (the only member of the family who hated the sea and had never learnt to swim) come in dripping wet and very white. We all wished it had been "the luck" of one of the children to "enjoy" that experience. As a result Dad bought a heavier, steadier yacht, the *Kandoo*, in which he sailed to France.' Sister Laura adds: 'As a past commander of the submarine base at Portsmouth, Dad had permission to keep his anchor-hold in a basin on the Gosport side. The basin was narrow and protected by a stone wall commanding the harbour entrance. From there he rowed us up to the naval jetty and out near Haslar Hospital. No one ever questioned this right of entrance to this submarine yard and the freedom with which we parked our bicycles therein. Daddy was sailing his yacht along Stokes Bay, east of the pier, in an area where submarines practised diving exercises. Buoys indicated their presence and activity. Daddy sailed across this area knowing that the submarine look-out should be aware of his presence. Just below him, almost upturning his yacht, a submarine began to surface; stopped while Daddy manoeuvred his yacht to safety. He then let out a suitable invective on the young commanding officer, "Neglect of basics; there should always be a look-out".' In turn the submariners berated him, learnt next day that he was an Admiral, and offered him an apology, possibly undeserved. As Laura says, 'After all, who was at fault? Both!'

———— ∞ ————

In 1924 General Smuts sent a handwritten letter to Ned:

Irene, Transvaal, 29 Dec 1924.

Dear Admiral Charlton, I was indeed pleased to receive your note about the East African Dinner. It was an added pleasure to find that you presided at the function . . . East Africa I always look upon as one of the unique and wonderful experiences of my strange life. With very kind regards and best wishes. J.C. Smuts.

———— ∞ ————

The author received the following letter from Ned's nephew, E. Oswin Charlton, in 1993:

Cornhill-on-Tweed, Northumberland, 14 Jun 1993.

Dear Frank, I only saw Ned twice. On one occasion he took my brother and I to Tynemouth. Nothing would satisfy us unless we went to sea with a real Admiral. Ned hired a rowing boat and rowed us round Tynemouth Harbour. We were thrilled. Then he took us to the big hotel in Tynemouth. He ordered three beers as he said that, as we had been to sea with an Admiral, we must have a drink with one! The barmaid was horrified as we were only 11 and 13. I don't know what Ned said to that barmaid but we each got our beers. Yrs 'Oscar' Charlton.

In retirement Ned participated in many functions:

- July 1923. Presided at the Annual Meeting and presented prizes at Wellesley Nautical School, Blyth, Northumberland – a school for boys from broken homes.
- September 1924. Proposed a toast to the 'Royal Albert Yacht Club' at the Portsmouth Sailing Club's annual dinner.
- 15 October 1924. Attended the unveiling at Portsmouth by HRH the Duke of York of a magnificent Royal Naval Memorial to the 48,000 British and Commonwealth naval seamen who were lost in World War I.
- 1925. Attended meets of the Gosport and Fareham Beagles.
- 23 October 1925. Responded to the President's toast at the Cornish Oyster Feast, Falmouth.
- 1 November 1929. Was Guest of Honour when the Royal Navy Torpedo Training was transferred from HMS *Vernon* to HMS *Defiance*.
- 2 December 1929. Attended an East African Campaign Dinner in London where General Smuts proposed a toast to the former supreme German East Africa commander, General von Lettow-Vorbeck, guest at the dinner.
- 11 July 1932. Attended the reunion dinner in memory of the fiftieth anniversary of the Bombardment of Alexandria.
- 6 November 1935. Attended a dinner given by the Lord Mayor of London for the Catholic Archbishop of Westminster.

Ned also undertook a number of duties in retirement including: serving as a county magistrate for several years; serving on the Gosport Catholic Education Committee and Gosport County School Board of Governors; and organising a charity dinner-dance for the St Dunstan's Home for blinded soldiers, sailors and airmen. Ned frequently sailed with his youngest daughter Rosemary and with his friend 'Old' Wylie, a marine artist, who lived in a wooden-frame house at the point where Portsmouth harbour entered the Solent. When Wylie died Ned and his daughter Rosemary stood together on deck as the artist was lowered into the sea he had so ardently recorded.

————— ∞ —————

Stamshaw, Portsmouth, 18 Jul 1932.

Sir, Your letter of 12 inst in the Evening News brought back pleasant memories of two years spent in HMS Alexandra. I must congratulate you on your appointment as a J.P. There are only two of us in the town alive of the 1880–82 crew. James McMenemy.

————— ∞ —————

In 1932 Ned's eldest daughter Audrey took her first child – me, aged two – from South Africa to Britain. Ned took us sailing on *Kandoo* and, in contrast to those still chagrined by the war, said 'he did not mind that his first grandchild was half-German'.

Apostleship of the Sea

The Apostleship of the Sea, or Stella Maris, was originated by Canon Bernard of Port-en-Bessin, France in 1926 to introduce seamen in strange ports to the families of other sailors and thereby save them from becoming part of the flotsam and jetsam of the city. Ned was inaugural Vice-President and, from 1927 to 1934, Chairman of the Executive Committee to the Co-ordinating Council.

In August 1927 Ned attended the first Congress of the Apostleship in Bayeux, France. The General Secretary reported that it had been formed to care for the spiritual welfare of Catholic seafarers throughout the world; its membership had reached 10,500. *The Tablet* reported 'Admiral Sir Edward Charlton, who had already won the admiration and respect of the fishermen of Port-en-Bessin, having specially navigated his little yacht across the Channel to attend this Congress, received an enthusiastic reception when he rose to speak on the conditions of Catholics in the Royal Navy and the facilities they now enjoy.'

In September 1929 Ned attended the second Congress at Boulogne when ships and seamen were blessed by the Bishop of Arras. The third Congress of this, by then, international organisation was held in St George's Hall, Liverpool in August 1930 and was attended by 3,000 Catholics. The proposed agenda for the Congress was set out in some detail in the *Daily Express* of 19 August 1930 by the Archbishop of Liverpool who commenced his article with these words: ' "They that go down to the sea in ships see the works of the Lord and His wonders in the deep." It is when they come into port that they need the help of man. Every day you may see them. They are shovelled off their ships like so much cargo. They wander about the streets, knowing no one, perhaps not understanding the tongue they hear around them. They fall into the snares of drink, gambling and immorality.' Ned addressed the Congress and said that when his brother-in-law Edward Strutt climbed Mont Blanc he had met Father Ratti, subsequently Pope Pius XI, at the top. When Edward Strutt later attempted to climb Mount Everest, his eighty-year-old mother was asked whether she worried about her son. She said she did not because, if he could meet the Pope at the top of Europe's highest mountain, there was no telling who he might meet at the top of the world's highest! In September 1932 Ned attended his last Congress of the Apostleship of the Sea at Volendam in the Netherlands.

The Final Tack

The last of the loose newspaper cuttings in Ned's papers is one from the *News Chronicle* dated 11 January 1937. It is headlined: 'Germany Re-fortifies Heligoland'. It describes in detail the refurbishment of the war harbour and the emplacement of six new eleven-inch guns. With what misgivings must Ned have read of the rearmament of Germany and of Churchill's unheeded attempts to awaken non-Fascist Europe to its peril. With what poignancy must he have reflected on Britain's 1890 decision to hand Heligoland to Germany in exchange for rights in his 1916 East African headquarters, Zanzibar.

About three months before his death Ned moved to the historic Haslar Naval Hospital in Portsmouth and it was there, on 23 October 1937, aged seventy-two, that he died from pneumonia. Freda was at his bedside. Following a Requiem Mass conducted by his parish priest, Father M.P. Murphy, Ned was buried in the same grave as his first wife Laura. A detachment from HMS *Barham* carried the coffin draped in a Union Jack from the church while blue-jackets from HMS *Vernon* served as pall-bearers at the cemetery. Mourners included Lady Charlton, four daughters, two brothers, Princess Blücher, Admiral of the Fleet Sir Reginald Tyrwhitt, Admiral Sir Richard Phillimore (a fellow cadet on *Britannia*), Air Commodore L.E.O. Charlton, Colonel Strutt, the Mayoress of Gosport, Mrs Graham, as well as numerous relatives, religious, magistrates' court and naval personnel. A plaque was placed on the wall of the little Catholic church in Bellingham, Northumberland where so many Charltons rest in the turf of the courtyard and which remained his spiritual home. It reads:

> 'OF YOUR CHARITY PRAY FOR THE SOUL OF ADMIRAL SIR EDWARD FRANCIS BENEDICT CHARLTON K.C.B.,K.C.M.G. WHO DIED AT GOSPORT ON 23RD OCTOBER 1937 AND IS BURIED AT FAREHAM IN HAMPSHIRE. R.I.P.'

Freda stayed on at 'Priddens'. Although much reduced from the fourteen servants she had known as a youth, and the eight she had known as a mother, she could afford the part-time assistance of one servant from Ned's limited estate. In stature Freda remained tall and in disposition forthright, her only compromise with luxury being to have heating installed in the bathroom of the house. She died on 1 September 1963, fortified by the rites of the church and is buried alongside Ned.

In the course of his fascinating career Ned tacked many leagues towards the 'broad vista of a world-state and universal communion' espoused by the Venerable Bede in Northumbria in AD 663. I like to think that as we, his descendants, continue that journey, he has a pithy word of encouragement for each of us.

Admiral Sir Edward Benedict Charlton's display of medals.

Admiral Sir Edward Charlton KCB KCMG leaving Buckingham Palace in full dress after receiving his second knighthood. He is accompanied by Lady Freda Charlton (centre) and her sister Monica.

Abbreviated Charlton Family Tree

b:born   br:brother   s:son   da:daughter   m:married   d:died

Hugh de Charleton of Hesleyside circa 1170
William de Charleton I – s of Hugh
Alexander de Charleton – s of William
Adam de Charleton I – br of Alexander
Adam de Charleton II – s of Adam I; d 1303
William de Charleton II – s of Adam II
Edward de Charleton – d prior to 1348
William de Charleton III
Edward Charlton – d prior to 1542
William Charlton – s of Edward
Edward Charlton – s of William m Elizabeth Heron; d 1614
Matthew Charlton – br of Edward
William Charlton – s of Matthew, m Dorothy Thornton
Sir Edward Charlton – s of William, knighted 1645
William Charlton – br of Sir Edward; d 1682
Edward Charlton – s of William, b 1665, m Margaret Salkeld
William Charlton – s of Edward, m Mary Croft; d 1736
Edward Charlton – m Teresa Swinburne; d 1767
William Charlton - s of Edward, b 1750, m M. Fenwick; d 1797
William John Charlton - s of William b 1784, m Katherine Cholmeley; d 1846
William Henry Charlton - 1st s of William John, b 1810, m Barbara Anne afterwards Tasburgh; d 1880
William Oswald Charlton – s of Wm Henry, b 1850, m Margaret Campbell; d 1894
William Henry Charlton – s of William Oswald, b 1876, m Bridget Purcell; d 1950

Mary Ellen Patricia Charlton, da of William Henry, b 1918, m Major Frederick John Charlton, previously Anne.

* * *

Dr Edward Charlton, 2nd s of William John, b 1814, m Margaret Bellasis; d 1874
Adm Sir Edward Charlton, 1st s of Dr Edward, b 1865, m1 Laura Strutt d 1909, m2 Freda Stapleton-Bretherton d 1963; d 1937
William Lancelot Charlton, Merchant Naval Officer, 2nd s of Dr Edward, b 1867, m1 Teresa Walmesley, m2 Ellen Young; d 1922
Elise, da of Dr Edward, b 1868, m Edward Doran-Webb; d 1949
Oswin Charlton, Solicitor, 4th s of Dr Edward, b 1871, m Mary O'Keefe; d 1941
George Charlton, Land Agent, 5th s of Dr Edward, b 1873, m Hon. Gladys Mostyn; d 1943
Frank Charlton, RN Engineer, 6th s of Dr Edward, b 1874; d 1908
Lancelot Charlton, s of William Lancelot b 1892, m Thérèse Byron; d 1961
Father Oswald Charlton, s of William Lancelot, b 1918; d 1996
Edward (Oscar) Charlton, E. African Game Warden, s of Oswin, b 1921
William Charlton, Professor of Philosophy, s of Lancelot, b 1935, m Anne Nichols of Lawford

Admiral Charlton's Descendants

Ned's family, as known to the writer in 1997, are:

First Generation:

No.	Name	Domicile/Interred	Born	Died
1.	Admiral Sir Edward Charlton	Fareham UK	1865	1937
1m1	Laura Charlton née Strutt	Fareham UK	1875	1909
1m2	Lady Freda née Stapleton-Bretherton	Fareham UK	1880	1963

Second Generation:

No.	Name	Domicile/Interred	Born	Died
2.	Mrs Audrey Urban née Charlton	Johannesburg S Af	1904	1994
2m.	Mr Victor Urban	Johannesburg S Af	1892	1981
3.	Mrs Marjorie Parkes née Charlton	Yelverton UK	1906	1978
3m.	Major Noel Parkes	Hastings UK	1891	1951
4.	Sister Laura Charlton	Hastings UK	1909	
5.	Mrs Nancy Morrogh-Bernard née Charlton;	Fair Oak UK	1911	1996
5m.	Colonel Joe Morrogh-Bernard	Fair Oak UK	1898	1994
6.	Captain Edward Charlton	Caen France	1912	1944
7.	Cadet Christopher Charlton	Dartmouth UK	1914	1928
8.	Lieutenant Brydget Charlton	Fareham UK	1914	1985
9.	Mrs Rosemary Acton née Charlton	Winchester UK	1917	1997
9m.	Mr Tony Acton	Winchester UK	1914	

Third Generation:

No.	Name	Domicile/Interred	Born	Died
10.	Mr Frank Urban	Comboyne Aust	1930	
10m	Mrs Patricia Urban née Fox	Comboyne Aust	1934	
11.	Dr Peter Urban	Johannesburg S Af	1932	
11m	Mrs Vivian Urban née Lungen	Johannesburg S Af	1933	
12.	Mr Michael Urban	Johannesburg S Af	1934	
12m	Mrs Wyn Urban née Weseman	Johannesburg S Af		
13.	Dr Martin Urban	Oxford UK	1941	
13m	Dr Jill Urban née Reichman	Oxford UK	1941	
14.	Ms Claire Reid née Urban	Bury St Edmunds UK	1942	
14m	Mr Alan Reid	Bury St Edmunds UK	1938	
15.	Dr Alan Urban	Pretoria S Af	1946	
15m	Mrs Ros Urban née Brown	Pretoria S Af	1946	
16.	Ch Inspector Charles Parkes	Somerset UK	1931	
16m	Mrs Angela Parkes née Clarke	Somerset UK	1933	
17.	Mrs Ann Russell née Parkes	Pretoria S Af	1936	
17m	Mr Allen Russell	Pretoria S Af	1924	1985
18.	Mrs Sue York née Parkes	Staines UK	1937	
18m	Mr Arthur York	Staines UK	1932	
19.	Captain Tony Parkes	Isle of Man	1941	
19m	Mrs Jane Parkes	Isle of Man	1941	1995
20.	Mrs Sarah Macdonald née Parkes	Sydney Aust	1941	
20m	Mr Colin Macdonald	Sydney Aust	1930	
21.	Major John Morrogh-Bernard	Fareham UK	1934	1968
21m	Mrs Julia M-B née Calvert, later Lady Blewitt	UK	1939	
22.	Mrs Penelope Crawford née M-B	Winchester UK	1936	
22m	Mr Michael Crawford	Winchester UK	1933	
23.	Mr Desmond Morrogh-Bernard	Cirencester UK	1939	
23m	Mrs Jenny Morrogh-Bernard née Walker	Johannesburg	1946	1979
24	Mr Christopher Morrogh-Bernard	Fair Oak UK	1955	
24m	Mrs Sarah M-B née Steele	Fair Oak UK	1958	
25.	Mr Peter Acton	Melbourne Aust	1952	
25m	Mrs Sarah Acton née Bolton	Melbourne Aust	1954	
26.	Mr Mark Acton	Dorset UK	1957	
27.	Mrs Mary Acton-Edmiston	Dorset UK	1963	
27m	Mr Simon Edmiston	Dorset UK	?	

Fourth Generation:

No.	Name	Parents	Domicile/Interred	Born	Died
30.	Mr Gerard Urban	10	Bathurst Aust	1960	
30m	Mrs Julie Ann Urban née West		Bathurst Aust	1963	
31.	Mr Adrian Urban	10	Bathurst Aust	1961	
31m	Mrs Julie Maree Urban née Grey		Bathurst Aust	1963	
32.	Ms Karen Urban	11	Johannesburg S Af	1963	
33.	Mrs Ingrid Kettles née Urban	11	Johannesburg S Af	1964	
33m	Mr Robert Kettles		NE Transvaal S Af	?	1994 (plane crash)
34.	Mr Charles Urban	11	Johannesburg S Af	1970	
35.	Dr Michael Urban	12	Johannesburg S Af	1963	
35m	Mrs Anita Urban		Johannesburg S Af		
36.	Mr Brian Urban	12	London UK	1965	
37.	Mr Edward Urban	12	Johannesburg S Af	1966	
38.	Mr Richard Urban	12	Brazil	1970	
39.	Mr Malcolm Reid	14	Crewe UK	1966	
40.	Ms Gemma Reid	14	Bury St Edmunds	1972	
41.	Mr Paul Urban	15	Pretoria S Af	1980	
42.	Ms Natalie Urban	15	Pretoria S Af	1983	
43.	Mr Simon Parkes	16	Nailsea UK	1957	
43m	Mrs Hilary Parkes née Parker		Nailsea UK	1959	
44.	Mrs Catherine Carter née Parkes	16	Kingston-on-Thames	1961	
44m	Major Michael Carter		Kingston-on-Thames	1957	
45.	Mr Mark Russell	17	Pretoria S Af	1962	
46.	Mr Paul Russell	17	Pretoria S Af	1963	
47.	Mr Iain Russell	17	Swakopmund Namibia	1965	
48m	Mrs Milly Russell née Thole		Swakopmund Namibia	1963	
49.	Mr Jeremy York	18	Staines UK	1970	
50.	Mrs Phillipa Wilson née York	18	Ashford UK	1972	
50m	Mr Paul Wilson		Ashford UK		
51.	Ms Kate Bryant née M-B	21	UK	1965	
51m	Mr Keith Bryant		UK		
52.	Mr Dominic Morrogh-Bernard	21	Scotland	1966	
53.	Mr Edward Crawford	22	UK	1963	
54.	Mr Patrick Crawford	22	UK	1966	
55.	Mr Anthony Crawford	22	UK	1967	
56.	Ms Camilla Morrogh-Bernard	23	London UK	1968	
57.	Ms Helen Morrogh-Bernard	23	Cirencester UK	1972	
58.	Ms Laura Morrogh-Bernard	24	Fair Oak UK	1979	
59.	Mr Philip Morrogh-Bernard	24	Fair Oak UK	1981	
60.	Ms Gemma Acton	25	Melbourne Aust	1981	
61.	Ms Annabel Acton	25	Melbourne Aust	1883	
62.	Ms Camilla Acton	25	Melbourne Aust	1987	
63.	Ms Emily Acton-Edmiston	27	Dorset UK	1991	

Fifth Generation:

	Name	Parents	Domicile/Interred	Born	
	Ms Jayde Urban	30	Bathurst Aust	1995	
	Ms Kristy Urban	31	Bathurst Aust	1982	
	Mr Michael Urban	31	Bathurst Aust	1986	
	Mr Brett Urban	31	Bathurst Aust	1986	
	Mr Daniel Kettles	33	Johannesburg S Af	1986	
	Mr Byron Kettles	33	Johannesburg S Af	1989	
	Mr Timothy Urban			1997	
	Mr Thomas Carter	44	Kingston-on-Thames	1987	
	Mr Charles Carter	44	Kingston-on-Thames	1990	
	Mr Frederick Carter	44	Kingston-on-Thames	1993	

Bibliography

Anglo-Saxon Chronicle – AD 892 to 1154

Blücher, Princess Evelyn, *An English Wife in Berlin*, 1921.

Blücher, Prince Gebhard, *Memoirs of Prince Blücher*, 1932.

Bradford, Admiral Sir Edward E., *Life of Admiral of the Fleet, Sir Arthur Knyvet Wilson*, 1923.

Caesar, Julius, *The Conquest of Gaul*, Penguin, 1951.

Cameron, Nigel, *From Bondage to Liberation*, (China), 1975.

Caughey, John W., *A History of the United States*, 1964.

Charlton, Barbara, edited by L.E.O. Charlton, *The Recollections of a Northumbrian Lady*, (1815–1866), 1949.

Charlton, Major John, *Hesleyside Hall* (Brochure)

Charlewood, Commander C.J., *Naval Actions on the Tanganyika Coast 1914–1917*.

Childers, Erskine, *The Riddle of the Sands*, 1903.

Churchill, Winston S., *A History of the English Speaking Peoples*, Volumes I to IV, 1958.

Clancy, Robert, *So Came They South* (Australia), 1988.

Cox, Tom, *Damned Englishman* (Biography of Erskine Childers), 1975.

Craig, Gordon A., *Europe Since 1815*, 1971.

D'Abernon, *An Ambassador of Peace*, Volumes I and II, c1924.

Davidson, Basil, *A History of East and Central Africa*, 1969.

Drummond, Maldwin, *The Riddle* (Erskine Childers' voyages), 1985.

Fairbank, John K., *East Asia*, 1973.

Foreign Language Press, *People's Republic of China*, China, 1979.

Fowler and Smit, *New History* (South Africa), c.1943.

George V, King, *(Personal Diary) Extracts by gracious permission of Her Majesty Queen Elizabeth II*.

Gray, Edwyn A., *The Killing Time* (German U-boats 1914-18), 1972.

Hamerton, J.A., Editor, *Our King and Queen* (George V), c.1929.

House of Commons, *Report of the Select Committee on Marconi's Wireless Telegraph Company*, 1913.

Johnson, Paul, *Ireland, Land of Troubles*, 1980.

Jolly, W.P., *Marconi, A Biography*, 1972.

Kee Robert, *Ireland, a History*, (BBC/RTE), 1980.

Kochan, Lionel, *The Struggle for Germany 1914–1945*, 1963.

Liddell Hart, Sir Basil, *History of the First World War*, 1970.

Marder, Arthur J., *Fear God and Dread Nought* (Lord Fisher), 1952.

Marsden, John, *The Illustrated Bede*, 1989.

Mathew, David, *The Naval Heritage*, 1944.

Poland, E.N. Rear-Admiral, *The Torpedomen*, 1993.

Schermer, David, *World War I*, 1973.

Sibley, Major J.R., *Tanganyikan Guerrilla*, East African Campaign 1914–18, 1971.

Smuts, J.C., *Jan Christian Smuts* (by his son), 1952.

Taffrail (Captain Taprell Dorling), *Swept Channels*, 1935.

Thomas, Lowell, *Raiders of the Deep*, 1929.

Thomson, David, *Europe since Napoleon*, 1957.

Ward, Russel, *Australia since the Coming of Man*, 1982.

Wedlake, G.E.C., *SOS, The Story of Radio Communication*, 1973.

Younger, R.M., *Australia and the Australians*, 1970.

Index